Making Public Policy

MIA NASETH-PHILLIPS

Making Public Policy

Institutions, Actors, Strategies

Mark Considine

polity

First published in 2005 by Polity Press.

Polity Press
65 Bridge Street
Cambridge CB2 1UR, UK

Polity Press
350 Main Street
Malden, MA 02148, USA

ISBN: 0-7456-2753-6
ISBN: 0-7456-2754-4 (paperback)

A catalogue record for this book is available from the British Library.

Typeset in 11 on 13 pt Berling
by SNP Best-set Typesetter Ltd, Hong Kong
Printed and bound in Great Britain by MPG Books Ltd, Bodmin, Cornwall

For further information on Polity, visit our website: www.polity.co.uk

Contents

Preface

This is a book for both practitioners and researchers and as such it must walk a tightrope. Tipping too far in either direction promises disaster; failing to take both into account guarantees only a brief spectacle of flight. Keeping theory and practice closely connected is also more a journey than a destination, as I hope the method of the book will show.

I have tried to write an account of policy-making from the perspective of those who want to change the way things work in order to make them more efficient and more equitable, but without being too glib about the difficulties which face actors who seek new pathways. Policy institutions and the habits which help sustain them take some understanding. To this end I have included a series of discussions dealing with the theoretical underpinnings of policy-making. The selections and emphases involved in the various choices and strategies outlined in the book are the result of a number of interventions involving many other people, including the many policy bureaucrats and activists I have worked with over the years who taught me more than I can say.

My colleague Ann Capling and I teach a Masters course in Advanced Policy Design and both she and the students in that programme have endured my experiments and made helpful suggestions and criticisms of a number of the chapters. John Thompson, Emma Longstaff, Christine Ranft, Helen Gray, and the anonymous reviewers at Polity also gave very useful feedback and were supportive throughout. My colleagues Damon Alexander, Jo Barraket, John Cain, Helen Szoke, Michael Crozier, Rita Deamicis, Joanne Pagounis, Brian Howe, Jenny Lewis, Paul

Smyth, Antara Mascarenhas and Steve Ziguras gave essential encouragement and welcome dialogue on the issues treated in the book. Colin Crouch and the staff at the Department of Political and Social Sciences at the European University Institute provided a haven in which to complete the manuscript.

But the people who have taught me most about the subtle strengths of authority relations and the creative power of negotiation are my children Kate, Tom and Pat to whom I dedicate this book.

1

Policy Interventions

The policies of governments contain and express the conflicts and tensions of contemporary societies. Sometimes they do this well and we see new rights and opportunities being confirmed. At other times these same policies are themselves the embodiment of what needs to be changed. Policy-making is thus a unique institutional environment and a powerful political tool.

The policies of governments and the counter-policies of agitators and special interests groups each offer to make tomorrow different from today. They do so in a world undergoing cataclysmic change. Older industrial institutions and governance systems are breaking up, new ones are still at the point of formation. Some patterns are beginning to show through. As French sociologist Alain Touraine put it in a book aptly titled *Can We Live Together?* (2000:3), 'What is emerging from the ruins of modern (read, "industrial") societies and their institutions is, on the one hand, global networks of production, consumption and communication and, on the other hand, a return to community.' Questions of policy are therefore always also questions of institutional design (Goodin, 1996). Official gestures, rules, counter-rules and each new act of political imagination bring to light the structures holding societies together or driving them apart.

This is a book about the way these policy-making systems structure the choices and options available to elites, interest groups and citizens. That is the first important level of analysis. The book also seeks to understand why government may be nimble and effective at some things and 'all thumbs' at others. It aims to draw attention to the way in which political institutions create characteristic action channels through policy and programme fields (March and Olsen, 1989). And in the end, the purpose of all this analysis and interpretation is to show where interventions by real actors might become more effective and equitable in improving both institutions and the social conditions they help support.

This is a large task, too large for one book on its own. Books, like institutions, do their best work by being selective. This one takes as its frame of reference the work of policy institutions in structuring policy-making and then seeks to push this institutional frame as far as is possible towards a preference for innovative and fairer outcomes.

Why start with institutions? Because much of policy-making is embedded in the routine practices carried out by government agencies employing well-worn repertoires of action. Day to day, little that happens in these agencies is entirely new. Very few who participate are novices. Interactions frequently follow proven habits and customs about such things as 'due process', 'ministerial prerogative', 'adequate consultation' and many other similar precepts and norms.

In other words, both action and inaction are institutionally framed. The simplest way to think about policy institutions is to understand them as rules of engagement; 'In politics as in everything else it makes a great deal of difference whose games we play. The rules of the game determine the requirements of success' (Schattschneider, 1960:48). This is also the paradox of social structures. Actors and systems are often in tension but they also depend upon each other. So we need to think of policy institutions as acts of creation and not just as impediments or constraints. In practice they must be both things. In a famous dictum the American pioneers heading West in their wagon trains were advised: 'Choose your rut carefully, you will be in it for the next 500 miles.' Each action pathway cuts a track into the social terrain. These wagon-tracks provide both a short cut and a constraint for those who follow.

Looked at from a theoretical perspective, this approach to policy-making assumes that each intervention rests upon, and must negotiate, a deeper structure of 'multiple enterprises' (Ostrom, 1992:75–6). What may be announced as new policy is rarely written on a single sheet of blank paper. Instead, the new is pencilled in the margins and spaces of other, previously negotiated commitments. These commitments include formal, coercive laws as well as implicit, habitual conduct, or what Bourdieu (1990:52) has called the *habitus*, a structuring in the dispositions which actors bring with them to each new engagement. These commitments typically connect several agencies and a number of different actor groups.

For example, when road deaths began to reach crisis levels in the 1970s policy makers in most industrialized countries searched for similar solutions. Regulating car safety and improving road construction only seemed to make minor changes to fatalities. One by one they decided to require drivers to adopt a common set of safer behaviours by wearing seatbelts, drinking less alcohol and slowing down. These instruments assumed the existence of a certain kind of driver, one willing to be regulated in the common good and one willing to be inconvenienced by personal restrictions which would only be of direct benefit in very extreme and remote circumstances.

Not surprisingly the willingness of drivers to comply differed among countries. In the United Kingdom and Australia the wearing of seatbelts was well accepted but drink driving proved much harder to restrain. In Italy and France the seatbelt laws were more widely flouted, but on the other hand drinking was more easily curbed. Policies and institutions thus make sense when we understand the history and social character of actors. In this case the actors were car drivers, but the same could be said of citizens and their approach to government in each national system.

The history of engagements between state and citizen plays a critical role in what is available for policy design. De Tocqueville (1835:39) was one of the most eloquent exponents of this deep history of institutions. He points out that 'the growth of nations . . . all bear some marks of their origins. The circumstances which accompany their birth and contributed to their development affect the whole term of their being.' Often, de Tocqueville observes, these effects are at odds with current practice and 'seems at variance with the prevailing manners'. What one people will accept and another reject, the way one community will prefer local solutions and another central control, all speak to this issue of the historical *embeddedness* of institutions. Policies and the laws they create sit within a multi-layered context of habits and bargains between rulers and ruled, past and present.

To bring to the surface the habitual or systemic character of these policy processes, and to throw light on the occasional dynamics of more fundamental change, the book focuses upon the idea of the policy 'intervention'. Two things are suggested here. First of all, that policies already exist before contemporary actors step onto the stage, a point already made above. To speak of an intervention is therefore to bring to mind what already exists and into which the policy will 'intervene'.

And second, the term hopes to suggest that any policy is but a conditional, often temporary opportunity for changing a larger matrix of institutional conditions. Whether or not any specific intervention will alter the fundamental conditions of a policy problem or crisis will depend upon both the quality of the intervention and the degree of openness in the underlying system. So, an able minister of education might have a good plan to redistribute school resources to poorer districts, yet get nowhere if she has a weak understanding of the teaching profession's conservatism and the long time-lines for the state capital works budget.

Other methods have been used to capture the character of policy-making and there are some good books written in defence of those approaches. Peter John (1998) provides an excellent summary of the literature of policy-making and some of the consequences of choosing one approach over others. Jan-Erik Lane (1993) does much the same but with a focus on the role of the public sector and public administrators. Hogwood and Gunn (1984) give a compelling overview of what might be called the rational deliberation model, in which policy is seen as a series of decision rules and sequential processes. An introductory version of the same approach but with a manual-handling focus ('eight basic steps') can be found in Bardach (2000).

Some text books also provide a version of rational choice theory (or economic choice theory) to contrast with these other types, although interestingly there are few texts which recommend rational choice as a method (Laver, 1986; Harsanyi, 1969), perhaps because many rational choice propositions are designed to show why public policy is often a bad idea (Hechter, 1983; Olson, 1971; Alford and Friedland, 1985).

This book was written to assist actors in their efforts to become better analysts and analysts become better actors. What links the two is theory. Not theory understood as an elevated realm of contemplation above the world, but theory as distilled, generalizable and critically aware practice. This fits the definition of an interpretive social science of the kind Clifford Geertz (2001:1) has described. 'First you do it, then you name it, then you try and determine what sort of "family resemblance" if any, holds it intelligibly together.' A somewhat similar view is taken by Schmitter (1977:5):

> . . . eschew premature closure; emphasize the high degree of uncertainty, indeterminism and experimentation involved in policy choice; make very modest and tentative pretensions to understanding; admit a considerable plurality of types, concepts and motives; not be excessively concerned with or restricted to immediately measurable indicators; and to recognize clearly its limitations in dealing with the accidental and/or brilliantly innovative act.

Institutionalism, and especially new institutionalism (March and Olsen, 1989; DiMaggio and Powell, 1983) provides our starting point for building such a theory. Rational choice institutionalism takes some of the same interests and pushes the analysis to consider an individual calculus (Levi, 1997; Elkin, 1987; Ostrom, 1998; Sabetti, 2000). A critical institutionalism seeks to link formal rules and customs to different forms of social action, including the discursive (Habermas, 1986; Dryzek, 1990) and the networked (Kooiman, 1993; Larner, 1997; Culpitt, 1999).

Having put theory into the story it is then incumbent upon us to know something about what theory is, and what it is not. In this account of policy interventions, theory is first and foremost a normative engagement – a dialogue about what 'ought', as well as about what 'is'. How should those in power behave towards citizens or non-citizens? When should governments be obligated to care for others? And so on. Second, theory can be defined as a map of the expected landscape of policy against which we might compare our experiences. Some writers use the metaphor of the lens through which one looks at the world, here magnified, or there coloured by the manufacturer's preferences. This seems unnecessarily reductionist.

The map ought to be far enough from the mapmaker to allow some level of independent observation, but now we are straying into the core world of theory itself – the explanation of causes. Maps show the institutions, pathways and wagon-tracks by which actors seek to influence and make decisions. They also show the traffic flows around impediments and conflicts. Maps also calibrate distance and scale, indicating the kind of value system built into the social geography of a particular policy field. This at least is our first point of orientation.

Third, theory carries the heavy load of interpretation. As Geertz (2001:1) puts it, this involves looking for the 'family resemblance' in different experiences. This search for intelligibility is the core of all theorization. However rough, however faltering, the search for a generalization to capture the larger character of actions and processes is the bedrock of this work. It is this that enables interpretation to inform some level of evaluation, not just in the technical sense of making judgements about what works or does not work, but in the normative sense of what is preferred, what is less objectionable and what, for the sake of more X or less Y, might have been different.

Among more sectarian accounts of policy there is a good deal of bickering over whether or not quantification is useful, whether experiences can be thought of as variables, and whether such variables can be linked to causal explanations. On the other side of this debate is a series of questions about whether qualitative data such as partisan observations and interviews can ever be truly free of bias, exceptionalism and wishful thinking. Nothing in the pages that follow will eliminate the divide between these factions. Instead, the book assumes only that methods of inquiry should be adapted to the problems at hand, and so long as there is a recognizable method, there is an opportunity to interpret and learn from the analyst's and the activist's experiences.

Given these conditions it makes no sense to discuss theory at a distance from actual policy work or to have chapters dealing with theory on its own. While there is a good book to be written about the theory of policy theories, and an explanation of why some theories arise in one place or time and not in another (Scott and Keates, 2001), that is a different task to policy intervention. The grounded theory used here is intentionally synthetic. It seeks to draw a map which is both practical in its attempt to explain the actual pathways of policy enactment, but also reflexive in the kinds of judgements and arguments used to push the untidy world of practice into a shape we can debate, discuss and, in some cases, change for the better.

2

Analysing Actors:
Bill, Bruno and Anna

Living in contemporary societies requires us to consider the impact of large social and political forces. These shape our own life and the lives of families, fellow citizens and people in other countries. These larger pressures are ever present and titanic. They determine the jobs that the economy produces, the schools we go to and the television programmes we watch. Being born, going to school, entering the workforce, getting married, losing a job, being ill and becoming old are each shaped in very critical ways by the work of the embedded arrangements we call institutions. Many of these structures are beyond the influence of individual citizens. One of only a few places available to us to influence these things in a more or less deliberate way is through the opportunities a democracy provides for contesting and making public policy.

Of course the very idea of 'influence' is controversial. Among millions of different voices the individual's demands will seem irrelevant to the actions of elites, agitators and legislators. Yet looked at as an institutional process our policy systems do require engagement among the citizenry and other stakeholders. Paying taxes, voting, signing petitions, even engaging in political debate with colleagues all form part of this larger social process for shaping, resisting and responding to policy. Here are three scenarios that illustrate how this engagement may unfold (see Van der Heijden (1996) and Ringland (1998) for methodological information).

On a cloudy afternoon in a leafy suburb in London's south, Bill Walker contemplates his prospects before the local planning board. Sitting next to him outside the Council chamber are two of his neighbours and an architectural consultant they have hired to fight an office development at the end of Bill's street.

Sitting in judgement on whether their houses will soon be overshadowed by an office block is Maria Rivers, a lawyer appointed to the planning tribunal by the local Council. If they lose, Bill and his neighbours have already discussed an appeal to the courts and the possibility of chaining themselves to the bulldozers. More than once during the twelve-month lead-up to the tribunal hearing, Bill's friends and allies have raised the idea that he should run for Council at the next election. The level of solidarity among the neighbours is high and social events have been organized to raise funds and develop an organization. Passions are running free, on both sides. Skirmishes in committees, delegations and media conferences have been marked by strong talk. Fundamental values have been invoked on both sides, including 'property rights', 'the importance of community', 'self-determination', 'heritage values', 'economic development' and 'quality of life'.

In another European community, this time on the Adriatic coast, a group of fishermen gather in a care-worn coffee shop off the main square to discuss falling yields. In the past three years the catch has declined by almost twenty per cent. Bruno Hella, one of the senior boat owners, points out that there is no longer sufficient income to enable all the families to employ their sons, wives and daughters on the fleet or in the local processing factory. There is talk of loans being foreclosed and boats being sold to pay off debts. In desperation some of the families have been fishing longer hours and sailing further afield to take fish from neighbouring waters. The sabotage of nets by competitors has introduced a new level of violence into the community.

To make matters worse a recent report from the European Union has shown that the fish stock is failing and the survival of the main commercial species can no longer be guaranteed. It is recommended that the fleet be culled and that new, heavily mortgaged, sonar-equipped boats be restricted to only three months' fishing a year. Over coffee the talk among Bruno and his friends is of the end of local communities and traditions that stretch back hundreds of years.

A different predicament faces Anna Trikolidis. She has been the CEO of a new national regulatory authority in Australia called Invitro-Australia (IVA) for the past two years. Her job is to grant licences and permits to clinics wishing to become involved in the new industry of in vitro fertilization (IVF). A new science for creating life outside the womb became possible in the 1980s, and scientists and doctors then began to offer infertile couples new hope for having children.

Despite having successfully managed the first stage of IVF development through the 1990s, IVA is now facing a difficult future. The early developments of the new technology were directed at popular patient groups such as traditional married couples wishing to have their own eggs and sperm harvested, cultivated outside the body and then returned to the mother for an otherwise normal pregnancy. But in the past two years science has moved ahead and created opportunities to employ unused embryos to produce genetic materials, or 'spare parts' for use in treating disease. And to make matters even more complex, new patient groups have begun to demand access to treatment including couples too old to conceive normally, single women, and those in homosexual couples. Anna and her board of church leaders and lawyers are now being called upon to interpret the public interest in areas where no precedent exists and where the smallest of decisions provokes the greatest of controversies.

What policy actors do

For every member of a given political community, that is, in any collective where people participate in decisions, some kind of story is told about the role of actors and of collective action in shaping how important things get done. Even where this common narrative is one of large structures and forces bearing down on individuals, the preferred world that is implied is one of respect for everyone's right to influence what happens around them. In other words the realm of actors presumes a realm of structures too. How this is understood will be different in different countries and even in different regions. As Putnam (1993:182) argues, 'social context and history profoundly condition the effectiveness of institutions'.

In each of the three scenarios we see this conditioning. Bill, Bruno and Anna operate within a complex system of relationships and interests that have a history and a momentum that appears to dwarf each of them. Yet these same actors actually do the work of bringing these processes to life. The larger structures of the political world would not survive if real actors did not accept the need to use them, follow their codes of practice and speak in the language that such institutions understand. Yet even in the most constrained of public roles, where the tasks are mandated and each sequence of moves is scripted by law or convention, the actor still is called upon to bring interpretation and improvization to bear.

Each politician, judge, bureaucrat or citizen interprets their given role in a way which enables them to manoeuvre and strategize within this structured policy space. Each individual effort therefore helps to adjust, confirm or re-programme important aspects of the larger system of institutions and interests. Both the characteristics of continuity and of the struggle to produce change are therefore of central importance to the attempt to understand what happens during policy-making encounters.

The three policy scenarios highlight typical points of conflict and convergence among actors that inform our need to develop a theoretical account of policy (see table 2.1). That is, in order to make sense of this multi-layered experience we require a set of generalizations capable of enabling us to learn about the pattern of interactions. In each of the three stories there is both a thread of new action and a narrative of established process.

Bill seeks to use the local authority's planning appeals system to give voice to his own and his neighbours', concerns. He does so in a highly structured legal process. Bruno and his fellow fleet owners want to fashion a viable future by mixing their own individual economic efforts with some form of collective protection. They must deal with the national and supra-national regulatory system. Anna and her board have an existing legislative mandate but they foresee a need to reorder their resources and rules. To do this they will need to negotiate a new act through the minister's office, the cabinet and the parliamentary committee system.

Table 2.1   Scenarios and maps

	Actors	Discourses	Institutions	Systems
Bill	Lawyers	Property rights	Tribunal	Property market
	Neighbours	Amenity	Planning code	Law
	Councillors	Development	Council	
Bruno	Fishers	Community	Fish market	Ecology
	Fish	Tradition	Fleet	Nation state
	Experts	Resource management	Licensing agency	Trade regime
Anna	Scientists	Parenthood	Regulatory act	Health care
	Physicians	Rights	Research teams	Family
	Parents	Family values	Health insurance	Bio-science

But it will also be obvious that these three scenarios are too brief to express a number of other important characteristics of policy-making. Good case analysis requires 'thick description' using the actual experiences of different participants, including recognition that these will often involve conflict (Sabatier and Jenkins-Smith, 1993). In comparing such experience the analyst is required to evaluate what is presented. Policy analysis is thus a process of seeing both what is there and what is missing (Kingdon, 1984). Each of the three narratives is pointed towards an implicit account of policy as a set of possibilities for actors where the future is as yet unknown and somewhat dynamic. But there is another way we could look at this same set of predicaments.

We could make a case to show that the majority of the work that goes on in these public places is routine, even mundane, and certainly not very open to change (Allison, 1971; Steinbrunner, 1974). For every citizen with Bill's complaints, there may be a thousand who will never go to the town hall. Similarly, most of those employed in the fishing industry may work their whole life without seeking the collective action that Bruno's village are contemplating. And while IVF is a currently controversial issue, much of what happens in the health system lies outside the reach of popular debate and decisions about alternative pathways.

In other words the theoretical account being developed in this book, its underlying assumptions and argument, are directed towards the action side of the action/structure problem. For the policy analyst this is a position that tends to come with the job description. A certain willingness to believe that change is possible is a necessary part of the professional belief system. In other words this is a normative position as well as an empirical one. In examining the policy-making world from the perspective of these action possibilities one acknowledges that each episode, even where it is heavily fortified and encrusted with institutional habit and resistance to change, still depends on real actors accepting, embracing or colluding with established practices. At this deeper level then, social structures are also actions, including actions imagined, deferred and foregone.

Policy interventions beget institutions or structures, these structures provide channels for further interventions and it then becomes impossible to explain the one without the other. Put another way, policy structures are both a curb on some forms of action and are also implicit preferences that serve to privilege certain choices. When we know what preferences and biases are built into these action channels we know quite a lot about how public policy will be enacted (March and Olsen, 1989).

Another way to think about policy interventions is to notice that policy-making arrangements or processes perform a double service to the political system as a whole. These institutions are responsible for producing both a standard flow of routine decisions and outputs. But they are also responsible for dealing with exceptions, with new problems not yet tamed by routine, and with novel puzzles only dimly imagined at the time the codes and norms of regular work inside the policy system were being laid out. Deciding what constitutes a 'normal case' rather than an 'exceptional issue' warranting new forms of action proves to be the central place for policy interventions.

The key to the approach presented here is a contrast of system and (action) intervention. Since the term 'system' is somewhat loaded and open to contending definitions it is as well to explain what is meant. At its core the systems perspective is one that argues that the individual's or agency's actions become powerful in relation to the things that concern them when they are linked to a larger process for negotiating and perhaps mobilizing the actions of others. When this happens the resulting coordinated effort results in some form of patterned, valued conduct. At this point the actors have succeeded in producing *system* effects.

Not all systems are political systems. Not every collective issue in a community or society is destined to be resolved at the level of the political system. Left to their own devices the market and the best efforts of private associations will manage to sort out a variety of problems without public institutions or governments becoming involved. But the division of responsibility between these three realms – state, market and association – is more controversial than any simple catalogue suggests (Kooiman, 1993; Salamon, 1989; Ryan, 1999). Left to market or associational action (NGOs etc.) many policy problems will multiply and create situations in which opportunities become restricted, resources are concentrated among the few, corrupt conduct robs communities of self-confidence, or where good private solutions remain too localized to be of much value.

The book therefore argues that there is no 'natural' realm or partition for containing policy interventions. The border is a loose, tense and poorly regulated one. Communities and individual actors push this boundary back and forth as they seek to answer new questions about the lives they share or the futures they hope for. This means that public policy is always a debate about what governments do, but is always much more than this too. Finding the borders and understanding the traffic and tension across them is a central part of the puzzle. The borders are those constructed between public and private life, between things defined as individual matters and those we call collective or common property, and the other boundaries built to manage time – between things that are just questions in the present, and those that flow from here to the future.

What governments do

Policy intervention is always a story with a central question: What can governments usefully do?

In seeking a way through these complex issues, governments and their agencies have only a limited range of options. They can pass laws to prevent conduct viewed as undesirable, or to license things that people favour. The state can use taxes to curb some activities. Similarly, government can create subsidies to actively promote desired behaviour by firms or individuals. And in all these endeavours the state may choose to do things itself or do things through third parties such as self-help groups or churches. While there is an impressive proliferation of these various forms of state action, at its core there seem three kinds of strategy – interventions based on legal regulation, on the distribution of resources, and those designed to achieve normative change.

In theoretical terms this limited repertoire has an upside. Liberal democratic states and their agencies are bound by these rather limited opportunities to regulate conduct. This helps prevent more intrusive forms of government action. In practical terms too these repertoires are rather rudimentary. Laws and regulations are unpopular and often create high implementation costs. Taxes are hard to administer, not least because they can create perverse incentives for people to cheat and thus create a new generation of problems for policy makers. Strategies relying on normative change offer major changes in citizen behaviour, but they require sustained effort over time and the effects are difficult to attribute to any single policy initiative.

In seeking to understand the structural dynamics of policy-making it is important to allow for some important feedback effects among the variables. The act of deciding a new policy is both a decision about a particular outcome and a laying down of precedent for the next decision that comes along. Often this recursive dimension will be most plainly felt as the need to reform institutions before being able to deliver new policy. When Anna and her board resolve a difficult individual case by accepting that it is up to the woman's doctor to exercise discretion over whether she should undertake an IVF procedure, they are both avoiding making the actual decision themselves and they are also creating a new piece of institutional machinery, a new action channel for others to use. The next woman seeking access to the service will claim this right because her doctor said so. The next doctor to dispute IVA's ruling on a case will use this precedent to defend her right to decide.

While the three scenarios grant us a view of the particular dynamics of policy systems and will later reveal important aspects of the way strategy develops from the actors' perspective, the larger structural role of policy-making in a complex society should not be forgotten.

Public policy is more than just a number of stories about governments reacting to pressures, or citizens battling to exploit or resist pressures placed upon them. Public officials such as politicians, judges and bureaucrats also contribute to an overall system of governance. In other words, in addition to the specific individual effects which policies have for citizens, the total system of policy-making actions, rules and values contributes a key element to the overall 'steering' mechanism of society as a whole.

This means that policy helps define the things a community holds to be important, including rights to work and own property, rights to organize and the capacity of citizens to be informed and involved in decisions which are important.

When a society develops a role for any form of public action, whether expressed as laws or forms of organization, it expresses a certain vision of itself, a certain interpretation of its own future. It sets in motion an important set of ideas about the kind of world its citizens will inhabit. In this sense policy is a form of learning which impacts directly upon the kind of shared future its people will experience. What roles will citizens have? How will children be educated? How long will people live? How will happiness be defined? What kind of ecology will exist in the future? All these very basic questions are answered, in part, by the form and content of public policy-making systems.

When we think in this way about policy we can see that it contributes to the overall governance of society. The act of policy analysis must therefore include more than just an evaluation of options to solve specific problems. It should also seek to uncover and discern ideas about the nature of 'the good life', of 'fairness', of 'respect for difference', 'honouring our traditions' or whatever other larger value is being mobilized through what takes place. Whether or not these are the questions in the minds of the actors being analysed, each decision or non-decision has the potential to confirm some view about society's larger direction or potential.

Of course policy-making does not do all this work alone. The economic system and the mass media also play a very decisive role in steering smaller issues towards these larger purposes. But what is different about the public policy system is its obligation to accept some level of public input and accountability. Elections, interest groups, opinion polling and demonstrations are the most obvious manifestations of this set of conditions. So too are they ways we think and talk about the nature of policy and of the actor's opportunity to intervene. This discursive dimension is discussed at greater length below.

What institutions do

Public policy is the achievement of actors making use of institutions and being shaped by them. Understanding the nature of these institutions is therefore a central task for the policy analyst. Each institution has its own particular history and architecture and it is these that help create the action channels of any given policy system (Weaver and Rockman, 1993).

To start at a very simple level we can observe that the executive class in charge of much of the policy-making process is dominated by politicians who are elected by a particular system of laws and rules. This electoral system establishes a cycle of contests and bids. It also creates incentives for the formation of parties and for alliances or conflicts between them. Once in government these elected politicians are then distributed into roles by another institutional system which determines the composition of ministries, cabinets and the distinctions between different portfolio areas. The same is true of the budget process. It does not wait to be invented or enacted by each new cast of contenders. Instead it has its own cycle of submissions, estimates, legislative enactment and review.

In order to make policy and have it implemented the actors in this system must navigate successfully through the runnels of these established institutions. As we have noted already, they may also have to rebuild aspects of these same systems before being able to get the policy outcomes they desire. But always and everywhere their efforts will depend upon institutional processes and resources.

One useful way to draw attention to the impacts and opportunities afforded by this institutional architecture is to compare the effect of different arrangements (Lijphart, Rogowski and Weaver, 1993). For instance, we know that electoral systems which use proportional voting are more likely to result in coalition governments. One of the interesting things about coalitions of the type common in Western Europe is that the different parties expect to have to deal with one another and perhaps work with one another at some time in the future.

This inhibits some of the 'winner takes all' approach to electioneering and policy-making that we see in majoritarian systems such as the United Kingdom. So when governments change there is more likely to be a gradual shift away from previous policy positions towards new ones. Where the electoral system uses first-past-the-post, or preferential voting, there is a greater likelihood of majoritarian government: that is, one party winning the election and governing in its own right. This creates strong incentives for parties to exaggerate their differences and to swing the policy system around to a new position once they win office (Pasquino, 1990; Schmitter, 1992).

Of course this is only a superficial example of institutional impacts on policy-making. To get a more comprehensive picture we would also need to look at the way other institutional conditions moderate or exaggerate these effects. For instance the length of time between elections might be very important in promoting or impeding major changes of policy direction. So too might the effect of upper houses, or in the European case, supra-national levels of government such as the European Union. We will look more closely at these issues in chapters 6 and 7. For now it is only

necessary to position the policy maker's role within a suitable analytical framework, a framework of institutional convention and
discourse.

Policy interventions are defined by the use of some authoritative instrument or action channel. These tools have different properties, different costs and different side effects. What is more, the
continued use of a particular tool often leads to the enculturation
of this form of action into the institutional intelligence of the
policy system. Having produced a policy solution by a particular
method once makes it more likely that this will be tried again.
Once repeated the method may embed itself as part of a larger
system of conventions to the point where actors will expect this
method to be used and will resist alternatives (Allison, 1971).
Even apparently superficial conventions attract tenacious support
in this way, in part because they give the institution a sense of its
own history and identity, and in part because even the more obso-
lete tools in the institutional toolbox may be useful at some point.

The other important aspect of institutional architecture is that
each design option or different configuration has both costs and
benefits. The policy analyst may not be called upon to change the
basic features of the policy system and is more likely to be engaged
in reviewing or implementing particular policies. Yet a well-
developed sense of the way strengths and weaknesses accumulate
around each institutional path will be essential to an understanding of how to achieve results at whatever level.

In Bruno's scenario we saw a problem that seemed to require
some form of intervention. To keep fish stocks healthy and to
make sure the fishing community has a viable future, some
arrangement other than the market and larger than individual
strategies to catch more fish was needed. This is a classic example
of the need for institutional design to manage common pool
resources, or those things which everyone has a right to enjoy but
which, left to private action, will be depleted to the point where
everyone is worse off (Hardin, 1995; Ostrom, 1990).

If we consider the institutional options available in this scenario
we soon observe how the architecture of institutions plays a role
in determining outcomes, including some that are less than
optimal. For instance an obvious starting point in Bruno's case

would be to bring in a government authority to control fishing and to regulate the market. A government role would be independent of both fleet owners and consumers and could take into account the environmental issues involved, including the future management of the ecosystem. But to do this effectively will require a selection of appropriate instruments. We cannot just say 'get the government to do it' without knowing what exactly will be required (Ostrom, 1990:14).

A standard strategy in this case would be to set up an authority to issue quotas and licensing arrangements to find an equilibrium point where fish numbers are preserved and the industry will survive. But these instruments will also have their costs. Inspectors will be needed to check how much is caught every day. This may lead to a heavy burden of paperwork and reporting by the local industry. This will also create incentives for fleet members to cheat by landing their catch offshore and by marketing through black market channels. This in turn will require the regulator to develop a policing role and to pursue cheats through the court system.

The licence system will also lead to restrictions on other boat owners entering the industry. Those already inside the system will be protected and may become lethargic in regard to future investments in innovation. Most likely the total cost of this licence and quota system will be passed on to consumers in the form of higher prices. If there are competitors in fishing grounds that do not have such regulation, the regulated fleet will lose market share to cheaper foreign products and this will doubtless lead to calls for government subsidies.

In this way we can observe that policy instruments are never innocent. That is, their effects are generally much more complex than first appears. The analyst's task is therefore to think just as hard about the consequences of action as about the effects of inaction. This can only be done where the analytical framework is wide enough to include the context issues that will be influenced when any given solution rebounds into a second and third generation of effects. This will be the task in the next three chapters.

So to summarize, the policy analyst's task includes an understanding of the contextual structures and processes around or nearby the problem being addressed. This includes the way certain industries work, how services are created and used, how benefits and costs are distributed, and how these things are valued within a normative system of rules and habits.

What policies do

As a starting point we have tended to define public policies as responses to pressing problems. Although problems often drive the policy system towards action, we have also noted that problems are themselves produced by policy-making. They are the second, third or fourth generation of effects produced by previous policy actions and instruments. An even more important reason to extend the analysis beyond the focus upon problems is that policies may also be positive attempts to produce benefits or to seize opportunities to assist citizens.

In Anna's scenario the IVF industry has grown beyond a simple therapeutic response to the needs of infertile couples and has become a means for couples to exercise a greater range of controversial choices (Van Dyck, 1995; Lee and Morgan, 1989). These include choosing important characteristics of their children, delaying childbirth until later in life, having someone else carry and bear one's children, and gaining access to better genetic material than would otherwise be available. As new scientific solutions are invented public policy must develop frameworks for distributing these benefits in a way that meets community standards as well as the individual rights of would-be consumers. Of course the minute a solution is invented we can say that the policy problem becomes how to pay for and regulate it. At this point the term 'problem' has obviously lost an independent status.

This points us to the fact that we really do not always know as much as we should about why some things become defined as 'problems' and thus become the object of policy-maker attention. The other side of this coin is that other equally compelling issues can be identified as things that deserve attention yet never seem to get onto the policy-maker's agenda. So one of the first things we need to do in policy analysis is ask how problems get defined as subjects of policy-making in the first place. The best way to begin such an inquiry is to ask for whom the problem is a problem to begin with?

For Bill Walker and his neighbours the problem began as a feeling of threat when the developers of that London office block decided to buy land in their street. Bill's group defined the problem as 'inappropriate development' and 'loss of amenity'. Yet even in this relatively simple scenario the problem definition was no simple matter. Later in the debate they would add the charge of 'threat to heritage values'. For their part the developers also fought hard to win the war of words. They called the appeal to the planning board 'bureaucratic interference' in the free market and a threat to property rights.

What we typically find when we ask 'for whom is the problem a problem?' is that there are two kinds of answer. The first is a practical, material puzzle. Policy issues arise when limited resources and differing material interests among individuals lead to scarcity and then to conflict. Limited land for suburban development, falling fish stocks and changes in fertility involve dramatic practical consequences for those affected.

The second part of the definition of the 'problem' is normative, or value-based. Sometimes the reasons for an issue becoming the subject of policy attention have less to do with their objective material consequences and relate to the perceptions and ideas attached to these material issues. For example there may be no cost-benefit basis for explaining the preferences which policy makers hold about the available methods for providing housing for refugees and asylum seekers. The choice between placing them in high-rise apartments with other poor people, in rent-subsidized houses out in the suburbs, or in closed camps will most likely be driven by emotions, preferences and ethics (Wildavsky, 1987).

These norms act as a kind of 'short cut' or simplification through which many different actors and interests seek to find some common ground with others. It would be a mistake to dismiss this normative work as mere 'spin-doctoring' or 'public relations', although there is a good deal of that involved. Rather we can think of the normative realm as one in which actors manoeuvre and jostle to shape the expectations of others.

Complexity and limited time conspire to make these short cuts essential. Policy-making is a selective process. Decisions are made about what is to be included and what is to be excluded from public action. Leaders and advocates must decide quickly which things are most important, which ones can be treated effectively, and which ones are too hard for them to tackle. In other words the definition of 'problems' owes a great deal to the cognitive map which policy makers develop to evaluate and rank different issues and interests. Some politicians are highly sensitive to issues brought forward by those they already feel sympathy for, or with whom they have some history of interaction. Others may search more widely but may use media coverage as a cue for paying closer attention. Still others will enter the policy-making field with a value-lens or ideological commitment already in place and will then seek out 'problems' which confirm their normative disposition. So rather than focus only on the level of problems, the analyst seeks to understand policy-making as a mandate to act which can result from several different imperatives – material, normative and a mix of both.

What rules do

The golden thread that ties the context of policy to actual decisions, battles and outcomes is rules. There are rules in other parts of society too, but in policy-making rules do the heavy lifting. The idea that politics and policy-making are a game of rule-making and rule-breaking lies at the heart of any intervention strategy.

Rules are a dispersed form of collective intelligence for reducing complex problems to preferred solutions. In the case of public policies these rules are backed by the strongest forms of governmental authority, which in its ultimate form includes the power to deprive citizens of their life, liberty and property.

A rule could be defined in analytical terms as an instrument designed to limit human agency. In the simplest terms we think of rules to stop people doing certain things such as building office blocks in suburban streets, over-fishing the oceans, or buying and selling human genes. Yet the same rules also empower other groups to protect their current positions and to go on enjoying certain opportunities. So rules both grant and limit power. A rule like compulsory voting might expand the basis of human agency for everyone, while another such as immigration laws might confer radically uneven opportunities, protecting some people at the expense of others.

Perhaps the most interesting way in which this agency power of rules is evident is in relation to international trade. Left to their own devices the nations of the world would make a series of agreements about which goods or services they might allow into their domestic markets. They would also erect barriers to protect domestic industry from outside competition. At a certain point this system of domestic rules would prevent the international trade system from evolving past a limited form of bilateral rule-making. If we then look at the evolution of the General Agreement on Trade and Tariffs (GATT) negotiated after the Second World War we can see that collective rule-making by all trading nations leads to empowerment, or new opportunities. In other words a structure of binding, enforceable rules may actually increase the agency of all those involved (Capling, 2001).

So all methods of analysing the underlying structure and rules of policy-making begin with the questions: On what does the basic order and power of the policy system depend? Who has a mandate to act, and what are the rules establishing this power? What conditions are imposed on those subject to such laws? How do the rules empower these actors to pursue their interests?

Although legally binding rules or laws explain a good deal of what happens in the policy-making system, a second layer of regulated conduct is also important. As we noted in discussing the work of institutions, an informal or tacit level of regulations also exists. For example, in Bill's scenario the decision to appeal the planning permit granted to the developers required him to lodge a written request for a review by the tribunal. The Council rules merely state that all such appeals should be dealt with in the most expeditious manner possible. But because the Council receives many such complaints it has had to develop internal protocols for assessing which matters to deal with first.

These are largely invisible to Bill's group because they have never lodged an appeal before. The developers, on the other hand, are well practised at fighting off complaints and have learned quite a lot about this informal system. They know that the general rule is that appeals will be heard in the order that they were lodged unless the planning department believes an exception should be made. A number of conventions have developed inside the Council to justify treating a case as an exception. These unwritten rules include whether the disputed project is very high cost, whether or not the original judgement to issue a permit was made 'at the margins' of the current planning code, or whether the degree of public unrest is such that the overall legitimacy of the planning process could be threatened by prolonged delay.

Summing up, we can recognize a good deal of complexity in these different roles and routines. Interventions must negotiate existing institutions, and may even have to reform them in order to achieve an ultimate benefit. But all such interventions create the potential for feedback and undesirable side effects, forcing the analyst to take a wide view of the context for policy-making episodes or encounters. This is the subject of the next chapter.

3

Analysing the Policy Context

Policy makers in modern Western societies have never faced more complex challenges. The structure and organization of both the economy and society appears to be in a phase of profound transformation. Traditional institutions such as the family, the Church and the education system have undergone deep changes from which new patterns and roles are still emerging. As Amin (1994:1) has observed, 'It seems that capitalism is at a crossroads in its historical development signalling the emergence of forces – technological, market, social and institutional – that will be very different from those which dominated the economy after the Second World War.'

Concealed within terms like 'capitalism', 'historical development' and 'transformation' are complex processes and multiple enterprises. Analysing the structural context for policy intervention requires some understanding of these processes and the different impacts they may have.

Two things can be noted right from the start of this discussion of contexts. The first is the most obvious. Policy interventions must be understood within the social and economic conditions through which resources are identified and conflicts arise. We might think about this as the broad context. Much of the chapter will be concerned with ways we can analyse and appreciate the different contextual factors that play into the policy game. The second thing we note however is that background may also become foreground. Questions of social and economic structure not only shape the work of policy makers, they may themselves be the subject matter of policy interventions.

We can see this double role as we reconsider Anna's IVF scenario. Looked at in its social and economic context the question of assisted reproduction is a matter of medical capacity and personal choice for those women able to get assistance. A contextual, or structural analysis of this policy question would focus upon the way medical research is funded, organized and rewarded in order to see why some therapies become available and for whom they are produced. On the patient or consumer side we would also want to look at the class background of couples seeking treatment, the social and religious norms which make the treatments accessible, together with the ideals of parenthood driving the demands for these services.

What we will tend to find when we tell this story is that the larger elements of the narrative are similar in most Western societies. The medical research industry, the scientific institutions and the private hospital and pharmaceutical industries have a reach which extends beyond any single jurisdiction. This is the political economy of this particular policy field and this is the first part of the context to be understood.

However, in addition to setting the scene in which policy interventions might seek to enact change, the structural context is also made up of actors who react differently in different places. So, for example, while the United States and the UK have the same pharmaceutical companies they are actually different markets. One is much larger and contains more home-grown firms, the other is smaller and has a system of strong government regulation. The same is true of the IVF sector. The same kind of science is practised in each Western system, but in the USA there is a liberal approach to letting wealthy patients seek their own therapy, while in the UK there is central regulation through the medical profession and the National Health Service to equalize many opportunities and restrain some forms of profit seeking.

These various arrangements empower actors differently in each system and give them contrasting incentives to support public interventions. In the UK, for example, the main medical groups are broadly supportive of government regulation, while in the US the same kinds of groups are less willing to have the government set limits or regulate services. This specific context also rests upon a larger one. The way doctors, scientists and hospitals deal with IVF in each country is closely related to their practised methods for dealing with other disputed issues such as medical insurance, subsidized treatment and the role of public hospitals.

In other words, policy-making always combines a certain amount of local novelty together with an inheritance of things filtered down through the lessons of the past. When Bill and his neighbours confronted the local Council over an adverse planning decision they came face-to-face with more than a hundred years of legal precedent and several hundred years of UK private property law. Yet for them this was also an entirely new issue and as such full of possibilities.

In this chapter a number of these structural elements of policy-making are discussed. The purpose in developing this analysis is to provide a guide to the kinds of relationships and processes which typically constitute the context of policy-making. Of course 'structure' as we have seen in the introductory chapter, is a rather large and controversial word for what are often small, subtle practices, customs and protocols. In some ways the term structure is also out of favour in social analysis because it may seem to denote the inevitable, the impregnable or the supra-human. That is not the intention here. There is a world of difference between a position which takes structure as a settled, unified equilibrium of social forces and laws, and one which views it as an historical resultant with dynamic and conflictual properties (Stinchcombe, 1975).

For example, if we consider how education policy is structured we will want to include structures such as budgets for schools and laws requiring pupils to attend. We would also want to include the forms of knowledge that teachers use in the classroom since these too are part of the structural context that will influence policy-making options or outcomes.

In setting out to map this context we need to pay attention to the larger processes of social change which drive advanced capitalist societies. An understanding of social formations would include considering how important social structures impact on the local policy system including:

- changes in the economy
- gender relations
- racial and ethnic relations
- organization of mass communications
- current claims of social movements
- levels of democratization.

These larger pressures have important local effects including impacts upon key policy issues such as the distribution of work and poverty, forms of social exclusion, and the emergence of new demands for participation and protection.

These major forces also help set in motion the historical alignments which shape existing policy alliances and relationships. Each policy field needs to be viewed in relation to this larger macro context. There are no fixed rules about how these larger forces may act upon the local and it is one of the characteristics of policy analysis that it generally seeks to focus attention at the middle level, between this larger stage and the level of individual actors and agencies.

For this reason the bulk of this analysis of context will focus at the middle level, at the level of *processes* and *instruments* because it is here that these larger forces must be played out through actual institutions and decisions (or non-decisions). It could also be argued that it is here that possibilities for action are greatest because local actors have opportunities to link their efforts to the authoritative power of their governments. Naturally this depends a great deal on whether or not these governments are open and able to accept new issues and prepared to act upon them.

The analysis of this local context includes all the territory between large historical patterns and the milieu of episodes involving policy makers. Some cases involve a great number of factors and institutions, others seem to be driven by extremely specific interests and institutions. In some real-life cases such as disputes over departmental budgets, the key decisions may be made by just a handful of people such as ministers, senior bureaucrats and advisers. In others such as a major change in the organization of public schools, the cast may number many thousands

of individuals, including parent groups, teachers and local community groups.

The approach here is to draw a first circle of actors and institutions and then to focus down towards those actors most able to
exercise power. As the analysis develops it will then be necessary
to add a second dimension to this picture so that the full range of
potential interests are acknowledged, not just those who are easily
identified. This second is necessarily a more speculative group but
unless we seek to explain who is missing, omitted or marginalized
from the first we cannot hope to draw out the things which make
the policy context dynamic or conflictual.

This mapping strategy raises a key question. What determines
the boundary or edge of any given policy field? Given what was
said in chapter 1 it is plainly not good enough to simply let existing problem definitions, rules or customs govern the decision.
Problems are usually defined by interests, and often by the most
powerful and persistent among them. Before there is a problem
there are first issues and interests brought to life through their
own histories. And interests are formed in the fire of policy-
making, during the process of contestation over decisions, and
during the process of defining the values which will be debated.
By moving between the level of actual actors and the deep
description of their histories we must identify and interpret
the larger processes driving the policy field. Often this must
include a discussion at the borders where one field meets
another.

Identifying authority holders

A good starting point for the map of the proximate actors is to
identify the sources of authority and the mandate of authority
holders. Authority holders are those individuals and institutions
with a legal right to use public or state power. Ministers have
it, so do civil servants. Courts have it, and so do some
contractors employed by government. Authority is a warrant to
act with the force of law. But not all warrants are of equal value.

Governmental systems are made up of a cascading chain of unequal powers authorized by constitutions, parliaments, courts and regulations.

In Bill's scenario and the case of urban planning which we examined in the previous chapter the authority to grant building permits was invested in the local Council. By law this organization is permitted to allow builders to do some things and not others. The Council may alter the terms of this warrant, but most likely they will have to answer to other levels of government when they set in place rules for the density and style of buildings. For example, they may be prevented from allowing historic buildings, sensitive environments or sacred sites to be built over by new developments. The Council authority is also subordinate to any national priorities enacted by the national parliament.

While it is always defined as a legal warrant, authority is less a fixed quantity of power poured into a mandate, and is more like a negotiated relationship between unequals requiring interpretation and testing. Each instance of authority is a mix of certain rights to act, plus a boundary with more contested issues. Once we see that authority is subject to significant movement and flow, to the process of intra-governmental politics, we can see that policy-making rests not on a fixed foundation but upon an alliance of forces among separate agents who must agree on actions before a result can be achieved. Each attempt to enact or change policy is therefore a means to interpret a prevailing distribution of authority.

In traditional pluralist accounts of public authority such as those of Polsby (1960, 1980) and Dahl (1961) the driving force of action is an embedded consensus handed down by law and precedent. Each new episode simply adjusts this consensus to fit new conditions. If a democratic system of laws can be discerned within this history of agreements then the pluralist will happily accept any outcome which has followed a well-worn path through these institutions. A policy becomes acceptable if it is arrived at through open contest among well-represented, opposing groups. And even if these interests are unequal in their possession of money and other resources, the outcome may be considered democratic if a wider public is seen to take its turn in blocking or supporting a more general system of values through elections, leadership battles and regular opinion-testing by the mass media and other organized interest groups (Lindblom, 1988).

Despite the fuzzy boundaries and the need to re-establish itself through contest or review, authority in most contexts is more or less hierarchical. That is, the right to act is layered into a set of subordinate ranks where those above are able to review and veto the decisions of those below. Participation by ordinary citizens and by non-citizen groups is limited. Even if the ultimate source of authority is the sovereign power of the citizen, in most cases the actual capacity to act is located in agencies and offices that form into different jurisdictions and separate fields of responsibility. For example, in health policy there are national insurance and funding agencies with budget authority, hospitals with authority over the main technologies of the system, and medical professions with authority over the knowledge that is used to drive these other processes.

In order to identify the public policy influence in this health case we need to search for the basic legal *warrant* that links health services to democratic institutions. Public authority is first expressed in a constitution which grants the government of the day certain rights and responsibilities. These include powers to tax, regulate and redistribute certain important goods and services. In addition we may also locate authority in the bureaucratic agencies of government that are charged with carrying out any government decision. This includes agencies required to check the safety of medical practices, regulate the sale of drugs, or train medical staff.

Summarizing then, the territory of a policy field starts with the shape and purpose of a specific kind of public authority. Which agencies or institutions must agree before action can take place? Where are the office holders who can decide on what will happen? Which other agencies of state have the power to block and amend? Who are the office holders whose compliance or com- mitment is needed to assure successful implementation? In answering these questions we find the institutional skeleton around which the muscles of interventions are developed.

Following the money

Intimately tied to the question of authority is the question of policy resources. The exercise of authority and thus the making (and unmaking) of policy always involve the deployment, mastery and modification of some kind of resource base or economy. Resources are both a means and an end in policy-making episodes. They are the tools which policy makers employ; they are also the things which are always in dispute.

When a tribunal decides to award a permit to a developer its decision is backed by legal force. Those who stand in the way of that decision are at risk of action by the police or by the civil courts. These enforcement authorities have the means to impose decisions upon unwilling citizens. The resources being deployed here are human and organizational. The tribunal itself is a resource and so is the permit. One is means, the other is an end, or outcome. When a hospital manager accepts a patient's claim for assisted care, authority is manifest as the granting of a service. This involves certain medical technologies, forms of expertise and particular kinds of financial resources.

Once we have a picture of the authority being used in a particular episode and the resources in play we can begin to search for the patterns which link them together into a system. Systems are interactive processes among common organizational actors which persist over time. They are made up of the regular relationships between authority holders, interests and ordinary citizens. The form which these processes take can vary a great deal. Sometimes systems are very hierarchical. In other cases they are loosely connected networks of different agencies. To understand what is going on and to begin to imagine alternatives we need to know how the character of the prevailing processes pulls different actors into play.

Defining public goods

In each policy field there is a characteristic set of activities undertaken by government. These provide the backbone of the analysis. A common way in which economists and others have sought to distinguish the norms that are unique to public policy is through arguing that the key to any policy system is its role in producing public goods.

To define a public good various writers have pointed out that in every community there are basically two types of needs, those which individuals can meet from their own efforts and those which can only be provided for everyone. For example an individual may choose which food to buy but only a whole community can protect the environment to ensure that the food is not contaminated. Similarly, clean air cannot be provided for individuals for their own exclusive use unless we foresee a world in which people carry oxygen tanks! Much the same is true of water and other important natural resources. A public good is something that is indivisible.

Other things usually added to this list include security, a stable currency and a universal law to enforce contracts between individuals (Samuelson, 1985). Without a central power to provide these things any single individual is prevented from prospering. The point to note about this way of defining the role of public policy is that it is not a principled position but one based on pragmatic considerations. Since clean air is equally needed by rich and poor, by old and young and by those of different ideological orientations, a state role is presumed to be required without need to achieve a more elaborate normative consensus.

The idea of a special group of activities called 'public goods' is often used by economists to support the idea that government 'intervention' in private conduct should only be attempted when markets or individual efforts prove inadequate to ensuring basic questions of human survival or prosperity. In some hands this account leads to the idea of the minimal state, that is, a form of public policy-making which takes every chance to turn responsibility over to the market, the family or other private institutions.

While it is appealing to think there may be a universal proposition like this one to guide all policy-making, in practice the definition of what constitutes a 'public' good is rather more complex than the 'indivisibility' rule suggests. For one thing it may not be true that even these basic needs are indivisible. If rich people choose to live in a part of the city or the country where air and water are clean it may suit them to allow polluters to spoil the environment in other regions.

Equally the ideal of a single security force to take care of public order is fractured when affluent communities build compounds and employ private security companies to police them. Perhaps the same could be said of those countries where affluent citizens choose to hold assets, trade, and plan their future using currencies other than their own.

The idea of public goods therefore rests upon particular conceptions of 'the good'. Those favouring markets argue that efficiency is achieved when most questions of production and distribution are left to the private market (Mises, 1962; Hayek, 1935). These accounts use a rational choice framework to justify the idea that individuals make better choices than governments. A counter-case is put forward by those who argue that efficiency of production is not the criterion to use in deciding whether public or private control is the optimum method.

They point out that equity is just as important (Goodin, 1996; Lindblom, 1988; March and Olsen, 1989). Without the state to even out the effects of markets, individuals will be excluded from participation, even in notionally private acts such as the purchase of food. Obviously this does not mean that governments must therefore go into business growing fruit and vegetables. Instead the equity principle might be honoured by the state granting income support to the poor, by giving them food stamps or by regulating the price of basic commodities such as medicine, bread and milk.

A further development of this argument also supports a wider definition of public goods. Even in cases where the private market dominates the production of a valued good or service, and does so efficiently, the particular cost structure or ownership pattern in that market may lead the firm to prefer fewer sales at higher prices rather than many sales at lower prices. An example would be the provision of telephones to individual consumers. If a profit-driven organization took a rational decision about the best way to sell telephones in a large country such as Canada they might well decide that it was not worthwhile to run cable to far-flung provinces and communities. In strictly economic terms this investment could not be justified by the prices that could feasibly be charged, since ordinary citizens would be unlikely to be able to afford thousands of dollars for each phone bill. The market would fail to deliver service to these people at an affordable price. While this may be an acceptable outcome if what was being produced was BMWs, it may not be acceptable for such things as electricity and roads.

This reasoning leads to the conclusion that there are imperatives for government involvement and thus for the development of policy interventions. A provisional list should include:

1 *Indivisibility*: goods or services that can only be provided to whole groups rather than individual consumers (e.g. public parks);
2 *Administrative ease*: goods and services which if funded on a fee-for-use basis would impose heavy administrative costs (e.g. a system in which all roads were private toll roads);
3 *Common pool resources*: goods and services where individual profit maximization will necessarily lead to all being worse off (e.g. fishing stocks, irrigation water).
4 *Cultural goods*: activities which if left to the market would lose their cultural character as a result of foreign ownership or the dominance of overseas technologies (e.g. film and television).
5 *Equity goods*: goods and services which if provided only on a fee-for-service basis would reinforce serious inequality (e.g. medical treatments, education).

It will immediately be obvious that there are different criteria at work here. In some cases public provision of a good or service is preferred because public policy is seen as more efficient than private provision through the market. In other cases the resort to public provision is the result of market failure, as in the case of monopolies and the potential for exploitative behaviours. In a further set of cases goods are seen as part of the public realm because this is the only place where an equitable outcome can be guaranteed.

While these principles appear to suggest that a universal criterion can be applied to the definition of public goods, in practice countries have developed quite different mixtures of public and private provision in most areas. In some countries the mass communications system is viewed as a vital part of the public sector and so a major investment is made in public television and radio. In others this concern about culture is not expressed through the mass media but through the funding of alternative forms of cultural production.

So while we seek principled justifications for why this or that activity is left to private choice or is brought under government control, these are always filtered by local traditions and preferences. These develop over time and reflect the success which interests have in getting the state to assist them, or in preventing state action from limiting their opportunity to make profits.

In mapping the context of any given policy it is therefore important to identify which issues have traditionally been viewed as the realm of the state or the prerogative of the market. How settled are these boundaries? To what extent have new pressures or new opportunities opened the way for this boundary to be realigned? A good example of the movement that has taken place along this border is electricity generation and retailing. Many governments took over the electricity supply function in the early twentieth century because the available private companies could not assure a comprehensive service to all citizens. Once electric power came to be seen as an indispensable part of modern life the state was drawn into the provision and regulation of the whole service. In order to gain efficiencies and relieve budget pressures many of these same governments moved to privatize these services in the 1980s and 1990s. This produced very large dividends and helped these governments deal with pressures to raise taxes or manage large debts. However, it also reduced the capacity of government to restrain prices or prevent excessive use of electric power.

In places like California this provoked a serious crisis in the supply of power and in the prices charged to households. In neither case, the switch from private to public, or the switch back to private supply, could one say that the rationale was so over-

whelming as to disavow alternatives. Rather the more general issue
was managed well or badly in each context depending on exactly
how governments balanced the competing pressures.

Locating policy instruments

Having identified these major allocations of resources and
authority to public goods, the analysis of contexts then must
examine the instruments being used to produce outcomes. What
is a policy instrument? In order to influence any outcome governments must develop practical methodologies for getting actors
to cooperate. Each local system will use one or more of these
instruments to organize itself:

- claims of entitlement
- rules about who is to be assisted
- protocols concerning the repertoire of assistance to be
  provided
- programme rules
- funding guidelines for agencies providing programmes
- budgets for providing those services
- contracts or partnerships between agencies
- procedures for termination of assistance
- provisions for appeal or review
- laws regarding accountability.

In the IVF scenario Anna and her board combined a number
of these ingredients. The board was charged with providing the
regulatory role. The demands driving the system were coming
from couples and individuals who believed they had a right to
parenthood and this included many groups not previously viewed
as having such a 'right' including older couples, homosexual
couples, single women and those with disabilities. The services
themselves were directed first of all at married heterosexual
couples with infertility problems. The first systems of service provision therefore created rules which reflected this type. Within a
short period of time the various anti-discrimination codes from

other policy jurisdictions were brought to bear on this field in order to widen the definition of who was to be assisted.

The small number of scientific teams working in the IVF area quickly developed protocols concerning the best way to provide this service. Screening tests soon became standardized and scientists shared information about how to harvest eggs from donors, how long to grow embryos outside the body before implantation, and which methods of storage were likely to deliver highest yields. This in turn helped systematize the process for treating patients and for managing the early stage of pregnancy.

The first successful pregnancies in Australia and the UK were achieved with the help of scientific research funding, but within five years these services had become part of the national health funding in these countries and were being performed in public hospitals. These budget rules establish what hospitals may charge for standard procedures and who they may assist. These guidelines also include specifications concerning the drugs that may be provided to stimulate and assist the artificial creation of pregnancy and childbirth. Within these same hospitals the total budget for services had to also be prioritized under national funding guidelines. These require the hospitals and regional health services to which they contribute to meet targets for a range of services. So IVF must be fitted into a series of target categories each of which has strong claims on the budget.

While the IVF programmes are often run from public hospitals because it is here that the strongest links exist with the medical research community, there are also private clinics in this field. They provide alternative means for couples or individuals to obtain services, usually requiring them to pay for all or part of this from their own resources. Contracts for the supply of these private services also exist between private and public agencies. Research institutions typically sign agreements with public and private hospitals to assure access to patients, theatres and nursing services, or to allow research to continue once more experimental services have been mainstreamed. These agreements cover issues of payment of scientists and clinicians, intellectual property rights, ethical treatment of patient data, ownership of research results and access to facilities.

For every rule governing access to a service there is an implied or actual convention for the exclusion or termination of such services. In the IVF case this has been a dynamic and evolving question. Homosexual couples have challenged the rules excluding them and a number of successful procedures have been performed for such couples and for some individuals. The age constraint on women bearing children has been more widely observed in most systems, although at least one case has been recorded where a private Italian clinic assisted a woman in her mid-fifties to have a baby. Hospitals and individual doctors have continued to advise such patients that the risks of failure are too high and thus to avoid treating them. However this is less a rule than a fragile convention which could soon collapse in the face of complaints of age discrimination or improvements in techniques for older women.

The regulatory part of this system is managed by Anna's small team at IVA. They review standardized applications from clinics wishing to treat women using IVF techniques. They supervise the disposal of unused embryos and oversee research arrangements involving human subjects. These too require set protocols. Their policy provides penalties for clinics that perform procedures which have not been approved but their greatest power is to revoke the licence to operate, to restrict procedures to a limited range of cases, or to instigate reviews of activities inside clinics. Given the controversial nature of the procedures and the close media attention they receive, these relatively straightforward powers tend to be multiplied in their effects because clinic credibility, medical indemnity insurance and funding from research authorities can easily be influenced by a bad report from the regulator.

As we have seen, the main external instruments of significance include national legislation to outlaw sex and age discrimination, and medical ethics permitting clinicians to promote their patients' individual interests against those of broader public policy. These legal and clinical constraints establish new pathways into services or widen the interpretation of who may be admitted.

Finally the checklist of instruments must include those which establish the accountability of the service. In the IVF case there were several of these. Parliament had responsibility for scrutinizing these public expenditures through its committee system where bureaucrats and ministers were regularly required to explain the purpose and impact of programmes. Hospitals in both Australia and the UK were also required to submit annual reports to the Department of Health explaining how resources were allocated and showing how targets or performance objectives had been met.

Inside hospitals and public clinics the practitioners were obliged to submit plans for their activities, indicating the numbers to be treated and the procedures to be used. In some cases this also involved the nomination of numerical targets or Key Performance Indicators (KPIs) to give outsiders a means by which to judge the success of the programmes. These involved such things as the number of successful pregnancies, the per unit cost of treatments and the level of patient satisfaction.

Identifying power relationships

Having identified the main actors in each context and having developed a map of the key instruments being used to allocate resources and attribute value to programmes, the analyst is in a good position to make an assessment of the power relations in the policy field. While this is always a matter of interpretation, power is so important to the understanding of policy-making that we should not avoid drawing some conclusions about its effects just because it remains a very difficult thing to measure with any precision. If power means the capacity to act, to have others act on your behalf, and to influence behaviour in order to achieve a desired end, then policy is always an exercise and an artefact of power.

To see how the map we have developed thus far can be used to identify key power relationships we first need to cluster actors around the key instruments already identified. Who controls the definition of policy objectives? Which groups or interests channel clients to services? Who controls service agencies? Which actors play the key roles in regulation, accountability or appeal?

Within the service delivery part of the policy context we can usually 'backward map' the normal processes for delivery of a programme. So in the IVF case the infertile couple attend a consultation with their general practitioner (GP) where they are told that conventional methods of conception and pregnancy are out of the question. This makes the GP's relationship to the patient the first power dimension in this case. It is however a power exercised only at the case-by-case level.

The GP tells them that she has just read a journal article showing that trials of new IVF methods would fit the conditions the couple is experiencing. This shows the power of the research clinic and the scientific communication system to shape the behaviour of the GP. This form of power clearly has potential to raise expectations and increase demand for services, but it is less effective as a means to influence who should receive such services.

Furthermore the GP tells the couple that some of these procedures are available as part of the national health insurance scheme and so would cost only a few hundred dollars. This step shows how public fund holders have power to allocate access to services through their budgets.

This outline shows one path through this local policy system. Further paths can be added by examining the role of large pharmaceutical companies in funding and retailing the drugs needed to perform these procedures and by tracing the ethical debate among religious leaders and lawyers concerned about the creation of life by artificial means. And in addition to looking closely at the mandate of Anna's institution, plotting the regulatory path will also include an examination of the rules of the health insurance companies, the official attitude of the board of medical ethics, the law regarding parenthood and adoption, and perhaps the funding rules and budget protocols of public hospitals.

Finding sources of coherence

So far we have considered these various context dimensions as separate elements of the puzzle. The last important dimension to be added is the form of *interactivity* in the policy system. What institutions, practices or power relationships bring the different parts of the context into some level of coordination or self-development?

There are a number of recognized sources of integration of policy actors and institutions into a more or less coherent whole:

- a dominant profession
- an agreed technology
- government regulation
- consultative institutions
- joint funding arrangements
- external threats and crises.

Amidst the normal chaos of citizens, associations, firms and government agencies struggling to provide services and goods it is often difficult to see how any form of coherence is achieved. Indeed it is precisely the fact that these multi-actor systems undertake very complicated roles that policy analysis needs to spend considerable time understanding the nature of relationships.

Professions are one of the most important sources of relationship across policy systems. Members cross the borders of different agencies and bring to bear a knowledge base and set of interests which are more than those of the current employer. Where a profession holds a dominant position in the service delivery system this ability to bring coherence can also generate potential problems for other policy makers since such a profession will be in a prime position to impose its will.

Professions are in fact a mix of devices including possession of a common knowledge base, recognized standards of practice and codes of behaviour. The agreed technique or technology of a profession is also a device in its own right, since many other instruments are linked to achieve it. For example one of the things that creates coherence in the education system is the technique of dividing students into age cohorts and then into subject specializations. By gaining agreement across the system about these basic methods of managing the total population of students, educators give themselves a powerful common platform. Other common technologies include certification of who can work in the system, pay and promotion systems, information gathering systems and standards for assessing both practitioners and clients.

The regulatory devices and instruments developed by government are undoubtedly the primary source of cohesion in most fields. In fact it often makes no sense to think of the system as a system except that government is involved in regulating various activities and, in so doing, brings the various actors together. For example it is difficult to imagine that the various interests involved in the transport policy field would be aware of one another or likely to cooperate if governments did not force car manufacturers, bicyclists and train operators to consider options of highway design or petrol pricing.

In many cases these regulatory interventions by government result in the creation of formal consultative bodies such as ministerial councils, national advisory boards and participatory planning authorities. These have significant impacts in drawing actors together, establishing a common language for discussing problems and creating incentives to negotiate policy outcomes.

The most structured of these arrangements are those which involve joint funding of programmes or initiatives. Here we see government agencies at different levels of the system joining forces to produce programmes. This may also involve participation by firms or community groups. For example a number of initiatives to provide employment opportunities for disabled people use these joint contribution systems. The result is a more densely connected set of actors and a greater likelihood that policy priorities will converge as these actors find common interests.

The final two sources of cooperation – threats and crises – are far less open to engineering by policy actors (Kingdon, 1984). Yet it is important to identify the way such events galvanize the system and grant key actors opportunities to establish priorities and common outlooks. Economic crises generally have the effect of forcing key actors to rally around an agreed programme of action to fight off the threat. While there may be serious differences of view concerning the proposed solutions, once the debate has been aired there will generally be strong pressures for actors to agree to a package of reforms. Refusing to cooperate will be seen as a want of patriotic commitment. Much the same is true when national disasters strike or when serious military threats are manifest.

Obviously there will be opportunities for key actors to manipulate the terms of such crises and even to manufacture a sense of urgency or panic in order to reap the benefits to be had from this tendency for a crisis to generate converging pressures and common policy strategies.

The context as a 'system'

Beyond a few coordinating instruments and pressures of the type discussed above, what can be said about the systemic qualities of the policy fields we seek to analyse? To what extent do enduring power relationships and standard practices produce an overall system of effects? This concept of the 'system', raised in the last chapter, can now be made more explicit. There are many different uses of the systems idea in social analysis and in common language. To some writers the system is a firm, concrete structure which determines action within a whole field. To others the systems concept really only signifies a process of generalized and continuing interaction between individuals. Each of the theories we reviewed in chapter 1 produces a quite different account of these larger structures of influence we are calling policy systems (Lane, 1993; Considine, 1994).

David Easton (1965) pioneered the application of systems theory to Western politics. He used a simple concept of the system in which politics was viewed as a 'conversion' process for turning inputs (demands) into outputs (programmes). Like a biological organism, the political system was thought to interact with its environment in a continuous struggle to adapt to new pressures and opportunities. He called this a 'dynamic response model of a political system'. The chief attributes of the system Easton describes are environmental pressures and threats, programme responses, information or feedback, and effective adjustment.

For Easton the intention in defining politics as a system was to show how authority holders and citizens interact in standard ways. His account rests 'on the idea of a system imbedded in an environment and subject to possible influences from it that threaten to drive the essential variables of the system beyond their critical range. To persist, the system must be capable of responding with measures that are successful in alleviating the stress so created' (Easton, 1965:33).

The Eastonian system had much in common with the systems account provided by Talcott Parsons and his followers (Parsons and Bales, 1956; Parsons and Smelser, 1972). They too considered the primary virtue of systems to be their capacity to adapt and survive in the face of external pressures. Parsons gives a more general account of all human systems and defines them as having four common functions – adaption, goal attainment, integration and pattern maintenance. Adaption is the task of negotiating with the environment. Goal attainment involves mobilizing resources in aid of a defined purpose. Integration is the function Parsons defines as control and coordination of the different elements which make up any complex human system. Pattern maintenance is his word for the means used to motivate and mobilize actors to achieve common goals (Parsons and Bales, 1956).

These standard works display a particular approach to the use of the systems concept which should be distinguished from the conceptualization being used in this book. Where they use systems to define functions, we use them to identify processes of interdependence and self-organization. We will not assume that these activities produce a 'balance' or equilibrium among actors and interests. The Eastonian and Parsonian systems prove to be too rigid for explaining policy episodes for three main reasons.

First, the idea that policy success is in some respect a function of the matching of internal activities and what an external environment may dictate is highly problematic when applied to human conduct. Political systems are not whole living things which obey a central, hierarchical intelligence in the manner of an organism or a computer program. Therefore any discussion of the way systems respond to pressures must be broken down into more specific terms so that real actors can be identified. Second, the notion that systems seek their own survival is tautological.

Since there is no functional equivalent in politics to the organism's need to find food, shelter and reproduction, the attribution of 'goals' to human systems is problematic.

The fact that the health system survives over time does not imply that it obeys some natural survival instinct or method of adaptation the way a plant might adjust itself to different weather conditions. Actors within a system of relationships may seek to preserve certain aspects of those relationships, but the system itself is merely a resultant. Systems do not have goals, thoughts and strategies. These are properties which actors have. Systems are the patterns of interrelationship between actors and these emerge from actual conflicts and disputes, both internally among different parts of the whole, and between any one system and the others around it.

Third, it is misleading for the systems concept to be used as a code or disguise for assumptions concerning social equilibrium. The Easton model and its Parsonian cousin suggest that system survival results from the possession of successful methods for balancing demands and outputs (Lockwood, 1956; Burrell and Morgan, 1980). According to these standard models the political process merely converts these ingredients, it does not create them. However there is no particular reason why political systems might not display quite radical forms of disequilibrium, upheaval and disorder. The fact that actors are dependent upon one another in some way should not be taken to mean that there is harmony or balance in the effects of this dependency. Indeed, where dependency is based upon scarcity one might logically expect the system to encounter persistent conflict over who is to benefit and who is to pay.

Why use the system concept at all if many of its original proponents provide such flawed accounts of what really constitutes a social system? One obvious reason is that we always need a concept which can express the fact that policy is often produced through patterned, path-dependent activity among a complex of actors. In this simple sense the idea of a policy system is opposed to any analytical frame that presumes complete openness or chaos. It also rejects the idea that most policy results from chance encounters and from encounters among actors who are innocent of history. Therefore we need a theoretical frame which can cope with the idea that individuals and institutions have historically developed processes for guiding their actions and thoughts. These are often located below the general level of the society as a whole, but above the level of individuals making personal choices. So the idea of a 'policy system' provides a middle-level generalization for a given institutional field or social sector.

This usage is consistent with the way those inside the policy process often understand their world. They speak of the health system, the education system and the transport system. These descriptions imply several important things which we may use to develop policy interventions. For instance the education system in a given country is made up of:

- schools and universities
- teachers and other officials ranked according to task
- students divided by age and programme
- laws governing rights and responsibilities
- financial arrangements
- ideas and customs concerning the purpose of programmes
- community expectations in regard to outcomes
- power relations between these different actors.

This set of arrangements endures over time and develops its own character. The organization of the education system in a given country will be seen to differ from the organization of, say, the welfare system. Both the authority and the key resources will be arranged differently. To break these complexities down into manageable analytical categories we therefore started the chapter with an analysis of these middle-level clusters of goods, pro-grammes and actors. The first questions were about what kinds of goods and services are characteristic of the policy field being analysed? This was seen to involve a certain limited mix of policy instruments. We then sought to analyse how this cast of actors and preferences might be constituted as power relations in which dif-ferent actors exercised influence in different parts of the system. And then we noted that such effects could be magnified where certain coordinating devices were present, including several ways in which different actors and interests could be drawn together to develop well-understood expectations of one another.

Finally we have raised questions about the way these various levels of engagement produce systemic effects, that is, effects which express non-trivial dynamics that are recognized by the actors involved. At its most extreme level the notion of 'system' suggests a level of self-production in which a policy system is capable of supplying most of its own means of intellectual and material survival. This idea of self-production can also include the notion of a system being self-referential, or capable of generating its own internal standard of what is good and what is to be valued. In this sense all material systems are capable also of generating a central value by which they organize the boundary between themselves and other systems. Luhmann (1984) has made such a claim for the legal systems of advanced societies because they do not 'import' notions of what is appropriate from outside, but generate their own definitions of what is legal or illegal.

This question of the source of coherence or 'system-like' character is important for those involved in interventions because it calls into question the main ways in which a system can be structured. For various reasons we cannot afford to assume that coherence is due to a general 'unity or purpose' or agreed goals. Yet we often find systems working in a more or less coherent way, even while major differences seem to bedevil the different parts of their roles. It is often the case that systems have a kind of poly-contextuality (Stichweh, 1999:135).

Take a hospital as an example. The formal context is made up of board members, government funding departments and insurance companies. However the internal parts of the hospital each have contexts of their own in addition. Professional groups provide different points of reference and possible coherence for nurses, accountants, radiologists and surgeons. Theorists speak of the distinction between the medium and the form of the system – the medium being the stock of symbols and relationships which define a system, and the form being its internal organization (Baecker, 1999).

Why does this matter? One reason is that, as we saw at the beginning of the chapter, the macro-context for policy is undergoing a major transformation. This raises questions (and new possibilities) about systems we have been used to taking for granted. It may no longer be the case that terms like 'hospital', 'university' or 'welfare agency' refer to a common medium, or a similar form. Some may retain the same internal form but be recast in the medium to which they relate. Some may stay in the same medium and undergo diverse changes of form. While there are several theoretical debates about these issues of form and self-reference, there is also an important sense in which the questions themselves are important to how policy systems may be better understood and, once understood, improved.

4

Analysing Policy Values

In 1997 the managing director of the International Monetary Fund (IMF) went before a major United Nations committee to announce a significant shift in policy towards countries requiring financial aid. A new protocol called 'Good Governance' informed governments around the world that future financial assistance from the IMF would henceforth be dependent upon them adopting new values for structuring their public sector activities and their roles in stimulating their economies. The stated motive of the new policy was to address the 'contribution that greater attention to governance issues could make to macroeconomic stability and sustainable growth' (Camdessus, 1997:1–3).

Central to this strategy was an explicit goal to 'limit the scope of *ad hoc* decision making, for rent seeking, and for undesirable preferential treatment of individuals or organisations'. The norms or values being advanced by this new policy included reference to other jargon terms such as greater 'transparency' in government dealings with citizens and firms, 'free and fair market entry' for corporations, and public enterprise 'reform'.

Within these simple objectives lay a major change in the way this important international organization proposed to administer its aid and assistance functions. It also spoke to its intended targets in the language of a particular type of institutional analysis – one based upon the norms and practices of free markets. We can quickly see that this policy rested squarely upon the authority of an agency empowered to redistribute funds from rich to poor countries and on its mandate to manage the new world economy. And nor were the resources in question difficult to identify. Those seeking IMF help were left in no doubt about the 'economic consequences of not addressing these issues' to the satisfaction of those driving the new agenda (Camdessus, 1997:4).

The new policy expressed an important normative move in the IMF's relationships with others. And given that its power structure and authority is based on the willingness of rich countries to continue funding its activities, this value-base was also an expression of the way dominant US policy makers and their allies in other advanced capitalist countries proposed to treat other nations. To make sense of the formal doctrine one needs to look carefully at the complex set of assumptions and expectations about the options available to governments in developing countries.

For example, the policy made it clear that government intervention in the economy was now to be regarded as a 'second best' option to be justified only in exceptional circumstances, and even then to be considered highly problematic. And by using the force of external financial aid as the lever, the IMF position raised continuing doubts about the independent sovereignty of countries receiving aid, moving the balance of power decisively away from local parliaments and institutions and delivering authority into the hands of this and other international agencies. Claims of cultural specificity or unique traditions of governance would now be much harder to make if that meant restricting the power of either local or foreign businesses (Strange, 1988).

Theories and techniques

There have been several different theoretical approaches developed to account for this normative aspect of policy-making. Murray Edelman (1977) analysed what he called the symbolic basis of politics and showed how issues obtain meaning and salience because of the link to structural (economic) interests. Grice (1975), on the other hand, provides a framework for understanding communication exchanges, showing that talking is usually a cooperative effort in which participants come to recognize some common purposes or, at a minimum, some accepted direction. Policy communications can therefore be seen as asymmetrical exchanges in which a dominant participant seeks to lay out the terms and direction of discourse, but must keep other participants engaged for this to succeed.

This constraining and directing role is also present in the approach taken by Rein and Schon in their (1991) notion of the policy 'frame', in Haas's (1992) theory of the epistemic community, Peter Hall's (1993) concept of the policy 'paradigm' and Jobert and Muller's (1987) *'referential'*, each of which acknowledges the link between expressed ideas and dominant interests. A good example of how these ideas can be applied to power relations in a specific setting is Mishler's (1984) account of the language and normative bias in medical communication, a theme also developed by Fisher and Todd (1986). These works show how patients are contained and directed through characteristic speech acts, by use of technical terminology, and by the hierarchical contexts in which communications occur.

One of the most interesting of these accounts of policy values is Sabatier and Jenks-Smith's idea of the Advocacy Coalition Framework (ACF). They define belief systems as the deep structures of policy-making and use content analysis of documents and speeches to measure consistency and consensus in the beliefs of different individuals. They extrapolate from these results in order to generalize about the 'deep core of fundamental normative and ontological axioms that define a person's underlying personal philosophy' (Sabatier, 1993:30). Like the other structural accounts, this one posits a theory of policy in which intellectual or cognitive maps and codes are more or less stable and consistent with political position and with objective interests. The two are parts of one structural account.

Power/knowledge and policy

But the larger movement in social theory which gave rise to the break between such objective accounts and a new subjectivism was provided by post-structuralism (Best and Kellner, 1991; Smart, 1993). The hallmark of this account is the relationship between power and knowledge. Because knowledge is seen as

always constructed through the history of institutions, no
objective claims of truth or validity can be trusted. In particular
the fundamental intellectual nostrums and concepts of modern
politics have their taken-for-granted status removed through a
process called deconstruction. Concepts such as 'citizenship',
'state' and 'market' are disqualified as settled universal ideals, and
no longer have meanings which stand apart from their actual
applications. The history of each concept is instead to be found in
the micro-processes of particular institutions. In many ways this
approach is itself a socially contrived response to the excessive
confidence which social scientists and the social professions placed
in their own principles and programmes during the 1960s and
1970s.

> Given post-structuralism's scepticism about grand theory building
> and the claim of positivistic science to know all there is to know,
> it is not surprising that post-structural work has also tended to
> focus on the mundane, everyday practices which constitute our
> social realities. (Barns et al., 1999:4)

In addition to attempting to launch a critique of other ways to
understand and explain the social world, post-structuralism developed its own object and method. The subject matter is what its
proponents call the 'discourse'. Discourse is a philosophical term
used to describe a formal speech or written exposition of some
important thesis or homily. It retains this notion of a more or less
coherent act of speech in its post-structuralist meaning. The
French philosopher Michel Foucault popularized the term as a
way to show how social knowledge is always bound by a set of
statements used to explain the world in a particular way. In epistemological terms this means that the world of the policy maker
or the citizen does not exist outside the terms which define them
as actors and which give their actions meaning.

A discourse in this sense is a larger narrative used to control
what is said and what is understood about what is said. Action is
therefore first and foremost a linguistic property and other things
such as authority and resources only obtain meaning by being
understood as part of this world of structured meanings. So the
language of policy would begin with a set of terms which first

define what can be called a policy and what is excluded from this realm. But a language is only possible because of the existence of rules or codes to organize concepts and attach values to issues and to the actors being described.

Power is therefore understood as a capacity to act within and on behalf of this established framework of signs and values. According to this approach, power cannot be separated from this local syntax and nor can knowledge itself be free or independent of the powerful logics or rationales which organize thinking and acting.

Unlike other subjective accounts of politics and policy, the Foucauldian approach does not set out to provide a general or universal theory of language and meaning: 'I am a pluralist,' Foucault says, 'the problem which I have set myself is that of the *individualization* of discourses' (1991:54). Instead of a total system of common meanings or laws, he proposes that we look at the specific system of knowledge, or *episteme*, of a period or place in history. And this system is 'not the sum of its knowledge, nor the general style of its research, but the divergence, the distances, the oppositions, the differences, the relations of its various discourses' (1991:55). In other words, not a system in equilibrium, or balance, but a system made up from various disequilibria.

We begin to see the wide scope of discourse analysis when we also appreciate that the post-structuralists use a quite different focus from others in seeking to undertake policy analysis. For them the issue of governance (and therefore of policy) is not simply the conduct of governments and their agencies. Rather it is 'the government of oneself and others' (Gordon, 1991:2) and of the 'conduct of conduct' itself. Apart from being a clever turn of phrase, what does this signify? An example might be the best way to show what is intended.

If we examine the efforts which governments go to in order to meet the needs of people who are unable to gain a livelihood by working in the paid workforce we see that in a given society welfare is provided only to certain groups. The unemployed, the disabled and those of a certain age are deemed entitled to a state pension of some kind. For the post-structuralist the issue to understand here is not simply the payments made to those in need, or the organization used to deliver such payments. Rather the idea of welfare itself is subject to deconstruction. That is, the construct or explanation put forward about the programme by its leaders and participants is broken down into its implicit and explicit components and these are questioned.

Each of the basic conditions or criteria employed by those in power are then open to question and to alternative possibilities. This brings to light the values used to define entitlement. Who are deemed worthy of support and who are excluded? What social characteristics are portrayed as virtuous for both recipients and programmes? This approach quickly reveals that in some systems the discourse of entitlement plays upon the thrift, compliance or industriousness of claimants. In others the language is one of inherited disadvantage and in still others, the threat to social peace is used to justify granting income support to otherwise dangerous classes.

These underlying meanings organize a local power through which pension schemes, payment systems, measures of need and programmes of action by bureaucrats create the identity of subjects – in this case those on welfare. Both governors and governed are described and fixed by these cognitive and linguistic systems. When fitted into an overall account of institutions this leads post-structuralists to generalizations about what they term 'rationalities' of government. Gordon (1991:3) interprets Foucault as follows:

> A rationality of government will thus mean a way or system of thinking about the nature of the practice of government (who can govern; what governing is; what or who can be governed), capable of making some form of that activity thinkable and practicable both to its practitioners and to those upon whom it was practised.

The application of these insights to actual policies involves two different sets of analyses. At the level of ordinary, so-called 'mundane' practice, the analysis of discourse is a powerful method for seeking out the customary or anthropological basis of power. Queues to get food relief, tolls on highways, forms filled out in a hospital casualty department all provide a rich source of insight into the control of populations and the definition of a pro-gramme's real, lived significance for groups of actors. At the larger level these micro systems of signifying the circuits of power may also be used to analyse whole systems of knowledge, such as medical knowledge or a welfare philosophy. But this general level of analysis also brings into question bigger problems for the post-structuralist.

The underlying assumptions of a discourse approach involve certain understandings about how power is used to suborn indi-viduals and define the complicity of institutions to bigger imper-atives. The deliberations and actions of real actors are never more than expressions of an *episteme*, which they do not control and may not fully appreciate. This weakens the capacities not only of ordinary clients within these systems; it also undermines confi-dence in the capacity of practitioners, such as government offi-cials, to do good.

The sword of deconstruction is thus a weapon used with equal weight against the powerful and the powerless. Both are routinely cut by the same language blade in which historical patterns of subjugation underpin programmes and change strategies. Thus the governing mentality, *governmentality* to use Foucault's term, of policy-making is always a matter of deep suspicion and a source of real threats to liberty. The human capacity to reason and delib-erate upon new and better ways to create the future is therefore never free of traps and pitfalls. The only hopeful sign in this analy-sis is the fact that no complete or total ideology is possible. Knowl-edge remains tethered to local forms of power and knowledge, a process Foucault calls 'a complex relationship of successive dis-placements' (Foucault, 1991:55).

Embedded decisions

This cultural analysis of policy therefore turns attention to the methods real actors use to sift and sort the opportunities and threats within a context, and in this process to invent and express their own identity. The solutions to emerging problems are very often pre-packaged before events create the need to act. If this were not so, very little could be accomplished in the complicated and pressured environment of the decision maker. A simple way to think about the strength of a cultural explanation is to look at the different ways individuals might choose to handle the decision to buy a new computer.

A simple version of economic or rational choice would require a careful audit of the various purposes to which the computer is to be put, followed by an objective assessment of the many available models. These would be compared according to a ranking of goals. Cost, speed and memory might rate towards the top of this preference list, colour would almost certainly rate lower down. Quite a lot of time would be needed to learn about the way computers work and to investigate magazine articles and consumer reports concerning reliability, ease of servicing and capacity to handle different software applications. Becoming expert enough to make a rational choice would be somewhat expensive in time and effort.

A different approach would be to do what a university colleague once described as his preferred approach. He has a friend who takes pleasure in working with computers, has an extensive practical knowledge of how they work in academic settings, and who uses them for much the same purposes as himself. When it comes time to buy a new model our decision maker simply finds out what his friend is currently using and buys that. This is not only a reliable short cut, it also provides him with a ready source of advice on how to use applications and sort out minor problems that arise from time to time. This is also a case of networked intelligence where decisions arise from 'know-how trading' among actors in different settings. To work effectively this decision strategy relies upon reciprocity, good will, expertise and trust. Every time this method works well, it reinforces the likelihood that it will be used again as a preferred short cut. The decision is therefore embedded in a set of customary rules that exist before any individual decision is called for.

This approach to decisions depends upon an intricate web of factors which may be invisible if we simply focus upon the moment of choice and upon solitary calculations. We need to treat decisions as part of a longer chain of social relationships and learned methods which come before the decision itself and which persist after it has occurred.

Embedded decisions are therefore structured by different factors to those which emerge from the simple forms of economic choice. They are not irrational, nor are they unreasoned. Rather they obey a different set of principles. Wildavsky (1962:718–19) defines these factors as 'issue contexts' and points out that organizations regularly use such short cuts in responding to new problems. 'Organisations would find life quite unbearable if they treated each stimulus requiring action as something new.' What they do instead is develop a repertoire of responses for 'frequently encountered stimuli'. Much the same logic applies to all forms of expertise. An expert is someone whose training has prepared them to recognize standard diagnostic stimuli and to apply to those facts a patterned response. Experience is therefore condensed into a long history of classification and induction. Engineers attempting to resolve the demand for a clean water supply have at their disposal a standardized framework for assessing the opportunities for building dams, pipelines and treatment plants. So expertise involves equipping actors to bring previously developed solutions and to apply them to each new decision problem.

Of course the virtues of expertise and other repertoires of action are subject to various limitations (Steinbrunner, 1974; Allison, 1971). Since no two cases are ever exactly the same, the expert must adapt a routine to fit new conditions. Essential to the success of this approach is the belief that certain underlying conditions persist in the natural world and in society. But what happens when something new occurs? Either the expert adjusts his or her framework to fit the new conditions, or they try to force an inappropriate remedy onto the problem. Since this happens all the time in most complex situations the expert is also trained to employ standard methods for reasoning about the path towards novel situations.

If it is a scientific profession the rules will stipulate how new facts are to be treated. Are they to be regarded as 'extraneous', as 'background noise' or as 'unexplainable facts', or are they valuable signals to be used to try and generate new theories? And if it is a case of the latter, there will be rules and customs concerning the manner in which new knowledge is to be validated. Most likely the practitioner will have to submit findings to their peers, to have them studied in a laboratory situation and then to have various explanations tested in experimental conditions before anyone attempts to apply them to new cases in the field. Otherwise there is no way of knowing that what takes place is any more than an act of random guesswork or crackpot theorizing.

No matter how detailed are these rules and practices we can quickly see that expertise must carry the weight of its own history. The same thing applies to the routines used by institutions. In seeking to punish the guilty and protect the innocent the legal system lays down certain mandatory forms of conduct for lawyers, police and judges. While no one supposes that these create a perfect solution to what can be known about an alleged crime, the regulation of the courts and the rules governing police work serve to create a standard pathway which is deemed better than any alternative method. We accept legal decisions as valid even if we suspect that many criminals go free. We do this because we accept the validity of the steps along the way.

Culture as constraint

This process of using customs and rules for structuring decisions carries with it the cost of creating a discursive framework which is capable of blocking other facts and resisting novel findings. Techniques and tools may become more powerful than the ultimate purposes intended or sought. The aphorism, 'Give a man a hammer and soon everything begins to resemble a nail' captures this sense of technique-dependence. The more decisions are embedded in such languages, the more we may ask how much is being omitted in order to make the new facts resemble those which initially stimulated the development of the repertoire.

An important result of the questioning of these embedded decisions is the critique of the independence of the decision maker's preferences. Why was the decision a decision in the first place? Were there not many things that might have become the object of attention? Even if we accept that the techniques being used were the best available, we may doubt that there was anything compelling about the goals which started the whole chain of actions to begin with.

Whereas the economic choice model assumes that actors already have preferences before they begin the calculation of possible means to an end, the cultural model puts the preferences back into a social context. Preferences are seen as being moulded by experience, including the experience of decision making itself.

In politics this approach suggests that the goals, wants and preferences of politicians, interest groups and citizens are formed within institutions, not prior to their development. For example, electoral systems do not just take pre-existing preferences and turn them into ballots. They structure what is available to voters and teach them through experience what is 'on offer' at any one time. Similarly, the information which decision makers have available to rank different options is also generated and communicated inside institutional contexts. An electoral system based on proportional representation generates different opportunities for both candidates and voters to that generated by preferential voting. These different systems impose a structure and a history upon any single episode, election or ballot.

> By a political structure we mean a collection of institutions, rules of behaviour, norms, roles, physical arrangements, buildings, and archives that are relatively resilient to the idiosyncratic preferences and expectations of individuals. (March and Olsen, 1984:741)

The building blocks of such institutions are made up of a mixture of elements in each context. Some are more heavily structured than others. Repetition and reciprocity are fundamental to this cultural framework. The more often decision makers face similar choice conditions, the more they will respond to what they learned before. The more often they face encounters with the same cast of fellow decision makers, the more likely it is that they will be able to expect a pattern in their responses or strategies.

The persistence of repetition and reciprocity among those involved in any one episode generates a language by which individuals steer their way through complex challenges. A policy language can therefore be expected in most contexts involving a regular set of actors, including organizational actors. Institutions achieve their coherence through languages and these in turn are made up of categories, boundaries, codes and rules.

Categories

One of the most important ways in which policy-making becomes a cultural rather than an individual achievement is through the use of categories and names. These practices classify and evaluate people and issues. They prioritize problems and then bend attention towards probable solutions. Naming is the surface level at which such systematic practices invest policy environments with meaning. Most organizations, for instance, will have a favoured set of terms which act as shorthand for more complicated events, resources and problems. For example a welfare bureaucracy may develop a habit for classifying their clients as 'poor people'. This suggests that they are individuals who lack financial resources and are vulnerable. Alternatively they may name them as 'unemployed' in which case the attention shifts towards the lack of opportunities in the labour market. Or they might well define them as 'job seekers' and thus focus attention upon their attractiveness to employers.

A useful way to identify such categories and boundaries is to observe the effort that goes into developing, maintaining and modifying them. Election manifestos, statements to parliament and replies to questions frequently show ministers working hard to establish where they stand in relation to conventional boundaries. Often such speech-making is primarily concerned with claiming the authority of customary thought, and far less interested in substantive outcomes. Naming policy problems is therefore a critical means through which actors communicate their expectations. As Edelman (1977) argues, 'the name for a problem also creates beliefs about what conditions public policy can change and what it cannot touch'.

Examining names and categories which are placed around bounded issues is a further aspect of this world of distinctions. By fixing a label, policy makers and the reference groups they wish to address collaborate in signalling the value to be attached to any given issue or problem. As Edelman (1977) points out, the name given to a problem immediately elicits expectations about the causes of the problem and the conditions which can be altered in order to bring about change:

> When we name and classify a problem, we unconsciously establish the status and roles of those involved with it, including their self-conceptions. If the problem is an economic system that yields inadequate monetary and psychological benefits, then the working poor and the unemployed are victims; but if the problem is personal pathology, they are lazy and incompetent . . . How the problem is named involves alternative scenarios, each with its own facts, value judgements, and emotions.

The choice of labels not only signals a positive preference, it omits other possibilities. 'In a situation in which a person is making a public decision about the category membership of an object by giving the object a verbal label, he [sic] is selecting a term out of a set of alternatives, each with classificatory import' (Frake, 1969:33).

Boundaries

Establishing boundaries and giving them names is a way in which actors are involved in 'making up' the policy world (Hacking, 1986). This is undoubtedly one of the most important ways through which cognitive work defines policies. The identification of distinctions between one class of problems or issues and another is historically determined and relies upon accepted exclusions. These structure what might be called the 'cognitive map' of a given policy field. Insiders always know where boundaries lie and where disputes about the edge of one policy system and another will occur. Much of the work done by planning and budgeting procedures, or by accountability rules, involves the setting of such boundaries.

To take a practical example, in some policy systems transport is defined as a separate concern and given its own department or ministry. In others it may form part of an urban planning office, and in still other systems it may be located with environmental services. This is no arbitrary matter. Where it sits shows how it is to be treated, who will get to make transport policy decisions and what form of accountability these decision makers will have to citizens, industry groups and other bureaucratic interests. Boundaries establish distinctions and distinctions direct attention to implicit priorities.

Luhmann (1995) also shows how boundaries enable systems to achieve coherence. In this case the boundary is not just a distinction between one group of problems and another, but between one core value and another. He points out that the legal system organizes itself through a boundary or distinction between what is either 'legal or illegal' and this paramount value enables everyone inside the legal system to make a contribution, whatever other differences they may have. Even more important, the legal system has the monopoly over this particular value, so other systems (the economy, the health system, etc.) can establish a compatible place next to the legal system and without overlap.

This is not dissimilar from Benhabib's (2002:7) claim that 'cultures are formed through binaries because human beings live in an evaluative universe . . . To possess the culture means to be an insider. Not to be acculturated in the appropriate way is to be an outsider. Hence the boundaries of cultures are always securely guarded.'

Codes

When organizational processes or customs work to factor or divide issues and experiences into valued distinctions, in ways which explicitly direct attention to important versus unimportant issues, or desirable versus undesirable behaviours, we observe the formation of larger narratives into codes. Codes are narrative rules that tell us how to notice what is up for grabs. For example, in the most structured cases such as in most technological systems, the code communicates a preferred method for ranking different problems and possibilities. We may observe a national language of symbols concerning citizenship, but then see that in some countries these are coded into ideals about the state (France, Italy), in others into ideals concerning individual property (USA, UK) and in others the code may refer to religious identity (Iran, Israel).

Codes define what is inside the realm of possibility and what lies outside. As Benhabib (2002:15) puts it, 'established narratives in various cultures define our capacities to tell our individual stories. There are only so many ways in which a cultural code may be varied; beyond them, one may run the risk of becoming an outcast or a convert, a marginal figure or a deserter of the tribe.'

Codes are therefore essential to the task of breaking down, or factoring, a complex world into more manageable parts. In any complicated decision context a code is the stage at which actors accept definitions of the kinds of facts to be accepted as relevant and begin to frame an appropriate range of responses. They not only reveal priorities but also impose both implicit and explicit sanctions on those being classified. In other words they perform a pre-evaluation of people and issues by attaching emotions to options. Political commentator Richard Barnet gives the example of national security policy during the 1960s in the USA (Steinem, 1974:136):

> One of the first lessons a national security manager learns after a day in the bureaucratic climate of the Pentagon, state department, White House or CIA is that toughness is the most highly prized virtue. Some of the national security managers of the Kennedy–Johnson era . . . talk about the 'hairy-chest syndrome'. The man who is ready to recommend using violence against foreigners, even where he is overruled, does not damage his reputation for prudence, soundness, or imagination, but the man who recommends putting an issue to the UN, seeking negotiations, or – horror of horrors – 'doing nothing' quickly becomes known as soft. To be 'soft' – that is, unbelligerent, compassionate, willing to settle for less – or simply repelled by homicide, is to be 'irresponsible' . . . it means walking out of the club.

Conventions

If categories, boundaries and codes form the building blocks of a normative world of policy, then conventions create the consequent methods for reaching conclusions about what to do with individual cases. Actors use 'conventional wisdom' to decide whether a given situation requires one form of response or another. Conventions fill in the gaps left by rules and boundaries and provide transportation through the available codes of conduct available in any complex situation.

Conventions are also habits and customs for carrying some issues forward from the past and leaving others behind. The way customary behaviour memorizes the past is necessarily selective and this selectivity is largely the result of a history of pressure and agitation from previous groups of people wanting their needs noticed and of the work of agencies trying to create order out of the potential chaos of unending demands.

This results in great variation in the form which conventions take. The same basic purposes which grow up around similar practices in different systems are mediated and filtered by inherited rules and customs concerning the methods to be used when reaching outcomes. Conventions may therefore be defined as unwritten regulations governing decisions. For example, in processes developed to channel many competing individual claims through organizational systems with limited time, we notice the tendency to use binding decision rules which have no formal status. Hospital admission staff may elect to filter more serious cases and leave less urgent matters to one side. Firms involved in reducing staff numbers often use the 'last on, first off' convention. Like the famous dictum from disaster management – 'women and children first' – such conventions reflect local assumptions about fairness which rest upon custom, not deliberation.

Conventions therefore work to pre-select and structure the focus of attention which decision makers will bring to any given issue. Rarely acknowledged or openly advertised, such selectivity is nevertheless an essential aspect of managing complexity and avoiding paralysis. Conventional wisdom may assist decision makers to manage such imponderable issues as who should be consulted, how much time to spend reaching a decision, what remedies to try first, or when to call for outside help.

Clearly, then, each convention has a double identity. It arises first and foremost as an authoritative practice inherited from previous experience, but it also has a defined status as an answer to present-day circumstances. Between these two aspects of its role the convention is subject to far more interpretation than is the case for formal rules. It may be set aside with fewer risks or threats, and even when it is invoked it is more likely to be a strategic response rather than one that is mandated. Furthermore the key decision makers in a given field may seek to invent such traditions or customs as a means to weave justifications from the past into contemporary events.

Policy languages

As the collective habits of mind reinforce one another as categories establishing boundaries, and these distinctions are linked by codes and conventions, policy-making creates its own language of meanings and signs. Schutz (1953:10) calls these 'a treasure house of ready-made pre-constituted types and characterisations' which turns the variable and the unique into a common language of decision and action.

General social norms may go some way towards providing the groundwork for this language, but in most cases a specific form of valuation will develop. The observer should expect this dialect or vernacular language to reflect the local experiences and histories that are common to the policy environment. There is always some established history in each field that consists of a mix of standard attitudes and beliefs together with particular values and standard responses developed to deal with the issues regularly encountered locally.

Every policy environment has its own vocabulary and grammar. These express a distinctive, if changeable, value structure. Often this is most clearly visible in the jargon and terminology of practitioners. In this sense it often helps to be an outsider for whom words such as 'termination' or 'separation' and 'early retirement' are less likely to be considered as descriptions of the unwelcome loss of paid employment.

We might ground this metaphysical puzzle of different meanings by pointing out that words are part of action. Socially created language embodies many exhortations and social evaluations. In policy terms the most obvious clue to the linguistic ordering of attention is in the prevalence of 'ideas in good standing' (Brown, 1986). In other words, those inside a particular circle will tend to develop an accepted repertoire of both problems and solutions. Often the power of such languages is most obvious when seen in the negative, that is when we identify the 'impure', 'unspeakable' or profane issues and solutions being named in a language.

An example of the emergence of a new policy language is New Zealand's programme of public sector reforms in the 1980s. As a response to various pressures the key decision makers, those involved in the senior bureaucracy, began to shift the key points of reference in all discussions of the role of the public service. Any positive references to 'procedure', or 'public service norms' or 'the public interest' were treated with suspicion and even hostility. Instead a new language of decision making emerged which stressed 'competition', 'structural adjustment', 'rent seekers', 'transparency' and 'outputs'.

These 'ideas in good standing' provided a means for aspiring young managers to recognize the new terms of debate being set by the Treasury and to avoid being stigmatized as yesterday's news. And the linguistic shift also signalled a new attitude to relations between agencies and the public service as a whole, with the emphasis now being put upon the autonomy of this new breed of managers to be 'left unfettered', to be 'free of red tape' and to 'get the job done' (Kelsey, 1995). This did not prevent all other views from being discussed but it loaded the debate against them by creating an unfavourable language and frame of reference into which they would have to fit. As Boston (1995:206) put it, 'those who reject the prevailing . . . orthodoxy are at a major disadvantage. For in order to have their views taken seriously they must first demonstrate the validity and coherence of their own intellectual framework.'

In each policy field or system we can observe some characteristic form of language to divide, decide and explain issues. Some
are stronger than others. In a few sectors there are competing discourses, driven by party differences or interest group conflict.
Some persist longer while others are evidently in an almost per-
petual state of flux. For instance in the health field we can trace
a language of doctor autonomy, professional independence and
patient–practitioner rights back over almost a century. Yet in the
neighbouring field of environmental policy a veritable whirlwind
of linguistic shifts and new narratives can be identified from 'pollution control', to 'ecologically sustainable development', to 'bio-
diversity' and 'species rights'.

Institutions again

To summarize these issues, we can now return to the issue of
institutions and look at them from the perspective of norms
and values. When customary decision-making is wedded to actual
systems of authority we begin to speak of the formation of institutions. In discursive terms then, an institution is therefore a
widely accepted treatment of a certain class of problems and
actions. It shows us not only what is to be recognized, but also
what is to be done. And it confers rewards and sanctions on those
involved in reaching decisions and on those defined as subject to
the rules being enacted. Institutions thus have three levels of
complexity – conventional behaviours or habits, special forms of
deliberation and decision, and socially prescribed symbols or signs
of success and failure. Anthropologists provide a rich source of
data about the social role of conventions. Mary Douglas (1987:9)
points out that the group behaviour upon which any society
depends requires that individuals 'share the categories of their
thought' and that these categories basically consist of the means
used to classify and interpret the world around them. She terms
these systematic cognitive processes, and, interestingly, she calls
them 'institutions'.

Institutions systematically direct individual memory and
channel actor perceptions into forms compatible with the

relations they authorize. They fix processes that are essentially dynamic; they disguise their partiality within widely taught principles; and they rouse our support by investing organizations with a defined status. The legal system, the health system and the education system are all examples of such institutionalized conduct. They are more heavily structured by the elements of mandated decision-making, custom and standard operating systems than, for example the transport system or the area of agricultural policy-making.

The degree and type of institutionalization is therefore a key aspect of the 'cognitive map' which filters and shapes the conduct of actors in any given policy system. How much of the traffic in issues and problems are handled by routines? How much is left to individual decision-making? To what extent do rules and strong conventions determine the way key actors interact? Just how regulated is individual conduct, and how much of this regulation is steeped in widely understood practices? These are questions which reveal the form and influence of policy institutions.

Obviously the institutional grid, which shapes policy-making, begins at the macro level. Constitutions establish formal relationships between legislature, executive and judiciary. Electoral systems place parties and interest groups in specific relationship to one another and the public. Systems which rely upon proportional voting will encourage different approaches to the stimulation and settling of policy debates than systems relying upon first-past-the post, or preferential voting. These arrangements lead to the formation of coalitions or single party governments, to consensual policy-making or strong party mandates. In other words they not only lay tracks for policy makers to follow in seeking to have issues decided, they generate different incentives for raising certain kinds of issues or for leaving other matters aside.

From the analyst's point of view, discourse is therefore a key building block in the structuring of a policy context. From an intervention perspective the mobilization of support is first and foremost an organization of words and a building of categories, new terms and imagined benefits.

5

Analysing Policy Discourse

As we have seen in the previous chapter, policy institutions are the layered histories of certain forms of received wisdom, cultural inheritances and locally developed short cuts. Such normative issues may cross boundaries between linguistic local systems and become part of the cognitive map of whole political cultures, as in the case of neo-liberalism in the 1980s and 1990s, or Keynesianism in the immediate post-war period (Benhabib, 2002; Edelman, 1977; Rose, 1996). It may even be that such norms underpin the very idea of politics and policy that make it possible for conduct, manners and an intellectual framing of issues to bring questions onto the political agenda in the first place.

But there is considerable dispute in the policy research literature concerning the exact status of these various filtering mechanisms and intellectual structures in shaping decisions and framing problems. For some writers in the post-structuralist tradition the emphasis is upon dominant discourses which explain the web of values and institutions that define attention and preferences. Nikolas Rose (1996:37) puts this most forcefully with the claim that 'in the name of national and individual prosperity, an "economic machine" has taken shape . . . through implanting modes of economic calculation.' This rather all-controlling calculus is seen to manifest itself in private and public life through 'techniques of advice and guidance, medics, clinics, guides and counsellors'.

But for others such as those in the rational choice school, ideas are important mainly in establishing preferences at the outset of the policy process. After this the normative domain refers mostly to the willingness of actors to compromise and bargain with competitors. According to this rationalist account, the trade-offs and bargains are learned incrementally and then revised in the light of each new encounter. In one version of this Axelrod (1984) accounts for the way people learn to cooperate. In each encounter, according to experimental results, they will assess whether or not the other person has assisted, acted neutrally or been damaging to their interests. By applying the idea of 'tit-for-tat' the potential cooperators will find that working together is usually more rational than being in dispute.

Others working from pluralist assumptions take it as given that elites will tend to develop shared 'road maps' or focal points, but these only involve the 'rules of the game' and not substantive issues of 'the good' or the general will. For pluralists the liberal idea of individual difference means that policy is only ever an approximation of 'least worst' outcomes and compromises among different interests (Dahl, 1982).

For the analyst seeking to understand and map the normative issues in policy-making these theories appear to be exclusive claims – that is, they cannot all be true. Rather than attempt to decide this matter on the basis of theoretical argument (for example, by comparing the consistency and sophistication of argument) the approach here will be to remain open to the possibility that ideas are a powerful source of pre-structuring of both issues and options, but to see what that means in practice we need to leave the *extent* of such structuring to empirical investigation.

To establish the existence of hegemonic intellectual systems, including a shared language and coding frame for policy-making, one would need to see common assumptions and valuations spread among the wide variety of actors able to influence outcomes. For example, in policies enacted in the transport field in the US in the 1980s one can see a wide agreement on the virtues of a new paradigm called 'deregulation'. Economists, consumer groups and airlines converged on a set of values and initiatives to do with reducing mandated airfares, opening access to restricted interstate trunk routes and a more flexible use of 'hubs'. But this consensus could not have been deduced from a reading of the history of policy-making in this field. Instead it emerged from competitive pressures within the airline industry, changed technologies, and pressures on government to reduce regulatory costs.

In assessing the form and impact of such cognitive or discursive structures we obviously face a number of methodological and epistemological challenges. The first relates to the extent to which we rank such arrangements as a source of system coherence on a par with, or more important than, material and legal arrangements. The further we go towards theories which attempt to encompass all action and perception as parts of a single mindset, the more we call into question the 'knowability' of such arrangements. In other words we call into question the possibility of there being an 'outside' person capable of knowing what those inside a system know. Since policy analysis is itself a form of cognitive mapping, we cannot be free of our own cognitive filters and embedded preferences. This reduces the value of truth statements to one of comparative advantage rather than one of objective certainty.

On the other hand, if we choose to regard perceptions as more or less visible elements and variables which have different weights or impacts, it may be possible to apply analytical rules and procedures which improve the reliability and validity of our observations. Those who are not themselves doctors may nevertheless be able to see how medical values influence responses to policy issues. So long as 'outside' observers can justify their assessments by openly linking such conclusions to actual statements by medical practitioners, the content of their training procedures and the positions they adopt compared to other actors, we may accept what is said about discursive practices.

The place and stance of the 'outsider' is therefore of great significance. In this case it may in fact be easier to recognize the discursive work of systems outside our own than to recognize our own position as partial or particular. A neighbouring country has 'unusual' methods for classifying different industries as part of the 'national interest', while we see our own as normal, obvious and even as a model for others to follow. And even when we acknowledge the work of habits, customs and classifications of our own group, it may still be difficult to imagine how it might be different. By their very purpose these discursive forms of ordering things are self-compelling. The task of bringing discursive devices up to the surface for analysis begins by asking questions about the nature of the justifications being used to explain how policy-making takes place.

- What is the problem being named?
- What is omitted from this formulation?
- For whom is the problem a problem?
- Which interests benefit from the prevailing definition of problems?
- Which actors are presumed to be part of this problem?
- How do the names and categories being used direct attention to solutions?
- How are exclusions being explained?

Explaining changes in discourse

A policy discourse acts as both a filter to remove unwanted issues and as a ladder to rank and promote some established account of 'current predicaments', 'emerging crises' and 'unique opportunities for reform'. Individual cases become parts of a pattern, things inherited from the past are grafted onto today's issues. The power of a discursive system is located within this tenacious orthodoxy. We are also aware that such systems of ideas neither float above the world of political interests nor do they remain unchanged by policy conflicts and the battering of new events.

The evident contradiction in a theory of discursive power is precisely this gap between the resistance to seeing individual cases as unique and the tendency for any discourse to alter and shift over time. Without the unwillingness to treat every decision as a unique and solitary problem, any discourse must collapse. There is no short cut if an individual actor, organization or institution determines every problem on its new terms. Classification, codes and the other methods for breaking the unknown down into accepted routines are ways to process many demanding facts and to give decision makers a chance to focus their attention.

Yet we also observe that no two discourses are the same. The Germans treat poverty differently to the Americans and we saw them doing this differently in the 1960s and the 1990s. How then do we account for change? Two general explanations are offered by the literature on the impact of policy ideas (Skocpol, 1996; Rein and Schon, 1991; Braun and Busch, 1999). One of these identifies external rupture, the other looks for the cumulative effects of internal contradiction.

The first suggests that policies exist in a context of 'external' pressures that are never successfully controlled or completely resolved by the discourses developed to explain them. For example the nature of poverty may undergo a transformation if world economic conditions alter. Eventually this will cause a rupture or crisis in the taken-for-granted assumptions of those in the welfare system. Whereas poverty in the 1960s may have been successfully defined as a condition experienced by working men unable to feed their families, the revolution in the role of women might explain why this no longer explains conditions in the 1990s. The same kind of case for 'external shock' might be used in regard to new patterns of immigration, the collapse of the Wall between East and West Germany in 1989, or the emergence of new technologies after the 1980s.

At first the old discourse may seek to impose old categories, to struggle to amend its lexicon but not its underlying preferences, but eventually even the most titanic normative frameworks are forced to capitulate. How this happens and when it happens might depend upon just how well fortified the discourse itself has become.

The second explanation provided for discursive change relates to internal conflicts within the normative frameworks being deployed. Having no objective status as a final arbiter of truth, any discourse will itself contain slides, elisions and silences. By definition the discourse is a selective device for simplifying the world and focusing attention. Facts, events, values and other material excluded or rendered unimportant always hover at the edges of the normative work of the discourse. Proponents of new explanations therefore have a ready source of counter-facts with which to challenge the authority of any accepted account.

Change may therefore occur when such facts are successfully mobilized as an attack on any dominant explanation. For example, the dominating idea of the twentieth century which saw industrial progress as a source of betterment for the advanced societies and which explained the need for large factories and a hierarchical division of labour always involved a class of employees whose life chances were less favourable than those able to own and manage such organizations. Industrial accidents, pollution and the depletion of the natural world were explained away by the industrial discourse as necessary 'side-effects' rather than as important counter-facts. But as these costs began to impact upon industry as forms of industrial disruption, threatened reserves of fossil fuels and a mounting bill for health and safety measures, the internal coherence of this discourse underwent its own crisis. Proponents lost faith. New norms such as 'environmental sustainability' and 'energy efficiency' emerged to challenge the old order.

This process of discursive transformation is obviously a political achievement as often as it is a triumph of learning or enlightenment. There is no guarantee whatsoever that change will be in the direction of improvement. So when a new international economy emerged in the latter part of the last century we also saw the emergence of doctrines based on regional competition, racism and the blaming of 'out groups' such as immigrants or welfare recipients.

A central question in both the theory and practice of discourse analysis is therefore the nature of conflict, including conflict between those who form part of one policy field or institutional system but may have quite different discursive positions. For example, in Britain in the mid-1980s the professions, practitioners and policy makers who made up the child-care sector were riven with important conflict concerning the basic norms of engagement in the child and family support area. What had previously been a system dominated by social work norms and values became conflicted as a result of a succession of child abuse scandals (Hallet, 1989). Key ideas and codes for assessing and treating children using a welfare paradigm were then challenged by law reform, legal aid and bureaucratic interests that favoured minimal intervention. Head of the Family Division at the Law

Commission, Peter Graham, summarized the conflicting discourses as follows:

> The Department of Health was very much on the welfare side. They believed the state should effectively improve the welfare of the child. On the law side we were much more suspicious of the state's powers, in a more liberal or Thatcherite approach if you like ... We believed that families should be left alone whereas the DoH was keener to take a therapeutic approach. (Daguerre, 2000:250)

In this instance the norms being contested included core beliefs about the nature of the problems being addressed, fundamental orientations towards rights and entitlements, and divergent assumptions about the likely effects of any intervention programme initiated to assist those in need.

Consequently, we require analytical tools and methods that enable us to recognize dominant or historically prominent sets of norms and linguistic closures, as well as a means to locate and assess the sources of internal difference which might provide the basis of dynamism and change. While such an approach does not deny the importance of discursive practices, neither does it relegate them to mere effects of other structures. A process of contextualization is required in which both dominant and challenging normative constructs are made visible within a policy analysis.

Rational choice as discourse

An important example of the valuation and identification processes in policy explanations and theories is provided by the rational choice account of policy-making. Here values sit at the top of a sequential chain of deliberations leading to decisions. Actors have preferences that they use to fashion consistent goals. These goals guide a selection of one of several possible means to achieve a valued end. The analogy of the market is always close to the surface in this account of action. For this reason we might also call this an 'economic choice' model. Just as consumers select the best goods to satisfy their wants, so too do citizens and other policy makers weigh and evaluate possible alternatives for reaching their policy goals.

To make sense as a legitimate path to action the rational choice model depends on this hierarchy of preferences, goals, options, evaluations and choices. Remove any one step and a decision is compromised. Actors who do not have clear preferences are apt to lose out. They will be incapable of selecting the best option and thus will bargain poorly and will waste resources. Similarly, if they have goals but do not have a menu of options to select from, they will not maximize their chances of success. And if they have options available to them but make selections which are not based on an impartial calculation of which is best suited to giving a maximum return at minimum cost, they cannot expect to make the most of their opportunities.

This model seems at first glance to honour an objective set of criteria for policy-making. Regardless of the problem to hand, this approach is apparently a robust method for moving towards better decisions. But the model is not without its own cultural meaning system and nor is it therefore free of distinctive bias. This can soon be appreciated if we question the foundation principle of the schema, the idea that all actors have goals which can be turned into explicit preferences. In many cases we find that goals emerge from the decision-making encounters between actors, and do not precede them, as would be required by the model. People learn on the run. Even in the market-place where this model is thought to explain a large part of human conduct we know that consumers may often find their preferences only after goods are presented to them. Advertising companies know this and spend a large part of the manufacturer's budget to prove it.

In policy-making the 'goal problem' emerges as a central puzzle which those in authority must resolve on a continuing basis. Cohen, March and Olsen (1972) show that in many cases solutions go looking for problems to attach themselves to, not the reverse. A policy system which is practised at running tribunals to resolve disputes will look for ways to attach this solution to any new issue coming within its purview. Politicians, bureaucrats and community activists may represent their communities by bringing forward problems brought to them by constituents. But just as often they take the initiative in defining such problems and then spend great effort in trying to convince the public that such issues merit the kind of action being proposed.

A similar problem exists with regard to the requirement that those with preferences should weigh available options without prejudice. A decision is rational if the option selected is the one which the evidence shows will maximize benefits and minimize costs in relation to the initial preference. So for example a decision to create public housing must consider only the optimal methods for giving the greatest number of people the best accommodation available, be that rented apartments, suburban houses or public hostels. However these 'options' are not free of values for both government and residents. The most cost-efficient choice might also be one which future residents dislike for non-quantified reasons. In other words the options in the paradigmatic choice sequence may also generate questions of their own, making it impossible to subordinate them to a single higher preference.

Finally, the rational choice process may simply be too arduous for most decision situations. There may be a lack of time or insufficient resources to create a menu of alternative options to be investigated and compared. The onset of a political crisis can render this process impractical. Or the need to make hundreds of choices each day can easily force an organization to resort to less taxing methods.

These criticisms of the alleged virtues of rational deliberation do not require us to abandon the model altogether, but merely to recognize that it depends upon its own unique cultural context made up of specific assumptions about the identity of 'consumers' of human behaviour, needs and capacities. This contextual frame may be limiting, but it does not follow that it automatically leads us to jettison the approach as false. What might apply easily to the choice made at a supermarket is just not so helpful in the context of many political decisions.

Example: drug discourse in Switzerland

Like most European systems, the Swiss have developed a complex set of ideas and theories to account for their experience of drug abuse. These norms have been the subject of intense conflict,

culminating in significant changes in both norms and actual policies during the mid-1980s (Kubler, 1999; Malatesta, 1993). By the
time the Federal Law on Narcotics was being revised in 1999 the
underlying discourse in Switzerland had shifted from 'abstinence'
to 'harm minimization'. This had its effect upon actual programmes and government commitments in the form of a change
of emphasis away from criminal prosecution of drug users to the
opening of syringe exchanges, safe injection rooms and rehabilitation centres.

Kubler (1999:119) defines the 'abstinence' discourse as one
focused upon the individual responsibility of drug users and the
definition of problems as ones of lack of respect for the law, moral
breakdown and individual weakness in the face of temptation. The
policy response to this language of restraint and rectitude was
therefore one of helping individuals 'back on track, even against
their will'. Public campaigns were used to emphasize the
voluntary option of 'saying no to drugs' and this was reinforced
by information programmes to show that drugs caused harm to
individuals and their families. Medical knowledge and norms were
used to reinforce this perspective, with evidence of physical harm
caused by drug dependence playing a large part in the language
of threats and the moral lexicon of self-harm, personal danger and
risk.

Policing the abstinence regime was also straightforward. Since
individual drug users were defined as harmful to themselves, to
their families and to society, every effort could be justified to take
them into custody, to force them into rehabilitation centres and
if that failed, to send them to gaol. It was also easy to make these
values consistent with traditional religious and moral precepts
which emphasize the seductive effects of sinful behaviour and the
need for wrongdoers to repent or suffer group sanctions.

While it can quickly be appreciated that the intersection of
these political, legal, medical and moral norms helped create a
strong cognitive map to steer policy makers, the discourse was not
unchallenged or robust in the face of external shocks. Internally
the 'abstinence' discourse was only ever as strong as its weakest
link and this was the invidious comparison which libertarians
could make with the treatment of alcohol and tobacco users. So,

while it might be possible to enrol large numbers of people in a discourse of abstinence when that was framed as a voluntary behaviour ('say no to drugs'), this would not be so easy to achieve when the legal consequences of drug use impacted heavily upon private, middle-class users ('criminalization') and non-users caught up in police actions ('repression').

The outside shocks magnified these fissures and inconsistencies in the 'abstinence' discourse. First, despite every effort by police and rehabilitation professionals, illegal drug use continued to rise in Switzerland throughout the 1980s. When linked to the issues of organized crime, youth unemployment, illegal immigration and urban crime, the drugs issues became harder to confine to matters of personal conduct. But undoubtedly the major fracture in the abstinence discourse came with the spread of HIV/AIDS. This disease multiplied the risks of failing to contain or reduce drug use. It created new imperatives to help users to manage their habit in a manner likely to keep the rest of the community from contracting the new virus.

From the mid-1980s onwards, Swiss policy-makers reversed the emphasis on repressive methods and began to embrace a 'harm minimization' discourse. In cognitive terms this placed greatest weight upon the health of the individual user. Rather than defining drug use as an unmitigated ill, the language and norms of conduct began to differentiate between better and worse kinds of drug use. And where policy actions had had the effect of driving users towards less safe methods, the new language adopted a code of 'decriminalization' and health assistance. Efforts to prevent needle sharing and other unsafe practices resulted in a decisive swing away from demonizing drug users and towards treating them as a class of sufferers who posed a threat to wider society not through the spread of drugs but through the epidemic of HIV/AIDS and associated diseases such as hepatitis.

The core of the new discourse was thus made up of a different set of medical categories and codes including the threats of 'epidemic' and 'pandemic'. Instead of defining the user as someone incapable of self-help and therefore in need of detention and compulsory rehabilitation, the new discourse sought to befriend users, to define them as individuals suffering from a disease, and to assert their right to use treatment services, or not, just as others in the community exercise such rights (Kubler, 1999:123).

The two discourses were clearly in competition for a period of time in the middle and late 1980s but it would be wrong to regard them as different ideologies advanced by competing interests. In fact the same sets of actors can be seen advocating abstinence in the 1970s and then shifting ground to harm minimization by the 1990s. Health professionals, city planners, legal aid staff and academic experts adopted the new discursive framework in part because the old one had not successfully managed its own inconsistencies and in part because external shocks rendered it useless. The task then became one of constructing a new discourse out of the ashes of the old. So in addition to seeing their contrasting perspectives we can also observe the points at which they converged. In particular we can see the prevalence of medico-moral judgements about the fate and value of the individual and his or her 'threat' and 'risk' to wider society. Both discourses framed drugs policy in these terms and both privileged the health model of treatment, first as rehabilitation and then as safe practices.

Summing up

Policies and the analyses we produce to explain them are intellectual constructs which have serious material consequences. How we think about a problem, how we name it, whose interests are 'included in', or 'included out' and which solutions are already in the shadows of such problem definition are matters of enormous importance. Just how firm or fatal are such cognitive maps and narratives is a more complex question. In general we know that deep conflicts produce the most intractable ideological differences. But so too do policy systems which are dominant or monopolistic in their reach.

Despite renewed interest in the formative role of cognitive and linguistic parts of the policy process we are no closer to resolving the longstanding questions in this field. To what extent do ideas follow interests? Do norms stand independently of the events they seek to interpret? How much of what we receive from the past still explains contemporary issues and problems? Can actors invent explanations and develop perceptions that break free of contextual bias or preferences?

These questions threaten to undermine confidence in the status of all observations. Since all observers are themselves participants in events they observe, the potential to be caught in the web of norms, signs and rationalizations is high. Thus the paradox of the subjective view of social life is that it renders everything, including itself, suspect. But even in the most radical of the post-structuralist accounts we see various strategies to attach discursive practices to real interests and institutions. This means that most, if not all, such frameworks posit a relationship between the way issues and problems are defined and the actual experiences of people in communities of interest.

Consequently we may view discourse analysis as operating at a number of levels and with different possible uses. For those examining the history of a policy field or institution, the comparison of texts and the self-descriptions of participants suggests a rich normative vein. Insulated from the urgent pressures of decision-making, the historical or archaeological method allows detachment of the observer from the immediate political context of policy. Protection is not so easy to find when examining contemporary episodes, although comparative analysis gives some counterweight against the gravitational pull of any single system.

The use of discourse analysis therefore requires careful methodological or analytical framing before larger claims about causation or inference can be assessed. This includes a clear specification of the sources that are to be used to deconstruct a discourse, the means to be employed to weigh differences within and between discourses, and the status of this subjective data when compared to other important sources such as budgets, legislation, external shocks and crises.

6

Institutions: Elections, Executives and Legislatures

Sitting astride the contextual and normative imperatives driving policies and interventions are the more formal instruments we use to make policy decisions and then to implement them. These usually take the form of public institutions and they are different in every system, including those at regional and local level. Knowing how they work involves learning the rules, but it also means understanding how groups of rules and sets of instruments fit together.

For example, in the Netherlands the means for addressing problems of unemployment include the use of a public agency for helping some clients, several private employment agencies for assisting others, and a complex contracting instrument for working out who goes where (Sol, 2000). In Germany those who are unemployed and wish to get help must first enrol with a national public employment office. In the USA the services are sharply divided between an insurance-based entitlement for those who have been in work, and a minimum welfare payment for those who have never worked or who have exhausted their insurance. And of course, both Germany and the USA are federal republics and that means these services will involve two levels of government and possible variation in different states or *Länder*.

The institutional architecture involved in these different agency arrangements and different governmental levels form a kind of organizational intelligence which enables a society to steer a forward path through very complex individual and group requirements. It also sets up barriers to what any individual or group may demand and achieve (North, 1990:3).

As Genschel (1997:47) says, institutions

> define what actors in certain situations are prohibited to do, and what they are allowed to do. They allocate information, opportunities, and restrictions, and in this way influence the distribution of power and *collective problem solving capacity* of a society. (emphasis added)

Policy-making is therefore a strategy for using these institutions to achieve changes in society, and it is also a process for changing those same institutions in order to direct the attention of actors who come forward in the future. With this in mind the analyst certainly needs to know what the rules say, but also how they are defined and interpreted by the dynamics and culture of the institution and by the intersection of a number of neighbouring institutional practices.

Governmental institutions might be described as the particular framework used to define present and future relations between governors and the governed. At its most skeletal level this involves several different institutional arrangements to deal with selecting representatives, forming governments, establishing law and order, defining citizenship and resolving disputes.

There can be no doubt that the precise form of these arrangements is central to public policy-making. In other words policy institutions are never neutral. Their purpose is to require some behaviour and to prevent others. They not only provide a common track down which new issues travel, they confer advantage on some travellers and block others. Policy analysis therefore needs to pay attention to the *evaluating* role of institutions, to understanding how they invest a certain preference about the conduct of policy actors. This will help us see that institutions have definite design characteristics.

Goodin (1996) points out that the actual process for such design of institutions may be either direct or indirect, but

> the things that contribute to the longevity of any institution and the chances for its successors surviving into the distant future –

those are all things that can and should be subject to conscious
social choice.

Perhaps the most obvious way to explain the work of policy institutions is to use the analogy of the rules of the game. From this
vantage point any institution acts as a kind of regulatory system
and the actors then occupy the rest of the available space, or
conduct themselves freely within that domain. But the game
analogy has some important limits. In particular it draws too neat
a separation between action and the regulation of action. In the
political world the umpire is also a player and the players regularly force the umpire to rewrite the rules.

But at an even more fundamental level the game analogy misses
the point about institutions as 'action channels', the March and
Olsen (1984) term used earlier. Rules of a game generally involve
constraints and only in a few cases do they mandate precise behaviour – the exception being rules about how to start the game or
resume it after goals are scored. But in the action channel idea the
institution actually directs the attention, behaviours or strategy of
the actors in important ways.

The point to notice about this distinction between mere constraints and preferred strategies is that it enables us to include in
our analysis of institutional practices the fact that such customs
involve positive repertoires and rehearsed actions as well as more
formal constraints. Government institutions not only impose constraints on policy systems, they also lay down pathways for action
and send signals to actors about how to move forward. They both
regulate and prefer certain types of change. It is for this reason
that we speak of institutions as having both a constraining and a
steering role, two functions which are not always easy for them
to combine well.

Regulatory and steering roles

The regulatory or constraining role of policy institutions can easily
be seen. Parliaments, political parties and bureaucracies are examples of organizations which lay down strict codes by which actors

engage in decision-making. A simple example of this is the common decision rule used in most public organizations which the law recognizes as *stare decisis,* or the law of precedent. This rule encourages decision makers to decide new cases in the same way that prior cases were decided.

Legal authority, together with power over important resources and some form of organizational capacity, give these institutions the actual tools with which to regulate conduct. For example, to run for a seat in parliament in most countries one has to be a citizen, must be of good character and must be of voting age. Obviously this leaves most of the population eligible to stand, as one would expect in a democracy. The means to enforce these restrictions is typically provided by a formal, written nomination procedure and by oversight of that process by an independent electoral commission or office with the power to check whether what candidates say about themselves is in fact true.

Institutions develop rules in a cumulative, historical fashion using a variety of justifications. As we saw in chapter 5, these rules also involve customary behaviour, or settled expectations that have no formal status but are important to getting things done. Customs are a kind of organized memory through which past insights and short cuts are reused. An example of customs in the electoral system is the practice in places such as Australia of candidates and their representatives standing outside the polling booth in order to distribute final encouragement to voters. Once a few candidates decide to do this pressure exists for others to match them. Once that happens a set of understood ground rules must develop to prevent disputes. These informal rules then help govern the space around the booths and each new generation of candidates are taught the manners or customs appropriate to this social space.

This systemic memory clearly has many advantages. Without it every issue, whether threat or opportunity, would have to be considered afresh and no action could be contemplated until the most basic of decisions about how to proceed had been resolved. In short there would be no established machinery with which to confront current concerns. The more these current concerns resemble previous ones, the more likely it is that custom will grow around the practices of actors.

This set of institutional short cuts and ground rules have their problematic side, however. Because these regulatory mechanisms carry past practice into present circumstances they represent a strong constraint on change. It is often said, in this vein, that military leaders are people who are always perfectly prepared to fight the previous war. Routines work precisely because they create expectations of conformity and restrict the attention span of actors to those things previously found to be appropriate. If circumstances change, institutions may be found clinging to routines which solve problems that no longer exist. If such customs also become embedded in the formal rules, this may slow the institutions' capacity to respond to new conditions.

For example the legislatures in countries like Germany and the USA were developed during periods when inter-state or provincial differences were a key form of social division. The founders of these systems were aware that without guaranteed state or provincial representation the national government would not be capable of generating wide support. The common method for assuring state rights was to use the upper house as a state chamber composed of equal numbers of representatives from each state or province. This meant that these upper houses had a quite different constituency to the lower house. It also guaranteed that the upper house voters were unequal, with small states permitting fewer voters to elect each legislator and thus influence policy outcomes. While this may have seemed appropriate in the eighteenth or nineteenth centuries when communities were small and more isolated, as mass society became the norm these provincial differences ceased to be the major social divisions of the day. But having institutionalized the state electorate it would now be very difficult to change it because all alternative methods would involve new costs and risks for the political elites who would have to agree to such change.

Because they apply a brake to the immediacy of current pressures and force actors to follow established patterns of behaviour, the adaptive skills of institutions are likely to be steeped in tradition. For example, most countries make it difficult to change the national constitution and insist that to do so a variety of safeguards are first negotiated. These procedural rules, such as Articles 79–81 of the German Basic Law, make it clear that the constitution can be changed to reflect new priorities, but in making the process somewhat demanding, they also send a clear message that any proposed change will have to be highly desirable in order to overcome the inbuilt preference for the old path.

In periods of rapid social change these regulatory devices become the direct object of policy change, a practice which institutions themselves are designed to resist, at least in the short term. In other words institutional change is not uncommon but it is rarely the result of single events or one-time actions by actors.

These are some of the general dynamics we look for in understanding the general work of political institutions. Now we turn our attention to the different ways in which electoral systems, elections, parties and legislatures operate. Because each individual state has its own set of such institutions it makes no sense to discuss the policy pathway in each and every instance. Instead we will use the literature and research on institutional dynamics in order to show the role they play in key tasks such as bringing together individual preferences, creating group positions, providing veto points, and authorizing the work of executive government. In the next chapter we will take the same analysis down to the level of courts, bureaucracies and budgets.

Electoral systems

Policy interventions in democratic or semi-democratic systems originate in electoral systems. The history of the regime is deeply inscribed by national ideas concerning the best way to 'empower representatives', 'create national identity', 'prevent factionalism', or 'respect regional differences'.

It is here that social actors seek authorization to use formal public authority to get things done, it is also here that the ideas or discursive work of policy-making undergoes its most dramatic test of support as candidates, parties and mass media all attempt to frame public debate.

The electoral system is therefore undoubtedly the formal institutional framework which has the most dramatic affect on policy-
making. Of course this is also a potentially controversial claim,
given that many electors feel that the mass voting systems of their
countries give little real power to individual citizens. So we have
a paradox buried in the centre of electoral processes: they are
devised to grant citizens ultimate power and also to prevent them
using it in ways that would make the country ungovernable.

The way this paradox is managed will vary in each country. As
Beck (1997:45) has pointed out, Germans, French, British and
American expectations of majority rule are all quite different.
Those derived from the philosophies of Kant will be concerned
to prevent despotic acts by ruling majorities. Those more sympathetic to the ideals of the 'general will' made famous by Rousseau
will expect consensus rather than dissent and disobedience from
majoritarian rule. And still others will follow Madison and the
American founding fathers in seeking ways to create a check on
majoritarian power, while still allowing factionalism to play a role
in decision-making.

Elections and electoral systems use different traditions to focus
attention on alternative policy packages and ideologies and deliver
decisive authority for new plans and proposals. Not all electoral
systems do this the same way, nor do all do these different things
equally well. Some give minorities a strong voice, some allow big
business to dominate campaign advertising, others assist single
parties to win majorities in their own right. Still others require
candidates to seek partners or coalitions in order to be successful.
Each type of electoral system delivers a different set of policy
opportunities and constraints.

Democratic political systems require a specific institutional
method for deciding who shall become the popular representatives, which leadership elite will obtain executive office and what
form of majority will hold power inside the legislature. It is obviously important to think about elections as windows of opportunity so far as policy-making is concerned, for once an election has
been called a wide variety of proposals begin to receive attention
from the formal institutions of government. It is also important
to view elections as forms of issue-structuring, since the type of

practice used to conduct and decide the outcome of the election will influence the kind of policy debate which is likely to take place (Taagepera, Rein and Shugart, 1989).

Electoral systems combine with patterns of social cleavage to produce different forms of representation. These often prove to be the most decisive factors in explaining the policy-making capabilities and styles of the entire system of government. Like all institutions these electoral arrangements set in place patterns which may be quite resistant to change. Lipset and Rokkan (1967) and March and Olsen (1989) point out, for example, that the European parties of the 1960s were based upon the social cleavages which had existed in the 1920s. Similar claims have been made about the Australian party system (Connell and Irving, 1980).

Voting systems

Even though most democratic systems provide for one vote for each citizen, they vary enormously in how that vote is registered, counted and attributed. Some make voting compulsory, some make getting registered quite difficult. Some demand electorates that are of equal size ('one vote one value') while others grant disproportionate value to those in smaller states and provinces, or among indigenous minorities. So voting systems include embedded assumptions about how interests should be aggregated.

In particular, we know that preferential voting causes parties and issues to cluster in different ways to proportional voting systems. Also important to amplifying or modifying the process of issue aggregation or conflict is whether the system has single or multi-member constituencies. And finally, it will be obvious that it makes quite a difference to the policy-making system as a whole whether the length of the term of office between elections is short (2 years in the US House of Representatives) or long (5 years in the UK House of Commons).

The form of representation which an electoral system sanctions always acts as a powerful action channel for the development and structuring of policy issues. Candidates seeking election will always scan their environments looking for ways to build support.

But the type of scanning will reflect the voting system being used. For example social movements will normally find it easier to gain a voice in systems which have proportional representation (PR). Katz (1980) shows that PR will lead to greater variety and to what he calls extremism. He follows Downs (1957) who asserted that parties in a preferential voting system would often converge in a two-party contest with the result that the range of issue differences will contract over time. In these cases parties will have strong incentives to concentrate their attention on 'median voters' who have no firm attachment to ideology or policy and can thus be bought off with short-term election promises.

On the other hand, PR will have a greater tendency to encourage multi-party activity because the method of calculating votes allows candidates to win seats with relatively small proportions of the total, regardless of how the rest of the votes are cast.

Paradoxically, smaller parties may tend to lock up or monopolize the issues with which they have obtained electoral success. They are also vulnerable to the charge that they render the system ungovernable which, as Schoonmaker (1988) has shown in the case of the West German Greens, may lead dissatisfied supporters to return to mainstream parties without a major gain in the policy area at issue.

Another important effect of elections is that depending upon the system used, encouragement is given to candidates to focus on local questions or to ferment internal party differences over policy questions. In the Irish Republic and New Zealand citizens elect their lower houses using a multi-member electoral system, using variations of the STV-PR, or Single Transferable Vote and Proportional Representation forms of voting. This means that a team of candidates is elected from each single district and the allocation of seats is in order of the number of votes cast for each individual on the team. To prevent very small parties from concentrating their vote and winning the last seat on the list, such systems usually have a quota of votes as a minimum before a party can claim its winnings (Weaver and Rockman, 1993:26).

Preferential voting systems allow parties to aggregate the national vote with the use of strictly managed how-to-vote cards.

Individual candidates are therefore dependent on the party leadership for the swing necessary to get elected and to form a government. Stable patterns in the composition of the ruling parliamentary elite are therefore common in these systems and even the use of coalitions is apt to produce quite stable governments.

The ability of party leaders to resist the pressures of key interest groups is also higher in such electoral systems. Median, or swinging voters play the decisive role in determining outcomes and local politicians have little to offer interest group leaders because centralization of the party platform is a precondition for electoral success, a factor which gives control to central party elites. When interest groups become involved in electoral politics in these systems they have incentives to maintain stable, non-opportunistic relations with the party they wish to support. Hence we find unions, business groups and farmers locked in to long-term affiliations with particular parties.

Multi-party coalitions of the European type result directly from electoral systems which reward vigorous competition among several parties at election time. This increases the range of policy issues likely to be promoted by parties and interest groups. It also allows greater shifting of support on the part of interest groups seeking maximum advantage. Since they are unlikely to be punished by a single winning party after the election, these interests will behave less predictably than in the two-party model. Party elites will therefore have strong incentives to constrain their maverick behaviour through the development of corporatist institutions and other means for drawing key interests into a predictable policy-making role (Lehmbruch and Schmitter, 1982).

Election campaigns

The calling of the election gives rise to a special period in which policy is of great interest to voters, competing parties and the media. This is a new space delimited by institutional rules and conventions, which have powerful effects. For example this is a period in which executive control and bureaucratic dominance by the government are temporarily suspended or reduced. Incumbent leaders search for a means to justify their rule and in so doing give special publicity and legitimacy to existing programmes which may have been languishing for lack of interest. They also encourage their staff to bring forward any proposals which they might be able to include in their manifesto, opening the way for hitherto unrecognized issues to receive attention. Such issues can travel very quickly while the system is in the grip of an election campaign, and if attached to a value position which can be made publicly appealing, these new issues may turn quickly into new policy regimes.

The institutional system itself influences the conduct of these campaigns, thereby structuring opportunities for participation and policy effectiveness. Several of these issues have been raised above. Voting systems shape party contests which in turn shape the kinds of campaigns that are fought. Preferential systems of voting for parliamentary representatives encourage aggregation. This creates strong incentives to run campaigns directed at a national audience and to select swinging voters for decisive promises.

Elections alter the opportunities for participation and, for a few weeks, change the relationship between the governed and the government. Depending upon the party system and the method of election, this period may see the mushrooming of new candidates with novel policy proposals, or the boiling down of issues into one or two themes around which two dominant parties organize themselves. This in turn will alter the role of the election manifesto. In multi-party contests some form of post-election bargaining is expected. Promises made during the campaign must be compromised in negotiations over coalition formation and the distribution of ministries. Manifestos or policy speeches are therefore less likely to become an institutionalized part of the policy-making process.

In two-party systems the manifesto quickly becomes an authoritative document which the future government expects to wield in the parliament, with interest groups and inside the bureaucracy. Commitments made 'in the policy speech' therefore take on great significance. Policy actors, advisers and party officials who are able to influence the content of the leader's election policy speech have great, if temporary, power to direct the future attention of the government.

The press and rival leaders will, during this period, take interest group spokespeople more seriously, thus granting a public audience to those who would otherwise be somewhat excluded. Issue constituencies not previously organized may suddenly find the incentive and opportunity to form themselves into pressure groups or action associations. Established organizations also find election time an auspicious moment to consider forming coalitions, popular fronts, etc.

It is obvious that this shifting and reorganizing of the terms on which individuals and groups participate in politics will always have a momentous impact on policy. It has been common to assert that these impacts fall mainly on what is called the agenda-formation part of the policy-making process and there is much common sense in this observation (Kingdon, 1984; Baumgartner and Jones, 1993; Lewis and Considine, 1999). New groups and old ones with new ideas certainly push forward with items or issues which they want addressed. But the chance to get things on the agenda is only part of the opportunity structure provided by elections. This is also a time when administrative issues bubble to the surface, implementation questions receive greater attention and financial considerations are addressed.

Each system has its own rules concerning the calling of elections. The longer the period between elections the less can be expected from campaigns and manifestos. Within a year or two circumstances will have changed so dramatically that much of what was said will be forgotten. Long terms in office are also likely to change interest group behaviour. When the government or president is to be in office for five or six years (e.g. in Britain or France) the stakes are very high and interest groups will need to find other ways to influence policy. Election campaigns will therefore be less important to structuring these relations than in cases where representatives face the ballot every two years (e.g. the USA).

Finally, the electoral system is framed by some institutional device or agency for fixing boundaries, issuing electoral information, enrolling voters and managing the events of election day. The independence of this electoral office is of great significance, as is the mandate established for it. For example, if rules and resources do not empower this office to actively recruit all potential voters, elections will be decided by those already well organized in a given society. And if the rules do not require constituency boundaries to be fixed impartially, various forms of malapportionment or gerrymandering may occur.

These arrangements, starting with the voting system and running through to administration of elections, all contribute to a characteristic form of responsibility among citizens and candidates, ranging from low turnout and scepticism found in the USA, to high turnout found in France. Plainly these forms of democratic character have a lot to tell us about policy-making interventions, including those which might be used to improve the electoral process itself through such things as advertising limits, campaign finance rules and candidate disclosure requirements.

Executive and legislative institutions

Electoral systems deliver two results in democratic systems – they provide the citizens with authoritative representatives and they create an executive to rule and make policy. While there is an important distinction to be made between executive and representative roles, in practice these are intertwined. We cannot identify the policy significance of the executive arm without also analysing the role of legislatures.

The executive arm is composed of two important elements and the means for bringing these two into harmony is of great significance to the overall architecture and design of the policy system. The two involve the political leadership of the system and the administrative apparatus, or bureaucracy for carrying out decisions.

There are many different models for combining these roles but to highlight the policy significance of their central differences we can compare the two main types – the parliamentary and the presidential, both of which will be familiar to readers.

In the standard parliamentary model the executive is a group of ministers elected by the people's representatives on the floor of the popular house. They then remain inside the legislature, answerable to MPs on a daily basis. Once in command of a majority in the people's house, however, such an executive is usually able to initiate whatever policy it deems appropriate. In the Westminster version of the parliamentary type the prime minister is the effective head of government and chairs a cabinet of ministers which acts as the coordination centre and point of integration for the political and administrative parts of the executive. In some European variants on the parliamentary type, the prime minister shares power with a separately elected president who has authority over key external policy fields such as foreign affairs and national defence.

In the pure presidential system the two arms of government – executive and legislature – are separate. In being directly elected by the people, the president has a unique mandate to present new policies to the legislature but cannot control whether or not they will pass. As even a casual knowledge of these systems will reveal, the executives in both systems require an informal set of procedures and conventions to assure themselves of a minimal capacity to govern.

From an institutional design perspective we can distinguish two sets of important conventions from the policy makers' point of view – those concerning internal coherence or discipline among legislators, and those concerning relations between the executive arm and the other legislative or parliamentary institutions.

In the parliamentary systems the principle potential threat to effective policy-making is the inability of the executive to convince a majority of MPs to support each and every item of legislation. Once the majority decides to vote against the executive it becomes impossible for this executive to deliver the resources needed to operate the apparatus of government (Rose, 1974; Olson, 1980).

Over a period of more than a hundred and fifty years these parliaments have evolved a series of conventions to counter this tendency for executives to decay. The most important is the emergence of strong parliamentary parties with strict rules governing the voting behaviour of individual members. In most cases these rules provide the absolute assurance that once elected as the parliamentary leadership, the top officials of the majority party will be able to form a stable executive.

From the policy-making perspective these party arrangements are critical to any understanding of the methods by which policy agendas are shaped behind the scenes, since much of what occurs on the floor of the legislature will necessarily be highly scripted by prior party agreements. As has often been noted, this system also limits the role of local MPs and local election campaigns as sources of new policy, and instead forces contests towards a simplified battle of two or three national positions.

In presidential systems the separation of formal authority requires the evolution of a different set of conventions and habits. These must address the principle structural weakness of this design which is the fact that both arms of government have a popular mandate to govern.

While party agreements help constrain the disputes between the presidency and the legislature, in cases like the USA where parties do not form governments, there are many opportunities for actors to default from the party line and still be successful.

This requires a more detailed set of rules and conventions concerning bargaining and barter between institutions and within them. The legislative process is more likely to involve 'tacking' of smaller issues onto larger bills so that a majority can be assured. Because the capacity to add, amend and renegotiate every piece of legislation holds the ever-present promise of deadlock, these systems have developed elaborate procedures for limiting who can bargain and how bargains will be honoured. In particular, these systems tend to evolve a process for authoritative negotiation in committee and a recognized means for bargains on one policy area to be traded for agreements on other issues.

From the point of view of policy-making capacities the parliamentary system presents a strong case of centralization of authority and accountability. It is also true that as a result of this centralization parliaments are thought to be able to perform a greater range of policy-making tasks, to be capable of better policy choices, and to be able to make sure that these choices materialize as consistent programmes and outcomes (Eckstein and Apter, 1963; Weaver and Rockman, 1993:12).

Legislative processes

These different capacities have their most obvious effect in the creation of new laws or the amendment of existing statutes. Most, but not all, major policy initiatives involve new or revised legislation. Policy makers inside and outside government must push and cajole various other formal participants, bringing them into sequence at just the right time in order to enact a new law. This is no small matter. Many a brilliant policy initiative has been left languishing on a parliamentary committee agenda or has been so poorly drafted that the need for subsequent amendments has destroyed its credibility. Frequently the new legislation which a department requires in order to commence a programme already promised by the government cannot be brought forward because of low commitment by other agencies which must give their clearance.

From the perspective of community groups with an interest in a given policy area new legislation is also vitally important yet inherently difficult to influence. Departmental officers with whom they may have had dealings will not be able to control this process. Politicians with no previous interest suddenly become critical actors. Technical issues to do with law and administration loom forward and often overshadow substantive goals and objectives. A new mix of horse-trading and gunboat diplomacy dominates several further rounds of negotiation.

In the IVF scenario, for example, those framing the regulatory legislation were at pains to specify exactly which procedures would be covered and to include a number of 'catch all' clauses to enable new scientific discoveries to be subjected to legislative oversight. In so doing they needed to avoid subjecting all work in genetic science and theoretical biology to government restriction.

Olson and Mezey (1991:10) provide a compelling list of the conditions under which a legislature might become more powerful in the policy-making process. This includes where: the system is presidential, has a more decentralized executive structure, has operating bureaucratic agencies that are strong, is candidate-centred rather than party-centred, has numerous parties, and has permanent committees directly shadowing the work of agencies.

What this points towards is a need to carefully analyse the intersecting effects of different institutional conditions such as rules, elections and parties.

Proposals

A common source of initiative for new policy, which is to be enshrined in law, is the minister or cabinet secretary responsible for the policy field in which action is required. In parliamentary systems this will be an elected member of the government with a formal ministerial portfolio, or a role as parliamentary secretary to the minister. In presidential systems the legislative initiative will typically come from the cabinet or from key members of the legislature such as committee chairs or party leaders.

It is as well to discuss the internal workings of these agencies in greater detail later under the heading of 'bureaucracy', for there are important differences in the way bureaucracies relate to the policy-making process.

In practice the minister or cabinet secretary rarely develops proposals alone. They employ a private office of staff with the responsibility to develop policy. During the electoral cycle these advisers will also include party leaders or experts from key interest groups.

Advisers have functions other than assisting with the development of legislation and the extent to which these other duties overshadow the legislative function appears to depend upon the specific skills of each adviser, the extent of their party affiliation, party faction obligations of the minister and adviser, and the degree to which the minister is able to find sympathetic support within the mainline of the department (Walter, 1986). There is also some indication that adviser roles may vary with the life cycle of the government, with policy duties being greater in the early period in office and less salient after control over the bureaucracy has been firmly established (Olson and Mezey, 1991; Considine and Costar, 1992).

Other than the ministry responsible for the portfolio in which a new initiative is to be proposed, the most common alternate sources of proposals are special inquiries established by the government, statutory commissions such as human rights commissions or equal opportunity boards, and parliamentary committees. Many important welfare reforms in Britain, Sweden and elsewhere have originated from Royal Commissions established to inquire into social problems.

Parliamentary committees are traditionally more enfeebled by strong party discipline by, and executive domination of, the legislature. Some issues are referred directly to committee with an invitation for members to research policy options and propose action but this varies specifically from government to government. Ministers and their departments generally prefer to keep such questions in the executive family. The exception to this general rule is the bicameral parliament in which opposition or corner parties are able to use upper house committees as a means to develop significant amendments to government programmes.

Since these parliamentary committees generally lack the research resources of government departments, corporatist institutions or Royal Commissions, the cases where they make a difference are often explained by the fortuitous alignment of a number of factors: the particular expertise of their leading members, the quality of proposals put to them by outside interests, especially functionally specialized interest groups, and the weakness of the agency responsible for the particular policy field. A long-serving parliamentarian, armed with research provided by an articulate lobby group, campaigning for an initiative which lies outside, or to the edge of the interests of existing agencies may have success.

And of course a great deal always depends upon the *salience* of the issues being contested. Institutions work to habituate new conduct to old tracks. But even the more enfeebled legislative systems will find voice when issues are new, when they do not fit neatly into current portfolio compartments and when they are of concern to a number of different groups in the electorate.

Deliberations

Once a government has decided that an idea merits action, has a high priority and is not deeply offensive to its supporters, a formal proposal will be announced. This can have several different starting points. The minister's office might issue a press release. A draft bill might be tabled in the parliament. Or the minister might make a formal announcement, either in the parliament or at a public gathering.

It should also be evident that for the government, and in particular the responsible minister or official, the costs of withdrawing or losing now become much higher. The making of public statements and the issuing of written proposals have the effect of raising expectations. Actors who had until now been resisting the proposal will be forced to offer some form of cooperation or to justify their opposition in a more detailed manner. The new level of public attention will generally have the effect of galvanizing supporters and opponents into more tightly organized camps.

In chapter 11 we will look more closely at the dynamics of public engagement in policy so there is no need to spend extensive time on that issue here. However it is vital to the careful analysis of the legislative process that we identify the various aspects of public engagement and observe how they impact on the key actors.

Two broad paths lie open before the government as it embarks upon a major legislative initiative. On the one hand it may choose to limit public involvement to the regular publicity and debate available through the legislative process. This will mean that the mass media takes the primary role in informing and educating the general public. Within this minimalist approach we may see a number of variants. It is common, for example, for governments to discuss proposals with key interest groups, including likely opponents, and for these to be put forward in debate as a form of public consultation.

This is a low cost approach in which governments seek to limit bargaining or the raising of new issues. Instead, they hope the power of debate and reasoning in the legislature will convince journalists and interest group leaders to carry a positive message back to the general public.

A critical institutional step in this deliberative stage is to gain the support of upper house members if the system happens to be bicameral. Lijphart (1999) points out that the nature and extent of policy-making power will depend upon three factors. The first is whether the upper house is directly elected. Appointed houses will have little legitimacy to do much more than delay the will of the democratic house. The second question is whether the upper house has powers that are broadly symmetrical to the lower house, in the sense of being able to initiate legislation, reject bills and so forth, or are asymmetrical in certain important respects. The greater the symmetry, the higher the price for gaining cooperation. And third, he points out that upper houses may vary in their degree of congruency, which is the term he uses to describe the extent to which special groups are represented in upper houses. This will tend to strengthen the upper house by giving it a special form of legitimacy.

At this deliberative stage the upper house will typically be in a position to make changes to proposed policies and may also be able to insert new proposals of its own as the price of cooperation.

In parliamentary systems the final stage of law-making is the signing of the bill into law by the head of state. While this is rarely an opportunity to re-open policy questions, the known preferences of the president or monarch may sometimes shape the framing of the bill. Heads of state with liberal dispositions may delay or debate restrictive laws and in some cases have been known to seek independent advice regarding the constitutional warrant for proposed legislation.

Example: the European Parliament and the budget process

The European parliament (EP) provides an interesting example of complex deliberative power. Composed until 2004 of 626 members directly elected in national constituencies, the EP reviews the initiatives taken by the executive which is made up of two institutions, the European Commission (EC) and the Council of Ministers (CM). If we take the budget process as an example of this deliberative system we can see that the EP has scope to exercise influence but cannot control these other key institutions.

The budget process commences early in the year with each of the three institutions preparing a budget plan. In the next stage a process of 'trialogue' (Corbett, 2003) takes place and each of the three seeks to communicate their priorities to the others. It is then the job of the commission to present a draft budget and in mid-year the council holds its first reading of this draft. Another trialogue takes place to resolve problems before the budget goes to the EP for decision in September. Any amendments go back to the council and another round of negotiations takes place before the second reading of the budget in the EP in December. Should the EP fail to pass the budget there is a provision for existing collections and payments to continue on a month-by-month basis. This means that the value of cooperation is high but in the end the EP must compromise or risk its own legitimacy in a dispute that the institutional rules do not intend it to win (Neureither, 1999).

The final element of the deliberative stage is the question of how the proposal is to be administered. Often it makes no sense to separate this issue from the proposal itself. The key administrative issues are likely to include decisions and debates about: which agency is to administer the new policy, how ongoing resources are to be found, how other jurisdictions will be affected, what form of accountability will prevail. These matters are further considered in chapter 7.

7

Institutions: Courts, Bureaucracies and Budgets

Our analysis of institutions in the previous chapter highlights the role of elections, executives and legislatures in framing the whole of the policy-making apparatus, including the all-important determinants of democratic legitimacy. These core institutions provide the method by which rulers and those being ruled accept some understood rules of the game and then seek to employ these rules to make policy.

And without diminishing the importance of such institutions we should also begin this chapter by observing that these foundation institutions are among the most resistant to change. Once set in motion the electoral system is necessarily difficult for any incumbent party to alter. So too the balance of authority between executive and legislature needs to be set deeply into law and convention or else it will prove too easy for disgruntled interests to pull down the entire democratic structure. This resistance to change is often called path dependence and there is an impressive theoretical literature on the reasons why institutions endure even when they may be sub-optimal (Pierson, 2000; North, 1990; Crouch and Farrell, 2002).

But when we move to the institutions under review in this chapter – courts, bureaucracies and budgets – we immediately notice how much pliability is available to policy makers acting as institutional designers. For example, in the past twenty years in different countries we have seen the growth of tribunals and courts to deal with special policy issues such as human rights, international whaling, war crimes, small claims against landlords, divorce and adoption.

Courts have arguably become more important in deciding policy issues in areas such as indigenous land claims, or access to new reproductive technologies and civil rights, but less significant in fields such as workers' health and safety and pensions. Of course there are major differences between countries, as there are with bureaucratic reform and budget changes. In these two areas there has been a proliferation of New Public Management (NPM) changes since the 1980s (Pollitt, 1993; Considine and Painter, 1997; Barzelay, 1992). As we will see, these changes have set in motion a major transformation in relations between bureaucrats and politicians in many systems, and also between the state and the market and civic sectors of some countries.

Courts and tribunals

The policy significance of the legal system cannot be reduced to a few paragraphs and since their role is largely indirect, at least when compared with executive and legislative institutions, less attention is given to them here. This does not deny the fact that higher courts in almost all systems have significant power to reject legislation as unconstitutional or unjust, the authority to create new policy by such things as the power to acknowledge new rights to citizens, and the mandate to force legislators to act, especially where significant wrongs have been identified. The form of policy-making most likely to emerge at the judicial level will vary with regimes, but as Rockman (1997:29) observes, 'an expansive judicial role has the potential to place somewhat greater emphasis on individual rights when placed in conflict with the police powers of the state'.

Perhaps the most assertive of these courts in policy terms is the US Supreme Court where many important policy questions have been decided in the period since the Second World War. Most famously in 1973 the court decided in *Row* versus *Wade* that a Texas law prohibiting abortion was a violation of the privacy law enshrined in the First and Fourteenth Amendments of the constitution. In the civil rights field too, the US Supreme Court has rivalled the other arms of government in shaping new public policy (Stidham and Carp, 1987).

It is arguable in these cases that the court was required to fill a gap left by formal legislative processes because those institutions had been unable or unwilling to resolve these fundamental social questions. No doubt the institutional architecture of the US system contributes to this tendency for the court to become a surrogate legislature, with successive presidents seeking to make appointments that suit their own policy preferences, and thereby increasing the likelihood that those who come after can do the same.

In other systems, particularly those that regularly produce strong legislative majorities, the policy role of higher courts is more measured. More common is the tendency to allocate only issues of policy implementation to tribunals, such as the one involving Bill and his neighbours, outlined in the opening chapter. This case of a planning tribunal is matched by various other case-based policy panels. Such bodies as administrative appeals courts, affirmative action panels and pension entitlement tribunals involve judges in policy-related decision-making.

Apart from the formal rules governing such inquiries, and their capacity to amend policy through precedent setting, these institutions also create distinctive forms of policy action. They require actors to present themselves in the roles of complainant, applicant or objector and to define a direct interest in the proceedings. Other than in these roles, ordinary members of the public or citizens do not have standing in such proceedings. Tribunals also create their own rules of conduct to shape the process of decision. For example it has become standard practice in many industrial relations tribunals for applicants to begin with large 'ambit claims' in order to maximize their opportunities to bargain later in the process, since rules generally prohibit introducing new issues after the initial stage of proceedings.

The policy architecture of these institutions can be summarized in three broad dimensions. First, the policy-making power of the court will generally be a function of the capacity of the legislature to maintain control of key issues. Second, the dispersal of policy-making power to tribunals will usually limit such authority to case-by-case interpretations of existing rules. Third, the process for making policy through either action at a superior court, or through a review at tribunal level, will generally involve specific conventions regarding who may participate and how issues should be presented. These conventions will have a powerful, and generally limiting, effect on the desirability of advancing new proposals through this path.

Bureaucracy

As we have seen, the power to bring forward new policy may originate in the minister's private office. Just as likely, however, is the probability that it will spring from work done in his or her department of state. Policy-making is therefore a principle concern of the central bureaucracy. Consequently, one of the key objectives of policy intervention is to recruit allies, convince opponents or avoid blockage among civil servants. As we will see in chapter 9, the organizing skills of actors also play a major role in determining how policy is implemented, but we will leave those issues until later. For analytical purposes we will concentrate here on distinguishing different bureaux according to the following distinctions: the nature of bureaucratic specialization, form of ministerial (executive) control, level of politicization, centralization or decentralization, and the nature of inter-governmental relationships.

In each particular policy system (e.g. national system, health system, transport system, etc.) the role of top-level bureaucrats in regard to policy initiation will be subject to local legislation, tradition and convention. For example in the French case these higher-level officials enjoy comparative freedom to engage directly with the political elite in the push and pull of policy debate in several different fields. Those who have been trained at the Ecole Nationale d'Adminstration (ENA) become known as Enarcs and they form a powerful network across the upper level of the French system (Hazareesingh, 1994; Robson, 1956). The line between politician and senior bureaucrat is relatively porous and as a result the capacity to initiate policy is more widely shared. In Germany, on the other hand, the senior civil service is more likely to be specialized in a particular programme area and only comparatively senior officials in central agencies would expect to be involved in initiating new proposals.

Within the UK civil service this same specialization is evident and is compounded by the fact that since the Thatcher government's Next Steps reforms in 1988, senior bureaucrats may be located either in central departments or out in executive agencies. In the latter case the presumption of 'sticking to one's patch' is much increased. This approach, like the Swedish reforms earlier that decade, represents a particular kind of institutional engineering by governments seeking both to limit senior bureaucrats to a defined set of tasks and targets, and simultaneously to raise the expectations concerning the steering and integrating roles of the most senior officials. We will return to this issue in chapter 10 where some of the more detailed aspects of New Public Management are discussed. For now it is simply necessary to note that a number of inherent differences exist in regard to the structuring of bureaucratic systems and to identify how these, like electoral systems or legislatures, establish a pattern for policy makers to follow.

The first important distinction to observe is the *extent of specialization* within ministries or agencies. Where bureaucrats are likely to spend most of their career in the one field – such as education or health – we observe a high level of specialization in regard to the local lore for formulating policy. In these cases the actual division of labour inside the agency tends to establish strong distinctions concerning those who may and those who may not become involved in policy-making. In bureaucracies with stronger generalist tendencies we observe a greater movement of staff between departments, especially at the executive level. Here the openness to policy initiative is greater but at the price of any given department being less secure about its ability to control its own agenda.

A second distinction is the one mentioned above between *direct or indirect ministerial control* of departments and other agencies. In the direct control type the minister and her senior advisers have a direct responsibility for all officials of the department. Conventions will determine whether this includes the right to allocate work, or whether this will be mediated through the office of the chief executive. In the indirect control type the ministers, or political executive, will establish the goals and objectives of the bureau, will determine the appointment of the chief executive officer, write legislation to direct the functions of the agency, but will then grant it autonomy to carry out its task.

In between these two different forms of bureaucratic organization lie a large number of variants, each with a potentially different role to play in policy-making. For example, in many line bureaucracies with direct ministerial control the chief executive (CE) will be appointed on contract. This is a device pioneered in New Zealand and designed to increase the CE's accountability to the minister. However the existence of a formal, written contract also increases the authority of the CE by giving greater power to direct internal resources in whatever manner he or she believes will enable them to meet the minister's targets.

Another 'hybrid' or mixture of direct and indirect types, is the common practice in direct control systems of granting the chief executive, or some other senior officer, specific responsibilities under an act of parliament. For example, in many welfare departments the law requires that someone be the designated officer for deciding adoptions and for deciding when a child will become a ward of the state. When policy disputes over the privacy of records of adoptions, or over child abuse cases, erupt in public disputes these statutory powers may see the responsible bureaucrat at odds with her own minister, or at the very least in a position very different from the rest of the line bureaucracy.

The third structuring principle of bureaucratic systems is *the level and nature of political control* – or politicization. This is a different issue to direct control by ministers, although plainly the two are related. Political control refers explicitly to the tools available for politicians to obtain a preferred policy recommendation from their departments, and to the role of the department in providing the minister with partisan support. In the most highly politicized systems, such as the USA, the senior levels of the department provide both preferred policy advice and partisan support. At the opposite end of this spectrum are the systems where career civil servants provide advice 'without fear or favour' and all political questions are left for the minister's private office.

Political control can be increased through a variety of institutional devices. We have already noted the rise in most systems of the independent role of the minister's private office. By appointing political advisers, and policy advisers with party affiliations, the minister can put pressure on the line department to produce the kinds of policies she wants, or the government wants. Political appointments in the senior civil service are the second common device for politicization. The third is the creation of authoritative policy councils or boards where the government's allies or supporters are appointed to give direct advice to the department.

The fourth design feature with real impact on policy-making is *the level of centralization or decentralization* and the role of central agencies in the overall map of civil service relations. In almost every system we expect to see the main budget agency – Treasury or ministry of finance – assert its authority over line departments and agencies. Usually this has its origins in the legislature's budget power and this is then delegated to the Treasury to make sure that the budget is enacted in the manner legislated.

Plainly this has enormous policy significance because budgets are also a form of priority setting and the agency in charge of budgets may well become the means by which a government assures itself that key policy goals are being taken seriously. There are however a number of other central agencies with significant policy authority. These include public service recruitment agencies such as Public Service Boards, which create the base of expertise the government must use to administer programmes and develop policies. Chief minister's offices or prime minister's departments are also a potential source of policy advice. An important distinction to be made here is between those systems which promote policy coordination at this level, not just for the prime minister herself, but often for the cabinet as a whole, and those which allow ministers to build up policy resources at the local department level.

In addition to showing how formal policy is decided and how key central agencies relate to one another in the setting of major government priorities, the power of central agencies also high-lights a broader question for the analyst – the degree of central-ization or decentralization of policy-making authority. Strong central agencies may choose to make policy themselves and thereby reduce the role of line agencies. Or they may elect to coordinate the policies being developed by others, thereby encouraging higher levels of local initiative. Or instead the system may be based upon decentralized policy-making in which all but the most pressing issues are managed by local agencies using their own authority over their programmes and staff.

In some systems the primary form of decentralization is from centre to region. In other words the central ministries cede certain administrative power to regional administrators who are employed by the national government to deliver services at sub-national level. The French system offers such a model (Brustein, 1988). This is a different form of regionalism to that practised in Italy, for example. Italian central departments also have regional offices but regional administration mostly refers to offices of the separate level of government centred upon regional legislatures (Putnam, 1993). Norway also fits this model while the United Kingdom has recently shifted from a form of regionalized central administration to a type of regionalism which also empowers new legislative bodies in Scotland, Northern Ireland and Wales.

The final important dimension is also the most complex – this concerns *inter-governmental relationships*. In all policy systems there are important institutions which attempt to systematize the relations between national and sub-national governments. In an increasing number of cases there are also elaborate institutions to formalize conduct between national and supra-national govern-ment authorities such as the European Union.

Since this is an indicative treatment of the institutional ques-tion we will do no more than highlight some key analytical issues and dimensions to be taken into account in any full coverage of this issue. The first issue to identify is one of jurisdictions. In inter-governmental institutions the first question to ask is about the mandates of the various participants, including which are domi-nant, separate, subordinate or overlapping and in regard to which matters.

In the case of policy dominance we may see one level of government with a virtual monopoly of policy authority and other levels remaining almost outside the policy field. These cases involve the least amount of inter-governmental institution building and need not concern us much. The only cautionary note here is that even in cases such as defence and foreign affairs, where the sovereignty of the national government is at its greatest, a wide variety of strategies may be used to force central actors to negotiate the terms of their dominance. For example, during the 1970s it became the practice of many local governments in places as far afield as New Zealand and California to declare themselves 'Nuclear Free Zones'. Energy policy is a state responsibility in California and defence is exclusively a national policy domain. In New Zealand the local authorities have control over some energy distribution issues, but everything else about the nuclear issue was exclusively a national concern.

Nevertheless many municipalities took it upon themselves to ban the use of nuclear power and attempted in some cases to ban the movement of both civilian and military nuclear instruments through their streets. This form of moral pressure obviously had some important effects in New Zealand because in the 1980s the national government banned access to its ports by US nuclear-powered ships. While these cases are more unusual than those in which authorities stick to their defined area of constitutional power, they show that movement may still be possible even in tightly controlled domains.

In some cases of actual policy subordination we find that different levels of government share formal power but that only one government has sufficient authority to shape outcomes. So in the case of federal systems such as Germany and Canada we see some policy domains where the sub-national government is little more than an agent for the national. In other words the state, province or local government is subordinate. This may be because of constitutional edict, because of agreement between the governments, or because the national level has used other powers to usurp this authority. In each of these instances the prospects for reversibility, or what Goodin (1996:40) calls 'revisability', are very different, with constitutional subordination usually being the most difficult to alter.

In other cases we find the different levels sharing the same authority and in this case of overlapping mandates the pressure exists for both to develop conventions of cooperation in order for either to enact effective policy.

Inter-governmental systems increase the number of political actors in any policy system and also create multiple levels at which policy games may be played. This has immediate consequences for those seeking to influence policy and for those wishing to hold the line against outside pressures. Interest groups benefit from such systems because they always have an alternative elite to whom complaints or counter-strategies may be taken. However, these same groups may be effectively shut out of normal policy bargaining where inter-governmental processes only authorize governments to speak on behalf of citizens, or where existing agreements between governments deny interest groups a chance to lobby their own, or some other government (Knill, 2001).

Budgets

Budget policies are critical and controversial aspects of contemporary systems. Before looking at some of the institutional mechanisms and processes used to create such policies, it is worth pausing to consider just how central the budget is to all of the other institutional processes that interest us. This centrality is not only structural, although it is obviously the case that payments and taxes underpin the whole of government. It is also because budgeting provides the first line of attack and defence in the struggle over the meaning of government and the norms to be used to drive it.

For example, the most important unifying theme in the policy battles of the 1970s and 1980s in the USA and elsewhere was the attempt to cut national budget deficits by reducing the size of government. This had a profound effect on other institutions as Barzelay and Campbell (2003:216) point out: 'The darkest periods in this era of hostility towards the role of bureaucracy have coincided with radical efforts to cut back the size of the federal government.'

The formal allocation of public funds to programmes and departments involves a complex local methodology for estimating costs, legislating permission, and auditing the spending of funds. Together we call these various processes 'the budget'. Of course there are many such budgets. The annual appropriation by parliament, the three-year estimates of congressional finance committees and the departmental budgets of public agencies can all be called budgets. But for our purpose the budget refers to the spending programme of the executive government which is approved by the legislature.

As Wildavsky (1964:xxiii) makes clear, such budgets serve many possible purposes:

> a budget can be many things: a political act, a plan of work, a prediction, a source of enlightenment, a means of obfuscation. A mechanism of control, an escape from restrictions, a means to action, a brake on progress, even a prayer that the powers that be will deal gently with the best aspirations of fallible men.

The budgetary process offers a prism through which to distinguish underlying values – political, economic and social – in so far as they are reflected in specific decisions about the raising of revenue and the distribution of expenditure. Cash values reflect political values (Wallace, 1980:13). In this sense the story of budget-making systems and the financial control systems they underpin is a 'function of their social and organisational environment' (Butt and Palmer, 1985:29).

Budgets are two things rolled into one. They are the annual appropriation needed to run public programmes and they are a government's major opportunity to signal its policy direction for the coming years. The comments made earlier about election policy speeches apply with equal weight to budget-making – those able to set the spending and taxing priorities of the government have unique power to shape its whole policy agenda.

To understand how a budget takes shape we need to consider two dimensions of budget-making. These are the continuing commitments of governments and the new initiatives of the current executive. In most systems the continuing commitments of the public sector will define as much as 90 per cent of the coming year's commitments. Programmes already in place, promises made in previous elections, legislative obligations which have continuing commitments each take a slice of the cake. Policies being announced as part of the new budget must compete with continuing commitments. Can the current programmes be cut back to allow space? Can some commitments be abandoned or handed over to others? Or will there need to be new revenue found to cover the new initiatives? These are the key questions that those framing the budget must address.

The first step in mapping the budget-making process is to comprehend the executive system which approves these core commitments in the budget. This may be a cabinet sub-committee or a special office of the president or prime minister. This process includes the departmental protocol for the presentation of departmental estimates of forward expenditure by departments. These sub-committees take advice on the economic outlook of the country or state, the major policy demands being considered by ministers, and the effects of elections past and future.

The budget process typically extends over several months and moves from wide-ambit bids towards actual decisions by a number of steps. In most systems an executive committee will attempt to set general guidelines, including spending targets of a general kind for departments. This group will then review the bids of large spending organizations. It is at this point that budgets involve a unique form of estimation and evaluation. Current and proposed programmes must be given a recommended budget, even though there may be no fixed costs or defined purposes. Writing about the American case, Wildavsky (1964: 42–3) points out that the bureau of the budget 'is put in the position of trying to decide how desirable a program might be on its intrinsic merits . . . Technical criteria like cost-benefit ratios would be helpful if they existed, but even so the determination of what may qualify as a benefit would be crucial.'

In most systems the annual budget cycle is governed by strict timetables with clear deadlines. By forcing policy makers to behave in a carefully proscribed manner and to obey general rules of conduct, budget systems hope to limit individualistic behaviour and special pleading. 'If we do it for you we have to do it for everyone' is the decision rule which propels this set of routines (Wallace, 1980:295; Hennessy, 1986).

Observations in individual case studies suggest that budget committee effectiveness results first of all from elite cohesion, which in turn follows from electoral laws and the other institutional constraints discussed above. Much also depends on what is at stake. Second, budget institutions are strengthened during periods of fiscal constraint. Governments which need to cut their budgets and restructure their resources frequently invest heavily in stronger rules and elaborate committees. Campbell and Halligan (1992:137) report the success of the Australian Labor government's Expenditure Review Committee (ERC) where the committee carried out a 'public choice approach to fiscal issues' at a time of 'severe economic pressure'.

The particular instrument used to formulate the budget also has an influence on policy and participation. Traditional line-item budgets which grant large sums to departments under vague headings privilege existing programmes but expose new bids to extreme pressure from above. They are somewhat conservative in policy terms because they conceal much of the policy intent of the budget, even (perhaps especially) from politicians. Programme budgets favour activities currently in harmony with management and political priorities but may reduce organizational flexibility. This is true wherever policy objectives cannot be clearly quantified or where they are apt to cause controversy (Corbett, 1992; Considine, 1990).

Interest mediation institutions

The final group of institutions that need to be identified and brought forward for analysis are those set up to steer, settle or improve relations between governments and key interest groups. For the most part the history of these institutions has been dominated by consideration of the industrial relations commissions and agencies developed to settle disputes between union and business interests. These consist of two main types. In the Anglo-Saxon countries we find a variety of pluralist institutions established to reduce strikes, moderate pay disputes and deal with demarcation issues between groups. These are termed pluralist because for the most part they are based on some form of voluntarism among the parties and because government attempts (often vainly) to remain outside the arena as an umpire or sponsor (Crouch, 1985; Lembruch, 1984).

In Scandinavia, Germany, and for certain periods in the Netherlands we see a very different institutional path, often called the corporatist approach. Here there is greater compulsion for all interests to join together to bargain, there is more active participation by government agencies, and there is a closer relationship between the bargained consensus of interests and the other key policy-making organs of government. This means that a bargain struck in relation to pay is more likely to draw upon other agreements in relation to the social wage or taxation (Streeck, 1992).

In addition to peace-making between key interest groups it is clear that such institutions offer significant opportunities both for social interests to influence policy, and for governments to multiply the points at which public policy can impact upon broader social conditions. For example a public policy in favour of supporting women to return to work after childbirth may change the behaviour of key civil service organizations. But such a policy when part of a broader industrial relations agreement may hope to transform the whole regime of policies in place within the society.

It is also important to note that a number of key interests in addition to unions and business interests are found in these mediation institutions. Environmental movements have been successful in countries such as Germany and the Netherlands in gaining a seat at boards and planning authorities charged with reviewing national policy. Important ethnic minorities and identity groups have also achieved similar status in Spain and France, while in post-colonial countries such as Australia, Canada and New Zealand there are authoritative institutions designed to enhance the rights of indigenous citizens and to mediate between their claims and the preferences of a majority white population.

In assessing the policy impact of these mediation institutions very little can be said at the general level without risk of trivialization. However, it is worth emphasizing the key design questions raised in the pluralist–corporatist debates which have raged undeterred over a forty-year period (Schmitter, 1974). As we observed above, the policy significance of these institutions depends greatly upon whether or not they are designed to require a common view and thus a form of 'social contract' on the part of interest groups. If their incentive structures promote inclusion and their rules support compulsion, the prospects for policy effectiveness are high. Of course the pay-offs to groups must also be high if defaulting and opportunism are to be avoided. The endurance of such institutions also depends upon their flexibility in accepting new interests at the bargaining table, and thus avoiding ossification. More pluralistic arrangements find this easier to do and are therefore preferred by governments wishing to alter the power balance between key interests, or hoping to avoid the veto power of such groups.

In these cases it is impossible to consider interest mediation without also considering the role of the electoral system. Enduring bargains and lasting agreements between interests are less sustainable where the political system encourages 'winner takes all' election contests, and party alignments in which the political world is always divided between enemies and friends.

Policy change and institutional adaptation

Finally, the policy significance of these arrangements is also dependent upon how easily their architecture, instruments and rules may be turned to other purposes, particularly by governments. Any institution with the power to influence policy has, by definition, the power to stop, slow or redirect policy-making initiative. Interest mediation institutions are therefore open to being used as buffers or shields by governments wishing to deflect pressure, distract interest groups and lower expectations by those seeking policy change. Where government regularly alternates between parties, where the prospects of coalition are small, and where government leadership change is frequent, the likelihood of such institutions surviving these effects is low. This serves to highlight the point made at the start of the chapter, that it is the intersection of different institutional features that helps shape a specific set of policy action channels, not merely the rules applying to any one institution.

Four types of adaptive change processes are identified in the research literature on institutional change.

Variation and selection

Standard practices or operating rules will tend to change through variation simply because each individual case will have some small scope for difference and each group of officials or decision makers will bring some local preferences to light. These small variations in implementation of rules will eventually lead to modification and adaptation of the rules if rewards flow to those whose modified procedures meet with continued success. In other words, if decision makers gain approval from those higher up, or from key outside funding bodies as a result of making amendments to current rules they will tend to use these amended rules the next time around (Pfeffer and Salancik, 1978).

It will be obvious that this idea contains a kind of Darwinian 'survival of the fittest' element. In practice there is no way to judge which practice is objectively better so in this instance the test is one of reward, including stakeholder support.

Policy failure

New rules and customs will also tend to develop where the key decision makers in an institution receive irresistible feedback or shocks suggesting that current rules are failing. The emergence of crises often results in a recourse to standard procedure because crises generate high risks which rules seek to minimize. But crises also expose normal rules to failure.

Rule failure may emerge in one of two standard forms. Current rules may be applied to new situations where they previously worked, but where they now prove incompetent. Or institutions may receive new pressures which simply cannot be withstood using existing procedures (Lindblom, 1959).

Diffusion and contagion

Evidence also exists to show that institutions may alter their operating logic or procedures as a result of contagion (Benveniste, 1987). That is, when neighbouring institutions adopt new routines which are successful, similar institutions in the local system will be more likely to succumb to pressures to do likewise (Kingdon, 1984). An example of this is rules governing equal opportunity. It is not usually necessary for courts to take action against every single institution to force them to change their hiring policies when new attention is given to disadvantaged groups such as women, gays or ethnic minorities.

Once one of these institutions has developed a successful method for deciding such cases the others will copy and modify this into their own local code. This suggests that public institutions pay close attention to one another and develop some known methods for learning from one another's experience.

Leadership change

We are used to thinking of leaders as people who bring forward new policies or programmes but it is also important to consider their role in changing processes and customs. Often the most obvious impact of a new leader is her determination to show the members of her team that 'things are going to be different around here now'. This determination to alter the culture of institutions is a comparatively recent phenomenon in the public sector but has been a key driver of change in private institutions for most of their history.

The optimistic view of this source of change might be that new leaders bring with them a knowledge of alternative procedures which have been successful elsewhere or which provide a means to respond to the unmet demands of key groups inside or outside the institution (Boston, 1991). It may also be the case that the imperative to generate one's own leadership agenda will also see valuable local rules and customs set aside.

8

Policy Interventions and Networks

If the industrial order driving twentieth-century public policy was based on specialization of tasks and the careful segmentation of life into sub-systems and functions, the new post-industrial order is generally taken to define a far higher level of connectivity, both across local groups and beyond the nation into the global realm. As Mulgan (1997:xiii) observes, 'This is very difficult for governments to grasp, since they prefer to focus on only a handful of indicators, and since few are well designed for a systematic view of the world.' While these are appealing ideas, and do seem to grasp an important truth about the way the political world is changing, the constant references to networks, connectivity and joined-up thinking are sometimes no more than intuitions. How would our understanding of policy institutions and interventions be improved by a better understanding of networks and networking?

In a popular dinner party conversation guests discuss the idea that all the world's people are no more distant from one another than 'six degrees of separation'. Examples flood into the conversation to confirm this pleasing idea. Someone knows someone who went to school with President Clinton's daughter. Clinton knows all the world leaders. That's four degrees. Another person went to school with someone who is now a leading criminal barrister who represents key underworld leaders. That's three degrees. The basis of this intriguing idea is a social experiment carried out by Stanley Milgram (1967). He sent 160 randomly selected people in Omaha, Nebraska, a letter containing the name of a stockbroker in Boston. Each person was asked to send the letter to someone they knew who might be able to get the letter closer to the banker. Milgram then tracked the number of steps and the nature of the ties along the way. He found that most people could reach the destination with five or six intermediaries, and it was from this study that the expression 'six degrees of separation' was born (Milgram, 1967; Kochen, 1989). The examination of the resulting pattern of contacts is one form of what became known as network analysis.

By the 1980s 'network' was also in wide use as a description of linkages between computers, especially personal computers. Here again the term described a beneficial world of interdependence in which 'stand-alone' machines could elect to download and upload information from other machines linked to them by cable and compatible software. The apogee of this new structure came with the spread of the Internet, a networking system in which machines could act as both a source of data for one another, or as an inter-mediary for data flowing between two other members of the network.

In both the communications industry and the computing sectors the network term suggested important new forms of orga-nization. First and most importantly in this new system each member remained independent. In technical and legal terms the network member retained an identity which could always be held separately from the rest and which, if necessary, could act without the assistance of the rest. Second, network members might come in very different shapes and sizes. There was no requirement that each should resemble the other, or even that each should com-prehend the other. Instead the relationships between members were explicitly utilitarian. Finally, the forms of interaction among members were open. That is, they could flow in any direction, unencumbered by formal imperatives.

Networks as norms

Relations between people and groups engaged in policy-making might once have been described by organizational boundaries, official mandates and interest group cleavages – now they are often said to be better understood under the rubric of network linkages, inter-organizational ties and a trust-chain of loosely coupled agencies. This is expressed in the new language of inter-action, partnership and reciprocal connections between actors. It is both an empirical and a normative achievement. As we saw in chapter 5, treatments of the role of ideas and discursive practices within policy-making are never free of representations which actors and institutions offer of their own preferred positions and preferences, and so it is with networks. They both describe a real change in relationships and signal an imagined virtue or desired set of norms.

The extent of overlap or conjuncture of norms and actors is however a matter of deep dissent among observers and practi-tioners. For example, in Peter Haas's (1992) much-quoted work on 'epistemic communities' the closeness of fit between profes-sional elites and their discourses is relatively tight. Professions remain a paradigm case for arguments which claim that knowl-edge and power are monopolized by relatively closed groups which enforce their standards and beliefs with a high degree of consistency and coherence. At the other end of the spectrum the work of Sabatier (1988, 1993) and his colleagues suggests a more open, even promiscuous, relationship between structural interests and the intellectual justifications or rationalizations available in any single policy episode. For these writers there is always a degree of flexibility in the way deeper values are mobilized and expressed in campaign claims and counter-claims.

If we look back over the brief history of policy analysis as a sep-arate literature we notice that the role of structured interests and groups is itself the subject of a great deal of reformulation and debate. Formal organizations and political parties are identified as having both embedded standard operating procedures (SOPs) and a good deal of open territory to be exploited by leaders, factions and opportunists.

Most of these early works treat organizations as the basic unit of analysis and this in turn reflects the prevailing influence of orga-nization studies in the first forms of policy analysis. It also reflected a prevailing form of institutionalism within political science and sociology where government or the state was often treated as a unified category and analysts made considerable effort to find the contours of a single unified 'system' of government. Public policy was widely regarded as the property and product of government institutions seeking to fashion solutions in the face of demands and pressures from an 'external environment' of organized interests. In other words public policy was the technician's guide to the unified theory of functions and rules.

But by the 1980s a major shift in focus had taken place both within policy-making itself and within the analytical disciplines seeking to explain and change public programmes. The new language of networks sought to open analysis to include a new 'mixed economy' of public and private actors. It also sought to understand the impact of new information technologies upon forms of production and communication in and around the state. Relationships were now seen as just as important as rules. At its most extreme were speculations that networks might involve 'governing without Government' (Rhodes, 1997:200).

Of course the use of 'network' as an organizational description pre-exists the information revolution. It is most commonly associated with corporate affiliations in the radio and television industries. From the late 1950s onwards locally owned and operated stations formed themselves into networks in order to benefit from the news-gathering capacities of larger organizations and in order to gain access to programmes which would be too expensive to produce locally.

The rise of these network ideas in the policy analysis literature signals a new kind of explanation of the social relations underpinning government. By shifting the focus from an older division of labour which separated the state from other 'private' activity and towards an environment marked by far greater fluidity, flux and an inter-penetration of groups and interests, 'network' seeks to identify both 'system' and 'individual', free of older institutional categories. In this new space we observe writers positing a stronger role for social movements, quasi-public actors such as non-profit agencies, and coalitions of interests joined together by their interest in 'building social capital' and creating stronger civic engagement in fields such as urban renewal, child care, and environmental action.

Some of these new formations retain strong organizational roots within established fields of state action such as health or education, but others cross the borders of ministries and departments and seek to promote policies with impact across government. So for example in many policy systems the second-wave feminist movements of the late 1970s began to agitate for equal opportunity and affirmative action in a wide range of service fields. Later, as neo-liberal campaigns took root inside and outside government we can observe such wide-ranging agendas emerging to cut expenditure, privatize services and open the public sector to new forms of competition. While business groups were central to such campaigns they were not the only such interest involved. Treasury departments, economists and management consulting firms also played a significant role, as did international organizations such as the IMF, the OECD and World Bank.

In other words the interest in analysing the work of networks comes directly from recognition that many policy domains no longer sit comfortably within the institutional histories which once defined them. Instead of thinking about policy as a routine engagement between certain public officials and a settled retinue of established interests, we are now forced to consider how a single system is constructed from semi-independent institutions and actors linked by resource agreements, joint projects and cross-border engagements. In Denmark this new structural type is sometimes described as the 'bear's paw'. Looked at from above the foot seems unified and whole, but underneath, the Danes say, it is really composed of separate pads of unequal size, each contributing to a characteristic policy 'footprint'.

The key to the network idea is its reliance upon communication, information processing, flexible modes of programme delivery and multiple points of engaging clients in services and activities. Policy makers can no longer be expected to articulate a single point of leverage on problems, but rather seek to act across several domains, using multiple measures. The network therefore defines both the form of action and the hyper-interactivity of actors and technologies deployed to change outcomes. The application of these ideals is evident in recent accounts of public administration.

> Public administration increasingly takes place in settings of net-
> worked actors who necessarily rely on each other and cannot
> compel compliance on the part of the rest. Yet the standard writ-
> ings to which most administrators turn for advice to improve per-
> formance devote relatively little attention to acting effectively in
> such situations. (O'Toole, 1997:45)

As an example we can look at attempts to address problems of
youth unemployment. Welfare departments once provided
income support and a brokerage service to steer applicants to
available vacancies. Now in the networked environment we would
expect to find health agencies, training institutes, schools, environmental projects, housing services and motivational experts all
clustered around a hub of decision makers seeking tailored programmes for different groups of young unemployed people.

These new conditions impose both new possibilities and new
problems on these actors, including would-be clients or customers.
Chains of producers and suppliers must be brought into cooperation. Their relations with one another cannot necessarily be
assured by strict rules of engagement or settled hierarchies of decision-making. They will have separate mandates and budgets. Even
formerly simple tasks such as defining who should get services is
now a complex achievement which depends upon negotiation,
local priorities, the forms of technology available to link actors
together, and increased self-responsibility for clients to navigate
and select their pathways and options. In other words the network
ideal requires forms of mutual adjustment far more complex than
that previously anticipated by policy theory and practice.

Network theories

To account for this change in the reality of a changed political
economy, and to recognize the weaknesses of the older interest
group and institutional frameworks, we note that by the mid-
1980s the literature on policy-making began to identify this new
class of group actions and organizational forms as networks. To
begin with the network was less a theory and more a convenient

analytical category into which one could place all the events, relationships and characterizations not able to be assimilated by pluralist, corporatist or Marxian state theories (Laumann and Knoke, 1987).

Networks became ubiquitous. They now described everything from a drink after work with colleagues to the structural relationships between public and private organizations. This popularity has unquestionably led to some weakening of the term, but was no more unexpected than the similar process of popularization which attends all ideas 'whose time has come'.

Perhaps most important to an understanding of the importance of network theory to policy intervention is the way in which networks also implied a separation of domains. They were also 'not' words. That is – not market, not state, not private, not public. In many early accounts they were seen as neither state nor market and some of the virtues previously reserved for 'third sector' or 'community' organizations seemed to be implied. Critics argued that the whole idea was therefore somewhat fuzzy and self-referential (Dowding, 1995). To some degree this is a consequence of the concepts and attendant methodologies being so new and lacking in grounded experience. Like any abstraction or generalization which seeks to explain the way complex actors interact, the network idea is only as good as the explanatory studies and strategies it helps generate.

In social theoretical terms, networks are defined by a qualitatively different means by which actors change the terms of their work, create and sustain new forms of technologically assisted production and reproduction, and alter the participation and identity of themselves and others.

In practical terms networks include non-hierarchical connections between firms, between governments and civic agencies, and between interest groups and social movements. Networking is also held by many social theorists to be a new condition of social connection and exchange among individuals. Rather than acting along a path determined by 'group or grid' (Douglas, 1987), that is by the organizational hierarchies or status groups to which he or she belongs, each single actor is seen to actively select and build a personal stock of contacts and these are believed to have fundamentally different properties to traditional affiliations such as the family, workplace or neighbourhood (Beck, 2000; Lyon, 1988; Postman, 1992).

When applied to issues and processes within the policy world, this notion of a personal stock of resources is expanded to include organizational contacts, alliances, favours and trusted ties. It is this that von Hippel (1988) and his colleagues had in mind when they identified 'know-how trading' across the lines of major competitive firms as a key determinant of innovation.

In addition to these positive roles as conduits of improved communication and increased social flexibility, networks are also identified with various negative processes including forms of veto or restriction on processes of policy innovation. For example, within the growing literature on policy interdependency 'conflicts of interests between interdependent actors are the main reason why policy processes give rise to chaotic and lengthy debates and stalemates, with the result that urgent societal problems remain unsolved' (Termeer and Koppenjan, 1997:79).

Since we are interested here in only one part of this more general debate – the particular contribution which networks make to policy-making – we can focus upon three aspects of network theory: the organizational basis of networks, the role of interest group theory, and the contribution of network theory to ideas of innovation.

Policy networks and joint action problems

How do these various ideas help us resolve policy problems or improve interventions? Perhaps the most important answer to this question lies in understanding the possible role they play in what might be called 'joint action problems' or problems associated with getting a number of actors with different interests to cooperate. Bruno's fishing fleet faced a joint action problem in trying to restrain exploitation of fish stocks.

Policy systems involve enduring sets of relationships that can involve thousands of clients and hundreds of governmental and

non-governmental agencies. Their patterns of interaction, cooperation and dependency frequently become institutionalized into
programmes, the procedures and regulations for which may run
to several volumes. We have discussed some of the major attributes of these systemic linkages in previous chapters. They may also
be based upon conflict where groups seek to act on their own preferred norms and have nothing more in common than agreement
that a certain issue or problem deserves attention by government.

Much of the theoretical work in the policy studies genre has
relied upon a state-centric definition of policy as the 'product' of
a division of labour in which various interests and institutions contribute to some authoritative action by the state. There is much
to admire in these accounts. They provide a rich source of insights
concerning the effects of rules, elections, mandates and constitutional imperatives. But they also provide a large target for those
who see policy-making as just one further arena for powerful
actors to capture and manipulate the organs of government in
their own interest.

In a curious way the focus on the state as the dominant actor
in this production process only serves to heighten the sense of
immanent betrayal once interlocks between state and private
interests are identified. In other words for critics, the state is less
an interest in its own right and more an opportunity structure
through which others seem to get what they want. Without
denying that public authority is always open to capture, the interesting thing about network theory is that it shifts the focus away
from this zero-sum framework of a public production system, and
instead creates a cultural framework in which meaning systems,
mechanisms of reciprocation, and brokerage between interests
loom larger than do the specific products or services under negotiation at any one time.

This is not to say that the policy network is never engaged
in production, delivery of actual programmes and so on. Clearly
this is one model of the network (e.g. health networks).
Rather the network may be less constrained by traditional, hierarchical methods for achieving such outcomes than the factory-
bureaucracies of the past. The normative system of the network

therefore assumes greater importance for binding producers together.

To realize the potential of network theory we need to specify some of the key elements which make up a network analysis in the policy field (Peters, 1998). The origins of the political theories that have influenced policy network analysis begin with a general dissatisfaction with the previous debate between corporatist and pluralist accounts. In these earlier theories policy-making was seen either as a production function based on the will of a certain power bloc of economic agents allied to the state (unions, business associations, etc.), or policy was seen as a bargaining game played by a large number of formal and informal groups seeking to influence their elected government (Schmitter and Lehmbruch, 1982).

Mancur Olson (1971) presents the most comprehensive critique of this interest group school. His classic study may be formulated as six key propositions:

1 The primary function of groups is to advance the common interests of individuals.
2 Groups seek to provide collective goods, which are those benefits which all those in the field, members or not, will enjoy.
3 It will often not be rational for self-interested individuals to contribute to the groups that deliver benefits to them.
4 Groups will often have to provide extra incentives or sanctions to get potential members to join.
5 The larger the group the smaller the value of participation by rational individuals.
6 Non-economic, or social incentives are important mainly only in the small group.

Olson's position differs from traditional theories of group association. In the writings of earlier political scientists and sociologists such as Mosca (1939) and Simmel (1950) groups were viewed as natural engagements which individuals sought because of 'herd instinct', natural sociability or other instinctive propensities. Olson (1971:20) rejects this view on the basis of evidence which shows that 'the average person does not in fact typically belong to large voluntary associations'.

The second more traditional account which Olson wishes to attack is the one which holds that group interests rather than individual interests are the ones which dominate politics (Truman, 1958; Verba, 1961; Galbraith, 1952). Arthur Bentley (1949:220) is perhaps the best-known advocate of this position. He argued that pressure between groups was the main force in politics and that the 'balance of group pressures is the existing state of society'. The democratic character of the political system was only preserved in these traditional group accounts by the fact that there were many groups available to represent the individual, the groups were in tension or direct conflict thus keeping the political system open, and the groups exercised influence which was roughly approximate to their numerical strength. Moreover, writers such as Galbraith and Truman argued that as one interest group grew and became influential there would be a tendency for others to enter the fray and counter this power, thereby producing a form of equilibrium among interests.

Olson's decisive critique of these accounts is based upon two central aspects of his own theory. Groups only exist to the extent that individuals within them find it rational to contribute, this same rationality being determined by the pay-offs they receive. But only some types of groups will be able to induce people to join. Large groups which are based on economic interests will find it more difficult than small groups. Olson uses this distinction to explain why business associations fare better than farmer organizations and trade unions. Most industry groups are composed of a hundred or so firms. Anything larger than this and the organizational costs plus a tendency for individuals to take a 'free ride' at the expense of the larger membership will make it difficult to mobilize the potential group into an actual one.

Since relatively small groups will frequently be able voluntarily to organize and act in support of their common interests, and since large groups normally will not be able to do so, the outcome of the political struggle among the various groups in society will not be symmetrical (Olson, 1971:127).

From individual to group rationality

The Olson model may suggest what the rational individual should do, but it is often unsuccessful in showing how they do in fact behave. For example, there seems little point, on the basis of individual gain, in attending large demonstrations or voting in blue ribbon electorates. No single individual could hope to influence the outcome by their actions. Yet demonstrations and mass voting have become a regular part of political life. In such cases it is obvious that something other than an individual calculation of probable success and likely cost is at work.

What do networks contribute to this debate? By focusing upon the recurrent or recursive nature of interactions between policy actors (including citizens) the network approach attempts to provide an account of how it is that individuals learn to solve group action problems, including the problems of 'free riders', short-term cost disadvantage and the behaviour of opportunists. It does this by viewing the network as having a certain kind of potential to regulate conduct.

The network localizes the place at which such regulatory issues are decided. If we return to Bruno's fishing village we can rehearse some of the properties of the network approach. Recall that in this scenario, outlined in chapter 2, the local fleet is having difficulty matching the individual interests of boat owners and the collective issue of maintaining the fish population.

The proposed market solution is to sell the property and expect the owner of the whole fishing stock to have a long-term interest in its survival. Provided there is genuine competition and thus a fair price, this solution is seen to create incentives for both management of the fish and efficient production and marketing of the catch.

But the risks in the market approach are also substantial. They begin with the cost of making most of the current fleet redundant, destroying local industry and damaging ancillary industries. They also include the possibility that the winning bidder might seek to make opportunistic gain from the deal, with the result that a large profit could be extracted by over-fishing and then quitting the field. It is difficult to use the market to force actors to make long-term commitments. The need to free the market from such obligations is summed up in the Greek proverb 'live like brothers, do business like strangers'.

The accepted alternative in this case is to develop some form of state regulation of the fishing stock and thus of the behaviour of the members of the fleet. This requires the state to develop an institution of some kind composed of inspectors, scientists and administrators. They take authority out of the hands of the boat owners and by limiting each to a quota and to a defined fishing ground, they seek to balance fish populations with the need for all to share in the catch.

But here too there are risks. Government regulators are not involved in the day-to-day work of the fleet and so must improvise when it comes to surveillance and regulation. Opportunities will inevitably arise for cheating and collusion among boat owners and regulators. Further, the costs of regulation will undoubtedly be handed back to boat owners or consumers in the form of taxes or licence fees. This may drive up costs and add a further burden to the industry and the local community.

A third approach, and one more consistent with the policy network model, is to view the regulation issue as a joint action problem for the community itself. In the way that Hardin's classic formulation of the 'Tragedy of the Commons' recognizes the benefits of cooperation, the key issue is whether or not the participants can trust one another to limit short-term profit in the interest of long-term gain. By developing a regulatory institution which involves boat owners monitoring one another and making collective decisions about quotas and penalties the group achieves a more rigorous form of regulation which has much lower costs, as Elinor Ostrom (1990) has demonstrated.

What are the network properties of such a system? First of all the solution assumes an ongoing and reciprocal relationship among the members of the fleet. No doubt they already share things like docking facilities and emergency rescue protocols. This reciprocal action produces an information-rich environment and a multitude of ways in which the benefits of cooperation (and costs of defaulting) can be realized. This alternative to state and market will be further discussed in chapter 13.

Characteristics of networks

Since policy networks are the actual, reciprocal linkages between individuals and groups in the policy system, and given that policy systems are differently structured, networks may vary quite profoundly. The linkages or ties may vary a great deal in strength. They may range from strong, dense intersections between all those in the system, or elongated ties in which one or two individuals form the centre point for clusters of other actors.

In addition to the patterns of connection between actors the network will also vary according to the nature or quality of the ties themselves. In relatively trivial networks the actors are connected by the fact that they use the same laundry service. In a stronger form they are linked by shared involvement in a movement such as environmentalism.

Emery and Trist (1965) describe these kinds of interaction as forming a characteristic 'causal texture', or a system of connections which is independent of the prevalent system of exchange, provision or regulation. This causal texture is based on the way groups and individuals are clustered and linked. This system can often shape the kind of action available to participants and can establish a characteristic kinetic property, by which they mean the degree of dynamism or inertia in the sector. This kinetic property is visible in the forms of action which participants see themselves as having available to them: how confident they are in reaching out for advice or offering assistance; how willing they are to reciprocate, especially where there is no immediate reward in doing so.

Network power is thus a crucial element of the overall map we are drawing. Unlike the market and bureaucratic forms of policy organization, networks lack a single irreducible value (money, rules, etc.) with which to define power. While it may be asserted that higher levels of connectivity (being linked to most other members of the network, possessing 'high centrality') equate to greater levels of network power, there are several problems with this simple calculus. Individuals may have high centrality by virtue of their role and not because of their power. For example the secretary of a top law firm may have more ties to top lawyers than any individual member of that profession, yet may have little decision-making authority in comparison with the most junior partner of the firm.

In order to understand the power dimension of networks it is therefore necessary to specify both the level and pattern of connectivity, and the use made of such ties to perform policy functions such as trading information, getting and giving advice, negotiating deals, resolving problems and gathering support for proposals.

Investigating networks

In policy terms the network is a political structure in that such ties or contacts may be activated to do important work. What the analyst needs to know is thus the character of the interactions within the policy field being explored.

How are the linkages between individuals and groups characterized? Some simple ways to understand the character of networks are to investigate the kinds of ties that exist between individuals and agencies. These can include both formal and informal ties. For example, it may be useful to map the connections between policy analysts to see who knows who, who calls who to get information, who has worked with who in a previous job.

It is also useful to map the agency level ties in a policy field. Which agencies share contracts, have members on one another's boards, or have memberships of the same trade organizations? In more elaborate networks it may be useful to explore how agencies are connected through third parties such as banks, professional associations or subsidiary joint ventures.

What values do networks communicate? As we have seen, there are numerous values to be found within networks. The easiest way to visualize this is to ask what is the likely basis of the ties that link actors to one another? The major links in the policy world are:

- authority
- resources
- professions
- programmes
- partisan commitments.

The mandate or legal basis of a programme or institution will often generate a series of relationships or ties that stretch across organizations and agencies, linking providers, suppliers and consumers. Similarly the shared dependence on a common resource will provide a powerful pressure for actors to get to know one another, share experiences and develop alliances of various types. Professions are a means by which experts are linked by shared knowledge and status. Officials in similar positions in different agencies will also find opportunities to form ties. This may help them solve common problems or it may simply be generated by the solidarity of having someone with whom to discuss common interests. And obviously we expect members of parties or movements to form quite elaborate links with others of like mind. These furnish the policy network with ample opportunity to generate a dense capillary system for the conduct of different kinds of business.

Until now we have sought to investigate the many ways in which links between actors may help and hinder policy-making, using ideas from a wider discussion of the nature of networks. Implicit in this discussion have been four characteristics:

- networks are based on actual ties
- networks extend across a range of actors
- networks are semi-formal or informal
- networks are not simply hierarchical.

In using the term 'actor' to describe the key players in the network we have merged two different kinds of unit of analysis. Actors may be individuals or groups. Networks in the policy field are typically made up of both. They are thus a hybrid form of organization. Of course all organizations also have people in them, but this is not the same thing. In the policy network the links between actors may be either based on personal ties (having gone to school together, having the same profession) or based on organizational ties (joint involvement in the same programme, use of same supplier). To adequately account for the way ideas, resources or decisions are influenced by these networks we therefore need to be able to map both the organizational and the personal onto the same framework.

There is no generalized method for deciding which aspects of communication among these actors is the key to understanding policy outcomes. This must be achieved empirically. Social network techniques allow us to work out individual ties, at least among the likely players in any case. We also have a wide range of techniques available to us to determine how and whether any group of organizations is connected. We can check the cross-memberships of key people, the joint membership of other organizations such as trade groups, and in the case of public organizations it may also be possible to identify contracts between organizations, or regulatory obligations which require them to be in frequent contact.

These ties provide many opportunities to understand policy and to explain how results are achieved. For example, such networks provide an obvious opportunity for 'interest group mediation' (Schmitter, 1974; Marsh and Rhodes, 1992), or the achievement of certain agreed outcomes. If we can show such ties as enduring and densely networked we might also have grounds to argue for the existence of a policy sub-system which governs a policy sector (Laumann and Knoke, 1987).

There is significant debate concerning the exact character of such networks and their likely policy impact. These issues cannot be settled by definitional fiat or normative assertion. They are empirical matters. The analysis presented here has attempted to provide a recognized framework for such an investigation by showing the factors most likely to influence formation and participation. Networks are therefore, before anything else, a system for recognizing the links between actors and the manner in which these generate a kind of *organizational capital* in any single policy system. Networks themselves are not actors and nor are they institutions. They are a kind of capillary system through which work is done, and in the doing they become a means for extending or modifying the paths available for the next expected encounter between regular participants.

9

Policy Interventions and Organizations

Policy interventions involve the skilful use of organization. Working between established institutional processes and across the rules and conventions of several different organizations, success in making things happen is much to do with organizing power. This capacity includes a wide variety of skills from the ability to research policy issues, to the planning of campaigns and programmes.

An important paradox is the fact that this organizing power must be capable both of effective critique of current practices, and of developing and implementing new structures. Among the many obstacles that actors face in trying to improve things is the ingrained resistance of formal organizations and the habituated preferences of official procedure. Yet once enacted, their own new programmes depend entirely on these same organizational processes for their success. What we call 'organization' is therefore an instrument sharpened on both sides and perhaps pointed at both ends as well. The noun and the verb are necessarily in tension with each other. When we speak of 'organizing' we think of a certain freedom of action and a capacity to contrive new effects. But once this turns to consideration of the role of the organization as a machine, we can see that size and scale produce unique challenges.

In other words the organizational side of policy-making raises important distinctions between the work of the activist or agitator, and the work of the manager. Activists are those like politicians, interest group leaders and analysts who seek to open the system to change, amendment or what Lindblom (1965:3) called 'partisan mutual adjustment'. Activists work in organizational spaces created by policy systems (i.e. health, transportation, urban planning) using their capacity to effect the actions of others through threats, promises, strong communication or unilateral action.

This suggests that policy is a form of organization with at least two sets of imperatives – a set of norms based on the formal legal-rational system for administering programmes, and a set of skills for bargaining with actors seeking to advance their interests. To devise a strategic approach to policy intervention we must have both an understanding of the way organized, systematic action is achieved among political players or interests, and we must develop an understanding of the principles of organization that drive bureaucracies and other parts of the public system.

Effective policy actors are those who read organizational life thoughtfully and shift attention to places where movement and novelty are most likely to be welcome. How do actors achieve this understanding? What are the dynamics of organization that inform and support transformation? In this chapter we consider the basic traditions of organizational analysis as they impact upon the policy-making process. We will start with the more formal approaches to organization and work back towards the activist and strategic goals that link formal organization to the political aspects of organizing and mobilizing for change.

The organization as a formal system

Much of the research in the organization studies field employs metaphors that liken organizations to mechanical or organic systems. The corporation and the local health centre are seen to share a common character. They import energy (or resources) from their environments, transform it into goods and services and then export those products to outsiders.

Starting from this simple model analysts then begin to identify the different influences upon the system. What shows through is a common set of structural characteristics – the nature of the control system, the type of service, the technology being used to communicate and process tasks, the legal framework and the labour market. Each of these is seen to be capable of shaping the organization and forcing it to adapt in a characteristic way.

Working from the inside, researchers find ample evidence that the ability of the system to successfully transform energy into outcomes is governed by a set of specific problems such as scale of operation, span of control by managers, and the nature of the communication and performance evaluation. Theorists like Henri Fayol (1925), Luther Gulick (1947) and Lyndall Urwick (1947) long ago developed recommendations for owners and managers that expressed great optimism in regard to the planning of these organizational activities.

The principles of organization driving these traditional accounts include some common recommendations. First and foremost they suggest that the work of the organization be divided into different elements according to functional specialization. So for example, the accounts department would be composed of clerks and accountants who focus exclusively upon ordering stock and managing invoices for customers. Next door the personnel department does the hiring and firing. Downstairs the operators perform the core activities of the agency such as assessing claims (insurance industry), seeing patients (medical clinic) or administering tests (driver's licence bureau). Each operator is given a specific, measurable task which he or she is then able to perform with maximum efficiency because he or she has achieved a high-level specific competence in a rather narrow range of tasks.

To keep all these functions properly aligned with one another the organization then creates various forms of supervision. This may involve the direct supervision by managers, or it could be built into the planning system, the performance payment framework or into the technology used on the job. Management's role is therefore to set the goals, allocate tasks and see that adequate supervision exists to make sure the jobs get done and in the correct sequence. The hierarchical authority of management is universally accepted as the only generalized coordination technique required in this kind of system. Issues flow forward from the functional divisions via their team leaders or other reporting systems and are dealt with by the senior executive. They have both the wide view of the organization – seeing all the functional divisions, and the long view – seeing the sequential consequences of local actions.

A summary of the traditional (sometimes called industrial) school of thought is therefore quite elegant in its simplicity. Authority is centralized in a hierarchical chain of command. Each level is subordinate to the one above, allowing purpose to be established at the top and to be communicated effectively to the bottom. Each supervisor must have a span of control over his or her subordinates which is adequate to fix this communication of purpose, without being so limited as to raise costs. Staff are given stability of employment and a remuneration and promotion system which is governed by clear rules and methods of appeal. The reward system and the actions of supervisors are seen as critical to encouraging compliance and commitment among employees.

F.W. Taylor developed this classical management theory to its most extreme form. Using precise measurements of the workers' actions, Taylor's work-study teams identified the least wasteful and most exact work methods. Training and monitoring of the workflow were then directed to ensure that employees and supervisors followed these practices. This relentless pursuit of routine and measurement distinguished Taylorist approaches to organization. They helped institutionalize the idea that owners and senior managers were responsible for the mental side of work, while those on the production line were employed as instruments of the organization and their independent capacity to think and act was explicitly subordinated.

Henry Ford (1924) was one of the most spectacular converts to Taylor's Scientific Management School and the success of his T-Model factories owed much to this form of organization. He went out of his way to try to legitimize the routine and repetition which Taylorism championed:

> Repetitive labour – the doing of one thing over and over again and always in the same way – is a terrifying prospect to a certain kind

of mind. It is terrifying to me. I could not possibly do the same thing day in day out, but to other minds, perhaps I might say to the majority of minds, repetitive operations hold no terrors . . . To them the ideal job is one where the creative instinct need not be expressed.

Many of these ideas found their way into the public sector where Max Weber's nineteenth-century ideal of hierarchy and strict subordination appeared to coincide with the management principles emerging from the industrial sector. The neat division of functions between policy at the top and execution within a subordinated organization also found favour with politicians and senior bureaucrats wishing to reassure the public that an enlarged bureaucracy held no threat to democracy.

In reality, as Perrow (1970) and others have pointed out, the adoption of these ideas often resulted more from ideology than from concern about good practice. Where Taylor's scientific management worked best, which is to say where it increased efficiency without major breakdowns in industrial relations, was in those organizations with simple products and compliant workers. Bureaucratic factories of clerks checking forms and processing standard payments also yielded to this approach, but not for long.

Many organizations faced greater complexity and change than this classical organization theory could manage. Routine was of no value wherever pressures demanded 'one-off' solutions to client problems. Moreover, machine technology quickly replaced much of the manual labour that Taylorism had worked to regularize. Finally, the dramatic rise in the use of technical and professional workers meant that lock-step compliance was no longer likely to be effective. These officials were trained to exercise professional judgement and were employed to do this whenever the problems required it. As organizations grew in size and complexity the struggle to keep the staff in a single line grew less feasible and less desirable. More and more the work of the complex modern organization came to rely on skilled workers exercising discretion and developing unique solutions to problems.

Ecological models of organization

With modern industrial and public service organizations becoming more and more dependent on the skills of professionals, theories of organization began to take an interest in 'organic' and 'ecological' models. These more sophisticated systems theories saw the organization as akin to a living organism attempting to adapt to its environment. In other words the external world was at last acknowledged as a critical determinant of the organization's behaviour.

In its simple form this 'open system' was described as a circuit of transactions which were not necessarily goal-oriented. Or more exactly, the main goal was seen in Darwinian terms – good organizations survived, bad ones did not. Instead, the key was found in the process of learning and adaptation which staff used to make sense of complicated, often contradictory goals. Nowhere was this more evident than in public agencies where goals and purposes were likely to include respect both for formal rules and the individual needs of clients.

In a key study carried out by the Rand group in 1972, the US federal government authorized a detailed examination of four major education programmes. What they found was that despite very different management strategies, these four programmes achieved equal outcomes. When they searched for sources of success in these cases the study found that most variance was due to the way local expertise was used, how local staff were included in shaping strategies, and the use of highly motivated participants (Berman and McLaughlin, 1975:22).

These observations confirmed an 'open systems' account of strategy formation. As the environment around the agency becomes more complex, open systems theory predicts that organizations will undergo greater focus on internal specialization and differentiation. That is, their internal structure will reflect the external world in its complexity. Simple, stable organizations will not survive in complex, turbulent environments. Overly complex organizations will be too expensive and troublesome in straightforward areas that demand simple, regular activities.

One important consequence of this shift to viewing the organization as a kind of living organism was that some of the simple certainties about the role of the employee and the manager were exposed to criticism. Although the head could still be said to rule over the body, none of the organs could be regarded as dispensable. So, without changing the hierarchy of importance, open systems theory promoted a reappraisal of the contributions that all sub-systems made to the whole's survival. Two consequences followed. First, greater attention was given to incentives aimed at compensating and motivating workers. The costs of high turnover rates, absenteeism, rule-breaking and variable work quality in the more rigid organizations helped justify the new concept of interdependence between management and workforce.

The second change was a shift towards designing the workplace with employee needs in mind. The Human Relations School initiated by Elton Mayo and implemented at the Hawthorne plant of the US company Western Electric argued that organizational performance was only partly determined by formal organizational structures. The other determinant was the human side of work. The sub-group of employees working on a specific set of tasks were now viewed as a sub-system in their own right and questions were asked about the conditions under which this organism would function best. Surely their needs and those of the wider organizational environment must also be in equilibrium? For this to be so, greater attention to individual needs would be required. The expanding field of psychology rose to meet this challenge in the 1930s. Mayo, following Chester Barnard and others, developed a new, more complex account of the conditions under which individuals would become committed (or motivated) to make contributions to the organization. Their emphasis was on shifting attention away from management's power and the force of routine and towards the full engagement of the staff – both head and hand.

Herbert Simon (1957) in his path-breaking book *Administrative Behaviour* viewed those in control as having a rational inclination to find out what employees want and to attempt to give as many incentives as might be required to gain employee commitment. No matter what the personal objectives of the control group, their decisions will be heavily influenced by the fact that they can attain their objectives through the organization only if they maintain a positive balance of contributions over inducements, or at least equilibrium between the two, Simon concluded.

In its most sympathetic form this human relations tradition was expressed by Herzberg (1966), McGregor (1960) and others as a determination to take account of the individual's full range of needs and desires. Work was viewed as a site for human development, not just a place to earn a living. Theoretically this shift widened the responsibility and the surveillance by management, an increase in effort they were often not equipped to make. Job rotation, job enhancement, re-skilling and team-centred control were all strategies which hoped to respect the individual's hopes for a more interesting work life. Of course, as Morgan (1986) notes, there was also the expectation that happy workers would become more productive employees and that the extra costs associated with humanizing the organization would be more than rewarded by improved productivity and better quality.

The liberation from stultifying bureaucratic work would now involve management intervention to control and organize the personal side of organizational life. Team building, the use of softer control skills by supervisors, improved physical environments and the expectation of greater team spirit embodied a new theory of psychological coordination.

Power and resource dependence

No doubt the human relations movement was a creature of the seventies, an era in which the ego returned to popular culture both as a consumer and a demanding political subject. But the idea that a 'balance of incentives' would produce equilibrium between workers, managers and external stakeholders such as politicians and owners was soon to undergo a new assault. The key to the conflict was a renewed appraisal of the power of different interests and in the fundamentally different ways these would be understood.

The resource dependence school pioneered by Charles Perrow (1970:1986) and others viewed organizations as elaborate mechanisms for creating, converting and distributing power. Organizations provided different conditions under which individuals or groups used power. The key variable was interdependence. That is, where units needed one another for the achievement of some task or outcome, a power relation would inevitably develop. In other words, power was viewed as endemic to both the internal and external economy of the agency. To say an agency is highly structured by rules or routines is to say that the outcome is fixed, set in a network of habits and unequal rights. But the focus on power, on the other hand, suggests that all these actors retain a capacity to influence what takes place, even if their role is small.

According to the resource dependence perspective, the chief source of vulnerability that causes the members of the organization to yield to the power of others was their reliance upon the flow of resources from elsewhere. Whenever one unit required information, money or authority from another it was subject to influence. The pattern of transactions that then took place would establish a power relation which would shape outcomes. Like many of those who work in this field Pfeffer and Salancik (1978) did much of their theorizing in regard to politics between organizations, not politics inside the organization. When organizations interacted with one another there was seldom a clear line of command and control to decide contentious issues. Suppliers were required to negotiate with customer organizations, and health and education ministries had to be cajoled into cooperating in some form of joint service. The thing that would always bind them was their common need to acquire and protect their resource base and only when official goals coincided with this reality would activity match the expectations of dominant policy makers.

This approach offered a politically sensitive analysis of organizational work. From dependence grows dominance and from dominance the possibility of resistance or conflict. As Hawley (1950) notes: 'Dominance attaches to the unit that controls the conditions necessary to the functioning of other units.'

Pfeffer and Salancik (1978:44) give a list of conditions that will cause an organization to comply with outside attempts made to control it. These include: awareness of the demand being made, the need for resources, the strategic importance of resources, lack of an easy alternative source for resources, lack of a retaliatory power available to the organization, and the technical and legal capacity to comply with the demand.

Other important assumptions are made by the resource dependence school such as the fact that the target organization must be aware of the demand being made, and the consistency of the demands made by different actors wishing to control the organization needs to be high or incoming demands will simply create confusion. But these are of less importance than the central dynamic of dependence. The key to this relation is that the organization will be controlled to the degree that others make offers that cannot be refused without high costs.

Benson (1977) distinguishes the explicitly political consequences of the resource-dependence perspective by setting it alongside the classical and human relations schools. These two are viewed as being concerned with goal achievement and need fulfilment, the first referring to the mental/manual distinction discussed above, and the second pertaining to the incorporation of individual needs into corporate strategy in the work humanization strategies.

The recognition by resource dependence theory that organizations contain diverse interests does not in itself threaten the earlier approaches. After all, much of the purpose of classical and human relations theory was to find strategies to bind the whole together, a project which would be neither intellectually interesting nor functionally necessary if the whole was generally compliant. The great problem in these theories, however, was their failure to examine the social basis of these internal conflicts and to recognize an abiding tension between them and any top-down view of organizational control. This was especially true in the public sector where democratic norms provide the justification for the ultimate purpose of organizations.

Feminists were among the first to see how much work must go into sustaining the organization's ordering systems and how great the tension may be between these objectives and the wider social aspirations and rights of citizens. Women employees, including women managers, cannot abandon their difference and as a result may find themselves excluded by the normal incentive systems used to structure the organization. For instance Game and Pringle (1983) studied six work processes and identified characteristic gender 'rules'. They noticed that when women worked on machines they were far more likely to involve stationary, repetitive tasks which created few opportunities for status or influence. Male workers were more likely to be found operating larger, more flexible machines and were 'able to represent the power of the machine as theirs and experience themselves as having "technical" expertise'.

Once raised in the open this question of social difference changed the ground rules for organization theory. As Silverman (1970:39) argued 'it would be more fruitful to analyse organizations in terms of the different ends of their members and of their capacity to impose these ends on others – it suggests an analysis in terms of power and authority'. But difference in itself is not enough to challenge the traditional perspective, for difference may simply be cast as the pluralism which allows there to be alternative methods for achieving a single goal. The resource dependence perspective claims more than difference; it identifies a key role for wider social conflicts. In other words it cannot be assumed that all those involved in the organization will want the same things, nor will they have similar capacities to achieve full participation. The same policy or programme may be driven by people with opposing values. These contests will then become decisive in struggles over scarce resources. In the end these often prove critical in determining what gets done.

Economic models of organization

While organization studies has mostly been the preserve of political scientists, sociologists and psychologists, in the mid-1970s this began to change and a small group of researchers began to alter the way economics treated problems of corporate behaviour. In particular this new interest became focused upon the (pathological) internal dynamics of the firm.

The first of these accounts – called 'agency theory' – produced a simple model based on the idea that all key problems could be reduced to a single relationship between the 'principal' and his or her 'agent'. The American political scientist Terry Moe (1984) has helped render this research in a form which makes it accessible to 'rational choice' theories of politics, but the foundation work in economics was produced by Fama (1980) and by Jensen and Meckling (1976).

The core concept of agency theory is that all important elements of the organization's work can best be understood as a 'chain of contracts' linking the principal (the owner, manager or political master) with the various agents he or she employs to carry out tasks. The agent performs this work in return for the rewards set down in the contract of employment or the other transactions used to create binding agreements.

Agency theory assumes that the driving force of the contract is the universal assumption that all these individuals – principals and agents – seek to maximize their own self-interest. Implicit in this notion is the idea that each individual's interest will be somewhat unique and that as a result each will need to perform his or her own calculation of what constitutes their best outcome and each will therefore be competitive in relation to the interests of others. The second important assumption driving the model is that these contracts will always be rather difficult to monitor. This difficulty arises from several different sources. In particular the agency theorists point out that the supervision of contracts is expensive. It takes time, effort and very good information to make sure that what is 'purchased' is actually what gets delivered.

The 'costs of supervision' argument is therefore critical to the model. When looked at from the organizational perspective this issue is commonly described as a problem of 'control loss'. When the principal contracts with someone to perform a task they concede a certain amount of discretion to that agent. The agent may work in a different agency or in a different part of a large corporation. Their work will therefore be invisible to the principal on a day-to-day basis. Furthermore, the agent may be employed because she has expert knowledge which the principal does not have and which they cannot easily understand or evaluate. So the task that is performed can only be judged by its ultimate effect on outcomes, not according to whether the principal judges it to be the right procedure at the time.

Two different 'control loss' problems have preoccupied the economists working in this field. At the top of the organization they observe a loss of supervisory capacity by boards of directors, owners and politicians in their dealings with chief executive officers (CEOs) and secretaries of departments. Highly skilled CEOs will know more about the method to be used to run large organizations than those employing them. Yet their role also requires a large freedom to manoeuvre in order for them to devise and implement a successful corporate strategy. Only when the results for the year are turned in can the board assess performance, and even here they may lack any objective benchmark with which to judge that performance. Several years may go by before a useful trend can be discerned by those outside the senior management group.

At the bottom of the organization we see the second form of control loss. When the senior managers employ staff to implement the strategy they too must concede a large degree of autonomy to staff members and local supervisors. Even where the CEO has a good understanding of the technical work being performed, the large number of employees and their remote locations will usually mean that the work remains shielded from the senior management gaze.

To try to overcome these two problems the organization will usually implement various forms of reporting and performance checking. Various forms of training and external evaluation will also be used to try to keep agents tied to the conditions laid out in the contract. All of these efforts, according to agency theory, are doomed to failure, at least to some degree. The reason, they say, is simple. Contracts only make sense if they are cost efficient, yet the more supervision and checking that are involved, the higher the cost of the work.

Given the starting assumption of the model it is not surprising that the chief source of this failure is that agents will behave in ways that serve their own interests and not those of the principal. This is termed 'opportunism with guile', or more exactly, cheating. The evidence for this is different at the two levels of the organization. At the top these economists observe a tendency in large corporations for CEOs to maximize their own salary packages and future employment opportunities at the expense of returns to the shareholders (or the voters and members in political organizations). They will also engage in dubious tactics to make sure short-term performance figures look good if this helps them win bonuses, even if this puts the future health of the agency at risk. At the bottom the opportunistic strategies are more likely to take the form of time wasting, carelessness in regard to quality and blame shifting to others, if this helps make life easier for them and is likely to go undetected.

The solution to these problems according to this model is for principals to act cautiously by drawing up explicit contracts for the work to be performed and by limiting the duration of such contracts. The closer the contract can be made to a 'spot market', the more power the principal will have to compel compliance. Long-term contracts such as tenured employment will foster excessive space in which agents may manoeuvre to insert their own priorities in place of those preferred by the principal. And if the terms of the contract are not explicit it will also be easier in these cases for the agents to avoid responsibility for their poor performance.

The second economic theory to challenge traditional accounts of organization is called 'transaction cost economics' (TCE). Pioneered by Ronald Coase and Oliver Williamson, the TCE framework shares with agency theory a belief that self-interest is endemic and that contracts are costly to enforce. However where agency theory assumes that the best system is one where contracts are short term and competitive, TCE provides an account of the conditions under which it will be efficient for the organization to choose hierarchy (internal) rather than market (external) allocation. Another way to understand this trade-off is to observe that for TCE there are many efficiency justifications for keeping activities inside the agency rather than buying them from contractors.

The cornerstone of TCE is the idea that agencies face several restraints on their ability to get the best from external contractors. In the first place they share with agency theory the belief that opportunism is rife and that suppliers of goods and services will behave opportunistically. So, for example, if the agency needs to buy paper and if the suppliers of paper realize that they can make money by promising high quality product but delivering average material, it will be in their interest to do so. Since they have no guarantee that the agency would be a repeat buyer, maximum profit taking would be best achieved by supplying the cheapest paper they could get away with.

The second assumption of this model is that agencies face an uncertain environment. They cannot know who will be around to offer contracts in the future and they have inadequate data upon which to assess their own need for supplies. This makes it difficult to strike longer-term bargains with other agencies with whom they trade.

A third component of the TCE model is the idea of 'inside advantage' which points to the inevitable benefit which current suppliers have in their dealings with the agency. These suppliers have a store of experience that they accumulate while serving the agency and this is always an advantage when it comes time to compare the bids of potential replacements. A simple version of this idea is that the incumbent employee is always equipped with specialized knowledge and experience when compared to a potential replacement, so even a well-qualified person outside the agency will find it difficult to be competitive in job selection.

Finally, the TCE model identifies the tendency for contractors (or agents) to develop what they term 'asset specificity'. The firm that supplies equipment to a hospital will develop exactly the kinds of beds and trolleys that hospitals need and which other firms supplying, say the hotel industry, will not have to hand. In many cases this will involve them in the development of specialized equipment to manufacture these goods, with the result that they will become dependent upon this kind of customer. And looked at from the hospital's point of view this will also mean that the pool of potential suppliers will grow smaller as the nature of these goods grows more specialized. In these conditions it is very difficult to use normal market interactions to guarantee efficiency.

The TCE school points out that when these conditions apply it will be more efficient for the firm to integrate suppliers into their own business through takeover, acquisition or by building up their own capacity to supply their own components. In other words it becomes rational to avoid the market and create a larger organization capable of performing these functions in-house. In fact the TCE school shows that there are relatively limited conditions under which markets will operate successfully. First of all they will work well in cases where transactions involve a once-only exchange between buyer and seller. There is a limited 'what you see is what you get' information flow in these cases and neither can know much about the other's needs, other than the obvious. So there is not much opportunity for either buyers or sellers to develop the forms of opportunism we discussed above.

A second place where markets will continue to flourish is where there is little in the way of uncertainty. That is, where the goods being traded do not involve any special knowledge and are easily compared with their competitors. Basic items such as pencils, pens and stationery meet this standard and so agencies will have little need either of continuing contracts or in-house production. The other condition likely to keep markets healthy is where costs of entry are low. In other words when it is easy for a new business to start up and challenge existing providers. Restaurants are a good example – the technology, skills and premises do not prohibit entry. Hospitals are at the other end of this scale as are chemical refineries.

If we turn these three conditions around we can see where TCE predicts problems for markets and the likelihood that agencies will prefer to perform tasks internally rather than risk being exploited in the marketplace. This applies when contracts need to be medium or long term, where there is uncertainty about the prices and quality available in the market, and where barriers to entry for new firms are high enough to give current operators a significant buffer against market forces.

Economic models applied to public organizations

The application of both agency theory and TCE to the public realm is subject to several conditions and not a few objections.

Some of these techniques and their virtues will be the subject of detailed discussion in the next chapter; we can focus the present consideration upon the implications for our understanding of the work of public organizations.

The obvious thing to note in this regard is that most accounts of public organizations are written as if market devices have traditionally been weak or non-existent inside the public service. Instead the principal method of allocation has been seen as rule-based hierarchy. This is the conventional view and it leads to a belief (and discourse) which distinguishes markets from hierarchies, and thus the public world from the private world of organizations. But when we look beneath the surface we can see a large number of occasions in which a typical public agency involves itself in market or quasi-market activity.

Public organizations employ labour and in this are subject to bargains and exchange relations concerning the market for labour. They buy supplies from private agencies and sometimes from one another. These range from buildings and other property to nuclear-powered medical technologies worth tens of millions of dollars. Equally, the public sector is the largest customer of the multi-billion-dollar-a-year pharmaceutical sector, most road-building products and of a large share of construction activity. All these activities involve public agencies in commercial transactions in the marketplace, acting as economic agents.

Yet we also know that despite engaging in economic activities of this kind, public agencies may also obey a different logic in pursuing such transactions. They may, for example, seek a purchasing contract which has goals other than profit maximization. State agencies might prefer to buy from local producers in order to foster employment or achieve reliable supply. Governments often support a national airline even if this is more expensive than allowing an international carrier to take over. They proffer all sorts of reasons for such non-economic (and perhaps uneconomic) preferences. They may want to keep access available to people living in remote and less economically viable cities or towns. They might want to foster tourism and to open up destinations not yet on the tourist map. Or they may simply regard a national airline as a sign of strong national identity.

While it is doubtful that agency theory would approve of such preferences because of the vastly increased possibility for opportunistic behaviour, there are some things the public sector can learn from economic theories of organization without surrendering to them the core purpose of public sector work. Assuring the regular supply of things like health care or airline services to government, and thus to the public, imposes upon the principal many of the dilemmas posed by agency theory. The more these transactions are governed by uncertainty, insider advantages and high entry barriers, the more it should suit government to self-supply. And where this is impossible for political reasons, the better it will suit government agencies to develop high-trust partnerships with like-minded agencies. The supreme paradox in all this is that TCE actually represents a powerful argument against certain forms of privatization of public assets, yet the public discourse surrounding the use of these economic theories of organization has been part of a more general assault on public ownership in some countries.

From models to interventions

These different accounts of how to organize public activity provide policy actors with contending designs for public pro-grammes and agencies. How might we compare the main options available? To simplify the problem we can start by identifying four attributes which all agencies must possess in order to operate a service or produce a programme: leadership, technical support, supervision and operating systems.

The leadership function is the place where a long view is taken and where the day-to-day issues of the agency are aligned to future capacities and demands. This might include questions of political support, or decisions about investment in people and technology. In current terminology this group will usually be called the executive management team or corporate management. The technical support sections of the agency will be the place where the specialist knowledge needed to design and run programmes is to be found. In a local council these will be civil engineers, social workers and planners. In an industry department they will be economists, agronomists and other resource specialists. The supervision work of the agency will be spread through a number of layers and roles, but its purpose will be to keep the different parts of the agency well coordinated and through coordination to achieve whatever targets have been set. Finally, the operating system will consist of all those roles that have to do with actually creating the services needed. This will include service delivery to clients and support functions such as cleaning and hospitality. In very large agencies the support functions are often segmented and treated as separate to the rest of the operating line, but in many public agencies the distinction adds little to the understanding of how organizational structures impact on results.

It should not be assumed that these activities are necessarily carried out by different people, although they might be. In particular it is controversial to imply that the strategic leadership tasks are divorced in some way from the operating line. Although this mirrors the reality in many factories and bureaucracies, it is a separation widely condemned even in the mainstream management literature. Peter Drucker (1961:250), for example, argues that

> Planning and doing are separate parts of the same job; they are not separate jobs. There is no work that can be performed effectively unless it contains elements of both.

This is a very simple starting point. Before considering how these activities might be structured it is also necessary to understand more about the work being done and the skills needed to do it. In most agencies there will be a spectrum of tasks that range from highly complex to more routine. The next set of design questions seeks to address the best way to group such tasks. Is it more efficient to have one person or group do all the routine jobs and a different group perform the complex ones? And if so, what should be the relationship between the two? Can they work independently of one another, or do they need close coordination?

Table 9.1   Design options in public agencies: ideal types

	Simple	Adaptive	Dynamic
Skill set	Routine	Technical	Scientific
Coordination	Direct control	Process control	Internal control
Stabilizers	Standard outputs	Standard techniques	Shared knowledge
Examples	Pension agency	Childcare centre	Court
	Insurance office	School	Emergency ward
	Tax department	Nursing home	University

The answer to these questions will produce a grid-map (or pyramid) of the kind of specialization the agency wishes to use in order to get the work done efficiently. This will range from strategic management at the core, then certain kinds of professional roles, technical jobs and through to the many types of operating jobs needed. The decision about how best to arrange these specialists requires that a path diagram first needs to be constructed to show how the various components of the work come together to produce a complete service. This flow-chart maps the order or sequence in which the contributions need to be made, and the different points at which decisions are made by staff or managers. The flow of work has a great deal to do with two external conditions – what supplies are needed, and what different client groups need at different times. In other words the grid-map of tasks and the work-flow diagram of work processes need to sit within a framework of external drivers defined as the agency's key relationships with suppliers and clients.

These elements may now be combined in several different ways, depending upon three conditions: the type of skills used to produce the service, the form of coordination inside the agency, and the source of stability (and dependency) in relations with the agency's environment (see table 9.1).

While all organizations require a mix of skills to achieve results, we can readily see that in each case a predominant source of skill will be evident. This will be closely related to the nature of the service being performed. Health services use medical skills of different kinds. Pension agencies use administrative skills as their core expertise. While the predominant skill or form of expertise usually shows up in analysis as a numerical superiority of staff with these skills, it may not be the case that the predominant skill set is aligned with the employment pattern of the agency. For example, in an agency established to assess consumer complaints the majority of staff may be clerical workers, yet the core skill will almost certainly be held by a team of lawyers who may number less than 10 per cent of those on the payroll. What makes the core skill so important is that it serves to define the value being created for clients and supporters of the service (including voters).

In order to see how different skill types will influence the design of the agency we can contrast three elementary forms of knowledge. The first is termed *routine* because it involves the repeated application of a stable set of tasks. The processing of applications for a pension, for instance, will typically involve a routine check to see that all data has been provided and that it conforms to standardized criteria for eligibility.

Technical skills involve the operator in more decision-making. The technician is someone who has a trained competence in a field requiring a selection of possible methods for dealing with cases. For the technician the reason for making one choice rather than another is structured into a set of protocols learned during training. The relationship between choice options and consequences is known to the technician. She can tell with great certainty that a given problem fits a given category and that within that category there are defined alternatives for action. Nurses have high levels of technical expertise, as do computer programmers and accountants.

Intervention by professionals

Scientific skills are those involving the application of a body of knowledge to problems which are ill defined and for which the likely outcomes can only be expressed as probabilities. Much of the public policy environment is shaped by such problems for two reasons. First of all the resolution of such problems is difficult to achieve using markets. Lack of knowledge, imprecise comparisons of alternative options and decisions with long-term secondary consequences make it hard for individual consumers to make good decisions. Second, many of these problems require collective solutions which only the state can easily mandate. A good example is public health. If all citizens are not inoculated against smallpox, and if drains and sewers are not covered and sanitized, the whole community is apt to succumb to disease, including those with access to high-cost health treatments. Engineering solutions for traffic management and public transport have a similar scale and universality element.

The scientific skill set requires that practitioners develop deep specialization which is capable of problem solving where information is limited. This process of innovation or improvization is of a higher order than most technical skills because many of the required procedures cannot be standardized. Each case is to some extent unique and therefore the professional has to develop a new strategy by using deep theoretical knowledge and long experience of diagnosis. For this to be sustainable the practitioners must belong to a community of practice outside the agency where new ideas and improved methods can be developed and where standards of performance can be maintained independently of local pressures to economize.

The skills used in different agencies thus tend to require different forms of coordination. Where routine work is common the training will tend to be on-site and the responsibility for coordination will tend to reside in a separate layer of managers or supervisors. In organizations such as hospitals the technical staff will more likely be coordinated by use of rules and protocols which seek to standardize the application of a repertoire for each type of case. In scientific agencies such as law offices, courts or medial clinics the staff assert internal control over the work through established ethics and norms of good practice which are to a significant extent held independently of local organizational imperatives. Managers may seek to ration these services and negotiate the kinds of cases they treat, but will have far less control over the actual work that is subsequently carried out.

What enables these different skill types to achieve some level of stability in their environments? Again we must generalize to see the important differences. The simple type is most likely to be associated with the routine treatment of a constant set of clients with standard demands, such as pensioners. Procedures and entitlements may change but the agency remains stable over time because it has a standard output that everyone can see and understand. In the case of the adaptive type the thing that brings stability is the technique-based programme being offered. Different client groups may come and go but the nursing home or child-care centre remains a distinctive agency because of the specific methods of care or service that these staff have to offer. In the case of the scientific type we have only the shared knowledge base to guide us to a continuing form of activity. A wide variety of different programmes may employ lawyers or engineers but wherever their skills are at the core of the agency, it will be their professional ideology and methodology which stabilizes the purpose of work.

It will now be clear that different agencies will have different organizational designs and that these should result from an intersection of the internal skills and external purposes of the group. Since both are open to manipulation by policy makers it is of great importance that the significance of different structures is understood. It hardly makes sense to employ professionals to carry out routine work, nor to expect them to move out of their area of training and undertake different tasks. Nor would it help the implementation of a new policy to treat a new and complex issue such as youth suicide by empowering technicians with skills from another field, such as teaching or nursing.

If we contrast Anna's scenario with Bruno's we can see that both involve a core scientific knowledge but in the latter case the fishing fleet have deeply embedded local knowledge regarding best networks and strategies. These needed to be made transparent before a successful regulation regime could be imagined.

Of course we must also acknowledge that no group is likely to act alone in treating a social problem or creating a new service.

Most policy fields are made up of a mix of agencies and it is the way tasks are divided between them that most affects the overall outcome for clients or citizens. It is to this question of interactivity that we turn in the next chapter when we consider how agency issues impact upon questions of governance.

10

Policy Interventions and Governance

Government reports, academic research and the soft-back management literature appear to have found agreement on the nature of new governance systems set to replace the older bureaucratic order. It is to be based upon the model(s) of the flexible firm, the Benetton network and the customer-oriented retail chain (Atkinson and Coleman, 1989). It is, of course, no easy matter to reconcile the various, often conflicting characteristics of these post-Fordist forms of organization, particularly in the public sector. But there can be little doubt that the previous order is under challenge and the new order is centred upon smaller, entrepreneurial units acting within some de-bureaucratized whole (Drucker, 1985; Powell and Dimaggio, 1991).

When social theorists apply these ideas to discussions of the welfare state they identify its core character as a shift to state support for 'organisational and market innovation . . . by intervening on the supply-side' (Jessop, 1990; Offe, 1984). In place of traditional welfare concerns to underwrite paid employment and productive accumulation, these theorists posit a welfare model based upon 'autonomous public spheres . . . that enter into exchange with one another as soon as they make use of the potential for self-organization and the self-organized employment of communications media' (Habermas, 1986: 15).

All these changes have in common the fragmentation of services and the multiplication of actors involved in their delivery (Capling, Considine and Crozier, 1998). Why are governments apparently opting to give up their dominant position in many sectors in favour of this 'new governance' approach? In each case the answer is a little different but some common causes can be identified. These range from critiques of any large organization, through to arguments against monopoly and to advocacy for private services (Mayntz, 1993; Kickert, 1993). Among a long list of reasons for moving away from the standard bureaucratic service type are the following: large bureaucracies cost too much to run, are difficult to steer, invite veto by unions and professions, require too many middle managers, and do not respond flexibly to consumers and clients.

Set against this stereotype is the imagined virtue of more complex governance systems in which public and private agencies form clusters or networks of service delivery capacity. It is argued that this new type of complex system provides hope for variety in organization type to stimulate innovation, for private participation to shift capital costs off the public budget, to compel competitors to regulate one another, or to generate forms of non-profit service delivery that is voluntary and responsive to local needs.

There appear to be serious gaps in many of the initiatives currently being taken in actual policy fields so far as the realization of these expectations is concerned. This may be a normal process of evolution and learning which is entailed in any large change. But it may also signal the prevalence of serious design errors in many cases of new governance. Breaking down bureaucracy can mean different things as the list above demonstrates. It rarely means all these things.

Anti-bureaucracy

Bureaucracy is a generic term applied loosely to any large organization with a layered system of authority and specialized ranks of officials working in separate divisions. Banks, insurance companies and manufacturing firms have tended to use broadly similar bureaucratic features to those found inside government. So too have the larger churches and trade unions. It is therefore important when discussing the antecedents of the current move away from civil service solutions and towards markets and 'mixed economy' arrangements to note that the anti-bureaucratic mood includes both public and private institutions. In both discursive and material terms, opinion seems to have turned against bureau-cracy, at least where that term signifies universal treatments and standardized methods of service. Flexibility, tailoring and other forms of individualization are now more in evidence in many systems than before. This suggests both a change in taste cultures, in identities and in the political assessments being made by elites and their advisers (du Gay and Salaman, 1996).

The alternative to the old (somewhat stereotypical) world of universal treatments is the world of multiple, alternate paths and preferences, usually with the state acting as guarantor of a minimum entitlement. There do seem to be, in theory at least, many benefits to having multiple-provider systems in places where once we expected a single public organization to dominate. In areas such as the delivery of environmental and social services where capital costs allow relatively easy entry to new operators or mobility by existing ones, this appears to open the way for greater flexibility.

There have been a number of attempts to introduce reforms which express these propositions in a practical institutional form. Barzelay (1992:110) identifies a post-bureaucratic model which champions the Minnesota STEP program as one plausible example of 'customer-focused' organization, citing the willingness and need of public servants 'to improve users' evaluations' of the service being provided. The more apocalyptic vision of Osborne and Gaebler's (1992:23) 'entrepreneurial governance' was expressed in Vice-President Al Gore's National Performance Review (1993) which involved a similar desire to achieve both downsizing and increased customer approval.

> We must turn bureaucratic institutions into entrepreneurial insti-tutions, ready to kill off obsolete initiatives, willing to do more with less, eager to absorb new ideas.

This more entrepreneurial form of public organization is defined by Gore and others as one in which managers have a greatly enlarged field of action in which to apply resources, cancel com-mitments, and do all that is necessary short of committing crime to satisfy the legitimate demands of customers. Contractors, markets and other competitive devices are viewed as the necessary instruments for empowering the new entrepreneurial actors. This consensus appears to be a consequence both of actual deficiencies and of the emergence of new anti-government ideo-logies associated with the stronger cultural power of business. As Fournier and Grey (1999:108) put it, the new vision 'seeks to stigmatise and marginalise bureaucracy, in general, and public bureaucracy in particular, as being outmoded and as functionally and morally bankrupt'.

It is also true that as this 'new governance' movement (and New Public Management as its principle instruments are often called) has gained momentum there have been a variety of attempts to privatize government utilities and services. The privatization process is clearly a harbinger of new systems of governance, although the one does not always follow from the other. Using private sector methods does not, of itself, change government into a private activity. It is here that discourse and organizational prac-tice need to be distinguished. The new movement for reform cer-tainly speaks with a corporate and market vocabulary, but this may also be tactical. Between the rhetoric and the reality may lie some sizeable distance, especially when these governments clothe their reforms with one eye on the credit rating agencies, international financial markets and currency traders. In other words the rhetoric may be partly a matter of how best to sell a reform agenda to external agencies upon whom one is unhappily dependent for support.

The rationale for reforming key parts of the old bureaucratic system using the new governance approach often highlights different aspects of its perceived inadequacy. The desire to increase political management of the core bureaucracy became a general concern in the late 1970s as a combination of the OPEC-inspired oil crises and the emergence of stagflation put major pressure on the spending capacity of governments in the OECD. Governing without budget growth entailed a new set of tensions between politicians and bureaucrats in many systems. As governments fell they often blamed an inflexible or malevolent bureaucracy.

This may have remained a localized problem capable of insti-tutional reform had a second series of pressures not emerged during the 1980s. New social movements and changing social life-course pathways became evident in many societies at this time. The relative security of the so-called 'baby boom' generation born after the Second World War was less available to the 'generation x' which followed. This group experienced higher rates of divorce amongst their parents, found the transition from school to work far more problematic, faced a less protected housing market, and a political system less cleanly divided by the Cold War and more attenuated by what Beck (1997) and Giddens and Hutton (2000) have termed the politics of risk.

The effect of these larger patterns upon actual bureaucracies is unknown and probably unknowable. What is more certain is that they seem to have resulted in a decline in traditional forms of status politics, that is in the expression of universal collective demands for assistance, and instead for the creation of individuated services (Streeck, 1992:43). No doubt elites inside and around the public service helped support this development, in part perhaps because the individualized model offers fewer veto points to unions, consumers and other outside groups. Instead the new service regime seeks to interpret itself to a world where 'one size' does not fit all. Sometimes this individualization implies the empowerment of citizens and in other cases it may justify the sudden withdrawal of support. But what is general to the type is the desire to govern through a more localized set of instruments for exacting measured performance, comparing the achievements of agents and increasing the flexibility and mobility of public resources.

An important part of this 'new governance' methodology is therefore to create a discursive ideal of the new individual, be she a bureaucrat, recipient of a service, or other 'stakeholder'. Elsewhere I have argued that the new image in the West appears to be one of the self-enterprising sole trader who creates their own public and private life and is entirely responsible for their own position, in much the way that the market-place risk-taker treats their own personal skills and personality as an object of investment and exploitation (Considine, 2001). Others have treated some of the same issues under the heading of 'contractualism' (Pollitt, 1993). We will return to these larger issues concerning the constructed discourse of citizenship at the end, but first it is useful to review the central instruments and institutions of the 'new governance' system.

The new public managers

A central assertion of the system reformers of the 1980s and 1990s was that the public sector was under-managed. Driven by the desire to cut costs, many governments sought to 'do more with less' by changing the systems of administration inside their various bureaucracies and between them and the political executive. The natural allies in this battle were the management consulting companies who quickly developed models and standard methods for 'breaking into', 'breaking up', or 'breaking down' bureaucracy.

The first wave of changes included those of the Carter administration in the US and the latter period of the Callaghan government in the UK where small experiments in improved budgeting and management training sent a signal of things to come. The two regimes that replaced each of these governments would do most to establish the break between the old and the new systems, in no small part because their political opponents had established a basis for bipartisan action. Reagan and Thatcher, separately and together, sponsored a major assault on what was now termed the old 'tax and spend' approach to government. Principles that had underpinned the Keynesian Welfare State (KWS) project were now dismantled, at least in rhetorical terms.

In granting new authority to senior managers these reformers were actually attempting two things at once. They wished to separate the senior managers from the ranks of the ordinary bureaucracy in order to make them more responsive to the political will of the government. The paradox, and the risk of this strategy would take some time to become obvious, but in essence the plan involved making senior officials much more powerful in the hope that they would use this new power to serve their governments better.

The management 'performance revolution' that took place in the 1980s saw a comprehensive set of changes attempted in most OECD countries, but with the Anglo-Saxon democracies leading the way. Programme budgeting, corporate planning, pay-for-performance, contracts for top managers, and the introduction of key performance indicators (KPIs) for both programmes and people were the most prominent reform instruments. Managers, and particularly senior managers, looked to business schools to provide training and to private consultants to model the organizational structures needed. Also driving the changes from above were central agencies such as prime minister's offices and civil service boards. They saw the performance system as a way to both increase control and to deal themselves into the new cost-cutting regime that was dominating policy debates everywhere and which, hitherto, was the sole preserve of Treasury departments.

Once the enthusiasm for management empowerment had taken root, it took little time for system reformers to look further down into the organization in order to question traditional practices. Most of the costs of public programmes could be found tied up in the salaries of middle and junior level bureaucrats. In most systems these employees were protected by career employment rules and by powerful trade unions. Using many of the nostrums of public choice and transaction cost economics discussed in the previous chapter, the new problem was seen as one of 'control loss' by shareholders. Two kinds of control loss were identified in this organizational economics literature – the top level where senior managers of the corporation were often able to divert shareholder funds into large salaries and benefits for themselves, and the lower level, where junior employees could escape scrutiny from their supervisors and substitute their own goals (including the desire for a quiet life) for those of the corporation.

Contractualism

Williamson (1975) and others had argued in the 1970s that an important dynamic in the process of growth in large private firms was the decision to 'make or buy'. Contracting slowly became an alternative to bureaucratization of the firm. Whether a firm should perform a function in-house or hire others to do it was primarily a choice about where it was efficient to commit scarce capital resources and when it was likely to be easy to obtain high-quality products from outsiders.

In this environment the firm had also to consider different options so far as the *range* of suppliers was concerned. Using a single preferred provider involves a greater likelihood of being able to negotiate exactly the product and the quality required but it may also lead the supplier to raise prices or adopt merely satisfactory, rather than optimal standards. Sharing the contract out among many suppliers reduces the level of confidence and reciprocity among contractors and this may harm trust and continuity. Multiple suppliers create price competition (or may do) but they also increase transaction costs.

'New governance' reformers now sought to deal with these issues by adopting as a core philosophy the principles of organizational economics which deal with the relations between 'principals' and 'agents' (Donaldson, 1995). According to this view, all organizations can be considered as a 'chain of contracts' between principals and their agents. In the case of the public sector that chain begins with voters, who are always the principals. They employ as their agents the elected politicians, who in turn have as their agents the senior public service. They in their turn act as principals when employing staff and hiring contractors.

When applied to actual institutions these ideas resulted in a wide range of reforms. One common outcome has been the attempt to divide the public sector into executive ministries and agency organizations. In the UK, for example, the process of civil service reform associated with the Thatcher and Major governments included separating policy-making departments headed by ministers from service delivery agencies headed by chief executive officers, and by linking the two through public performance agreements. This was an explicit institutionalization of principal–agent separation.

A similar approach is expressed by the popular resort to the contracting-out of public services. This seeks to bind contractors in both the public and private sectors into performance agreements in which the executive arm accepts a new role for itself as 'governing at a distance'. The division of management expertise into either steering or rowing rather than both promises a new specialization in which managers become expert at setting strategic direction and in devising contracts to achieve stated goals (Osborne and Gaebler, 1992). In other words the creation of public programmes now becomes an act of purchasing rather than a skill at day-to-day administration.

Once the chain of contracts has been extended to include the large number of potential agents we see a new kind of institutional architecture – the quasi-market. In the quasi-market the principal sets the objectives and specifies a time of delivery. There may also be procedural requirements such as quality assurance (QA) standards included. Through a system of competitive tender and independent assessment, the agents now compete with one another to win the bid.

The challenges for those using contracts have been well documented (Harden et al., 1992; United Nations, 1999; Blodgett, 1987; Alford and O'Neill, 1994). The most problematic issue is always the specification of what the agent is to produce. If the programme has complex goals or involves policy problems with multiple causes, agents will have many opportunities to shift responsibility for poor performance. A related challenge is where the effects being sought require a long time or a continuous investment before a good return can be expected. Here the quasi-market may give agents too much time to reap profits before the principal is able to measure their real impact. Finally, the quasi-market is full of just as many administrative problems as the traditional bureaucratic system it seeks to replace. The writing of agreements, setting fees, comparing different agency options, operating a commercial-in-confidence tender process, and preventing opportunism by agents and administrators are all issues for which no standard response is possible. Instead judgement, skill and experience will be paramount.

The entrepreneurial bureaucrat

When the various instruments favoured by the 'new governance' movement are put together there emerges as a core requirement of their success a new ideal and discourse for civil service leadership – the entrepreneurial bureaucrat. While much of the work surrounding this new conceptualization has an American orientation, the ideals of greater flexibility, tailoring of services and skilful management of resources are evident across the OECD. In a very real sense the belief in the virtues of the entrepreneur-manager are a necessary outcome of the 'new governance' movement because the older model and discourse no longer makes sense.

In the traditional approach to public service leadership the high-level bureaucrat offered impartial advice to the politician 'without fear or favour'. Rules and norms inside the civil service established an environment of constraints against these high-level bureaucrats abusing their posts. But the actual performance of the civil service as a programme and service delivery system fell between two stools. Politicians had formal responsibility but no direct control, bureaucrats had real control but little formal responsibility. Once the search for greater accountability had exposed this gap there would be no going back. The only question was which path to take?

The entrepreneurial ideal was best expressed in the Osborne and Gaebler (1992) handbook and subsequent Gore report (1993) in the US. In place of the view of public agencies that held standardized implementation as a primary virtue, governments now saw public organizations as having a responsibility to create their own new means to address problems and meet demands. To be entrepreneurial was to invent a range of different implementations, experiments and innovations. For example the US commitment to 'entrepreneurial governance', embodied in Vice-President Al Gore's National Performance Review, favoured bureau cutting at the top of the civil service and flexible innovation at the bottom (Gore, 1993).

A key feature of the new ideal has been the belief in 'flexibility' as an unquestioned value. At the most practical level this involves greater flexibility in the employment conditions of senior civil servants, allowing them to be brought in from outside the civil service, or transferred easily between departments. Implicit in this idea of flexibility is the lack of loyalty to any organization or sector. Loyalty is not valued and may even be a signal that the leader has been 'captured' by the local culture or by established practices.

A second virtue is the idea that these leaders need to be rewarded for 'taking risks' and that risk-taking itself is a key value in the service development process. Lack of fear, and thus being something of a pioneer, is also part of this new value-set. Implicit in this is the notion that the leader should prefer doing things differently to before – to have a bias towards novelty. In its extreme manifestation, as I have argued elsewhere (Considine and Painter, 1997), this reverses the old Sir Humphrey axiom 'never do anything for the first time' and substitutes incentives to 'only do things for the first time'.

The viability of these new ideals will depend in part on their reformulation into a lexicon suited to each specific country. The Blair government's preference for a language which favours flexibility within a network or partnership environment is one such modification. In places like Belgium and the Netherlands we see some of the same core values attached to notions of social harmony and partnership between key social groups. At the EU level there are also signs that the entrepreneurial ideal is being attached to notions of institutional innovation across borders and that maintenance of 'constituency support' among fellow bureaucrats in different agencies is a strong correlate of the innovator (Knill, 2001).

What is interesting from a policy development perspective is that 'new governance' appears to have brought the role of the senior public servants closer to that traditionally reserved for politicians. As they now take more risks, top bureaucrats must also be given and must accept greater responsibility. This in turn will mean more partisan appointment arrangements and more potential for disputes over accountability.

Regulation and 'new governance'

How should the analyst and those planning policy interventions seek the best advantage from the 'new governance' techniques and instruments? To begin, it is important to summarize the things about 'new governance' which offer the greatest challenge and the potential for both risk and return.

While different theorists emphasize alternative attributes, 'new governance' is primarily a method for managing services outside the normal or traditional bureaucratic system, but still within the public domain. In other words these are still public services and must therefore honour some basic public service principles. If a senior civil servant has a personal contract of employment this should not mean that he or she is left outside the norms and expectations of altruism and professionalism that should apply to this work. The same could be said of contracts with agents further down the supply chain.

Of course even if we can contrive forms of institutional design that preserve and support the altruism of civil servants, the fact remains that those responsible for implementation need no longer be public servants and they need no longer answer directly to the government for their day-to-day activities. What form of ethical behaviour can be expected from contractors? The first part of the answer to this is to recognize that in almost all cases the services being managed in this way continue to be authorized by the legislature and largely funded by taxpayers. In this sense they remain public services, no matter who does the ultimate delivery. This means that in design terms it is neither possible nor desirable to attempt to shift responsibility for these services off the shoulders of politicians and senior bureaucrats and onto the backs of contractors or a new class of 'quasi-consumers'. To do so will simply leave public policy objectives hostage to opportunistic games between actors.

In conceptual terms this problem relates to the earlier discussion of agency theory. In that framework the organization is depicted as a chain of contracts, and when applied to the political process the contract originates with the voter as principal and all other institutions as agents of one form or another. In the 'quasi-market' the governance relations between actors does not easily break down into a chain. Instead, many of the key actors have multiple identities which are in conflict with one another.

For example, the senior civil servant responsible for organizing a major tender for the contracting out of her department's programmes has at least three different relationships to manage. She is the agent of the minister and should act in accord with the minister's policy directives. She is a public servant, owes a formal duty to the public and is therefore an agent of the public interest. She is also the principal in the relationship with the contractors hired to carry out services. If the contractors behave badly or underperform for any reason, this senior manager will have an interest in protecting herself from the minister and the public by presenting a more positive image. This would also be the case in situations where the performance problem originated with a member of her own staff, except in the case of contractors the room to manoeuvre out of the line of fire is far greater.

The logical answer to this problem lies in treating certain classes of contractor as quasi public servants. This will involve certain forms of training and regulation. Much depends upon the nature of the service being contracted. The risks in hiring private firms to collect the garbage are lower (but not insignificant) than the risks in putting contractors in charge of a prison or an orphanage. If we consider the contractor as a source of risk we can identify the most likely places where breakdown might occur, and at the same time we can consider for whom a breakdown might be most problematic.

Contractors in the human services generally deal with problems that are hard to specify and use technologies that are imperfect and iterative. Assisting someone to overcome drug addiction cannot be achieved with routine applications of standard therapies. To assure the public, the client and the authorizing agency that risks are being minimized by the contractor hired to run the drug rehabilitation clinic, action will be required on the input and the output side. Inputs in the form of expert or trained staff will usually be certified according to some competency standard. The education of skilled staff remains one of the most powerful methods of organizational regulation.

Complex problems and unique cases can be brought within a defined zone of agreed strategies and responses, even where such actions have unknown impacts. This 'evidence-based' approach consists of reassuring key actors that 'strategy X' for helping heroin addicts is the 'best known and safest method' even if the results do not always involve a cure or a major improvement. These practised strategies can include the ethical treatment norms and altruistic objectives expected in public programmes. On the output side there are also opportunities to bind contractors. Requirements for ethical treatment can be enforced through case checking and audit procedures to assure the purchaser and the public that everyone in the programme got an appropriate form of assistance.

It will be obvious in these cases that contractors and contracting bring to the surface a number of competing values for different actors. Some but not all of these would probably be in conflict even if the service were in public service hands. The value not likely to be of major impact in the traditional public service model is the agent's desire to profit from his interaction with each client. Where professionals and administrators are rewarded by fixed salaries they can apportion their time without undue consideration of profitability. It is therefore important in considering the best applications of 'new governance' techniques to avoid creating unhelpful profit-making motives in situations where this is apt to lead to creaming, churning and other extortionate behaviours by agents. Particularly problematic are those contracts where agents are rewarded on a per-case basis and enjoy latitude in selecting which cases they will treat. Only the most saintly will decline the opportunity to cream off the easy cases and leave the hard ones to someone (or likely, no one) else.

By treating contractors as quasi civil servants the designers of new governance systems will have to accept higher costs and these may reduce the attractiveness of contracting out. Extra training and regulation might make the single civil service bureaucracy a more efficient option. Much depends upon why it is that the new governance model is seen to be successful. If the answer is merely that it cuts unit costs at the risk of reducing service quality, the decision is clear. But if the benefit is from flexibility, greater innovation and opportunities to bring new actors into the service chain, then even with greater regulatory costs, the multi-actor system may be preferable to the single provider model used in a standard bureaucracy.

Coordination and new governance

As we have observed, new governance involves many actors and agents becoming involved in public services. This multi-actor network includes different government agencies, some private providers and a range of non-profit groups. In some fields it might also include professions, unions and employer organizations. These networks are different from older interest group networks in that they actually get involved in service delivery and policy-making; they are not simply advocacy groups (Mayntz, 1993; Kooiman, 1993).

A key design challenge in these emerging systems is to achieve coordinated effort without excessive regulation. The logic of the quasi-market discourse, and the commonsense expectation of most observers, is that to get greatest efficiency from multi-actor systems the entrepreneurs must enjoy wide discretion. There is also a strong expectation that each agent will act independently of the others, and perhaps even in competition with the others. This behaviour needs to be coordinated if the different agents are expected to produce cumulative effects. That is, if one agent's efforts with a group of clients are apt to influence another agent's work with those same clients, coordination will be needed.

Governments may elect to provide coordination themselves or may invite others to do so. Experience of such networks in the health sector suggests that unless coordination is achieved through cooperative effort, various anti-regulation games are likely to occur. The most obvious of these is that agents will shift the blame for under-performance onto the purchaser or principal. The second thing that can be noticed in these systems is that the preferred method of coordination in the first generation of such systems is through the budget, and specifically through the budget incentive approach. While these systems produce high levels of transparency, on their own they cannot guarantee collective effort.

What needs to evolve in these systems is a capacity for joint decision-making and goal-setting such that network participants come to view themselves as having a shared future and a shared responsibility. In these cases governments may expect those in the system to engage in 'know how trading' and other forms of altruistic behaviour in order to assist other actors to maintain the overall integrity of the system and to avoid the network itself being ruined by the types of 'over fishing', or commons problems observed in the Bruno scenario.

Future investments and new governance

This discussion of collaboration raises the question of planning for longer-term opportunities. In some discussions of new governance there is a strong implication that such service and policy networks might become 'self producing' (Rhodes, 1990; Kooiman, 1993). This raises important questions in regard to the role of government in steering or directing such systems. Some of this discussion is too abstract or speculative for our present purposes. However the move away from simple bureaucracy and towards complex multi-actor systems does raise profound questions of control. The earlier discussion has identified some of the dimensions of this from the perspective of regulation and coordination. This third section asks what design objectives analysts should consider when thinking ahead to the future development of these systems?

A key to this inquiry is the frame of reference we use to model and evaluate these governance arrangements. Do we view the structures that deliver public services as a means to meet current obligations at the best cost? Or do we also view the policy and delivery systems as a particular kind of institutional capacity, which needs to be developed, over and above current demands? If we accept the capacity argument then we are forced to think about the investment side of the system from both the public and private point of view. How do we prevent the search for low prices resulting in a 'race to the bottom' in which skills and expertise are traded against immediate returns? How do we prevent critical 'memory loss' when key agencies leave the system? How can we encourage long-term commitment when one of the key things we value about these multi-agent systems is that we can replace or delete agents from time to time?

In the early period of industrialization firms struggled to reconcile the benefits of immediate low wages obtained through contract work and 'gang labour' and the opportunities available through permanent employment of a dedicated workforce. Gradually, all but the most basic tasks were made subject to management direction. This breakthrough enabled firms to do two things. First, they could now enforce quality standards which itinerant workers and gangs would be unlikely to adopt. Second, firms could require their workforce to undertake training in new techniques and to give up old, inefficient practices.

In the current period public organizations are seeking ways to shed labour. This pressure is likely to continue. The challenge therefore lies in finding strategies to guarantee high quality and high skill. There are a number of models which have not yet been used which offer interesting possibilities. Franchise development is an obvious way to keep control of quality, to allow investment in the future and to give private organizations and individuals opportunities to participate in the provision of services. The franchise system puts more pressure on public managers to keep a strong operational focus. It is more difficult for them to hide behind tender documents. Franchise systems also allow public organizations to maintain some outlets in public hands without recourse to unnecessary duplication of effort.

Another model which preserves some capacity to protect the investment in skills and other assets is the use of intermediary networks. Rather than engage a large number of small contractors government could sub-contract to another level of government, to private consortia with a track record of innovation or to overseas companies willing to establish local partnerships. By issuing a contract to a licensed network or consortium government has an opportunity to include requirements that such organizations establish accredited training systems, invest in world's best technology and use international benchmarks for best practice.

The risk with such systems is that networks may over-invest or over-service their government client. Regular reviews and new tenders both for network development and for subordinate participation offer a useful brake on such developments.

Empowering citizens and new governance

Implicit in all accounts of new governance is the idea that consumers will add their weight to efforts to regulate new multi-agent systems. In other words these arrangements are expected to grant consumer sovereignty to clients of public programmes, whether these are quasi-markets, networks or some combination of both. While laudable, these ambitions are little more than rhetoric and may be a shield for more sinister motives unless specific initiatives are taken to create consumer empowerment. The key task in this regard is to make sure citizens become more informed and more active on their own behalf.

Most quasi-markets assume that 'exit' options will allow client interests to apply pressure on the service delivery system (Le Grand and Bartlett, 1993). This is a weak influence in most public policy areas. We simply do not have the resources to duplicate service delivery outlets to the extent needed to make 'exit' a viable signal to producers. Instead we have tended to use the government purchaser as a stand-in for a kind of collective consumer interest. This is totally inadequate. Government agencies responsible for establishing contracts or regulating them have their own axes to grind and cannot be entrusted with the protection of individual citizen interests.

Disadvantaged people who depend upon government to protect their interests have need of more information, support and advice than is ordinarily available to citizens. Thus far, most reform processes have failed to deliver this support. This weakens the legitimacy of these public programmes as well as reducing the quality of the 'market' signals being sent to competitors and suppliers.

Some exit options may exist in systems based on large numbers of small- and medium-sized agencies, such as schools. But in other sectors the unit size of agents will need to be larger and therefore the number of providers will be small. For example, it is unlikely that most citizens will be able to choose between more than one or two hospitals. Rather than resolve the consumer sovereignty problem by seeking more and more agents, and a public realm of small business agencies, it will more often make sense to find ways to force larger agencies to support the development of consumer organizations. For example, Ralph Nader and his supporters in the US have pioneered a model whereby state power companies are required to allow their consumers to assign a few cents per month from their power bill to a registered consumer rights organization. Provided such organizations do not monopolize the consumer voice function, this offers the prospect of informed advocacy and a better balance of interests in these systems.

To summarize these issues we can observe that the policy analyst and the policy actor are now required to consider governance issues as a most central aspect of any policy design problem. This is much more than a choice about instruments, although it includes evaluating the impact of instruments upon actual policies. The new dimension is one of multi-agent and multi-actor interdependence. New networks of policy-making and service delivery create new policy priorities.

Summing up

In this chapter we have identified a number of key issues that policy analysts must now consider when confronting policy issues in a new environment. It must be said at the outset that great variation exists in these 'new governance' arrangements among and between countries. All generalizations are therefore set against a general type and that general type exists in only limited cases. Nevertheless we can identify a number of new institutions and instruments. The general propositions of the new governance movement concern the emergence of more fragmented, multi-agent systems for producing public services. These include stronger roles for non-government organizations such as firms and non-profit agencies. By actively seeking to open services to this kind of arrangement, governments have apparently sought to solve problems of rigidity and inflexibility in the traditional bureaucratic type.

The critique of bureaucracy continues to be central to the discourse of new governance and its more pragmatic twin, new public management. Using a number of propositions derived from organizational economics this new framework seeks to treat actors as agents and principals in a production chain relationship which begins with voters and ends with consumers. This has encouraged the greater use of contracts to define policy development and implementation.

When seen from a systematic perspective the use of these instruments often generates new models of conduct for civil servants, contractors and consumers. These include much greater emphasis upon strong public management, a willingness to separate design of policy from the work of agents responsible for carrying it out, and a more behavioural theory of administrative conduct.

Without suggesting how far any particular policy system might go towards these ideals, the chapter concluded with a consideration of four challenges for new governance. First, we saw that new forms of regulation will be needed to assure that services remain public in character, including their need to be ethical and altruistic. Second, we examined a number of coordination challenges which multi-actor systems pose for those previously used to dealing with simple bureaucracy. Third, the chapter raised a number of design challenges for analysts interested in capacity building within governance arrangements. The role of government in steering was seen to be linked to the need to anticipate the kind of organizational capacity that would be required in the future and not merely to use new governance methods to cut current costs or break up currently rigid structures.

Finally, the chapter considered how empowerment of citizens and customers would need to be designed into such systems. Since most of these arrangements involve fragmented government involvement it is no longer feasible to allocate all representational authority to government. This was a frail role at best in the older bureaucratic order, it is infeasible in the new one. While legislatures and regulators should be required to act on behalf of citizens as a whole, the new systems also require active support for consumers to enable them to assert a degree of sovereignty over contractors, agents or suppliers. This is all the more necessary if we accept the claim that one of the strengths of these new systems is their 'self-producing' capacities. Citizen-consumers need to be defined inside such boundaries and not seen merely as the objects of their activity, as the next chapter will explain.

11

Policy Interventions and Citizen Engagement

When decision makers in the private sector sit down to compare notes with their colleagues in public office the thing that all seem to agree is different between them is the role of the public and public opinion. Some go further and argue that the notion of a public interest underpins the activities of the public sector, while private interests drive the engine of the business sector. This last claim is probably too extreme. After all, there is presumably a private life of citizens which informs both state and market and who is to say it only feeds virtue in one direction? Some public interests can be served by markets, and certainly there are many cases where private ones have driven public life.

But even allowing for these points of overlap and for exceptional cases, the fundamental conditions which face decision makers in the two sectors are certainly very different. While a firm may lose part of its customer base and still prosper, may cut the number of its shareholders and still be strong, no public programme or decision can survive for long without public acceptance and none can easily prosper without public support. Even in relatively undemocratic systems a minimum level of tolerance is necessary for public institutions to function.

Participation in policy-making is therefore a simple term for a complicated engagement. Participation is itself defined and determined by policy, by the history of policy and by the climate of expectations about policy. Citizens take their cues about whether to participate from the things that have happened to them before, from the experiences of family and friends, from the ersatz experiences they observe in the mass media, and from their own imaginings about how their own situation, or that of those they respect, might become different.

In this way the participation question is no more or less than a keyhole into the social enactment of policy, its root and branch engagement with the communities and histories surrounding it.

In practice, participation in the life of a public organization or programme is achieved in a number of quite fundamental ways. Each country and each system develops its own habits and culture of engagement with key participants, including members of the general public. Like other factors we have examined, participation is both an intervention by real actors, and a discourse about what is to be valued and achieved through that engagement. And like much else this is a value with an obvious limit: just as a democracy demands a separate judiciary and an empowered legislature, it must impose constraints on just how much participating ordinary citizens can do. In other words there is both an explicit and an implicit division of labour to determine who does what. For this reason we will consider how participation fits within a more general notion of *responsive rule*.

In our IVF scenario Anna knew there was no way to get the issue of 'lesbian test tube babies' off the front page of the newspapers without a process for addressing the public interest concerns being stirred up by new scientific discoveries. Not only would some form of public consultation allow a more measured discussion of the facts of the matter, it would give people an opportunity to see how complex her own organization's regulatory problems had become. Equal rights and anti-discrimination laws made it illegal to deny public services to citizens on grounds of age, sex, race or sexual preference. At the same time the social security legislation defined families in heterosexual terms, as did the major political parties. She therefore advised her board to begin a nationwide public consultation on IVF and the genetic revolution in medicine.

The board debated Anna's proposal over two long meetings. Members expressed concern that ordinary people might not understand the scientific issues, that interest groups would use the process to raise tempers and create pressure for more restrictive regulation. Others worried that the issues would be driven by emotion, with the media likely to focus only on 'heartbreak' stories of women crying over lost opportunities to conceive. There was also concern that not everyone would have the same chance to participate in the consultation and that the major churches and scientific groups would drown out other voices. But in the end they could see no alternative. Without a renewed mandate their own power to regulate would steadily become eroded by doctors turning a blind eye to questions of age or sexuality. The scientists too would press on with new discoveries which they could easily claim were able to help those suffering congenital diseases. Anna's strategy was accepted: consultation would refresh the board's mandate and help it define the next stage of public regulation.

The institutional character of participation

Anna's case is not very different from those in most other policy systems. Participation by members of the public in decision-making over policies and programmes is a central aspect of public life. What is more, from the standpoint of democratic theory, the more participation we can engender, the better. If all other costs were held constant, the ideal decision would be one in which every citizen had their say. There is also an ethical principle at issue here. Some would argue that basic human rights demand that those likely to be affected by a decision should have first had a chance to vote on it, or in some equally valid way, make some input into its resolution. The American Revolution was in this sense a claim for direct participation. The slogan 'no taxation without representation' was not just a rally cry against colonial tyranny, but the assertion of a principle for all forms of public policy.

According to the inherited theories of representative (or 'responsible') government which shape most public policy, all decisions must be traceable to a mandate established through free and fair elections. So theories of participation and engagement commence with an understanding of the *opportunity structure* provided by existing political institutions such as the electoral process, the party system, the established interest groups and the legislature.

In democratic theory these are analysed in a number of different ways. Pluralist theory argues that institutions respond rather well to the pressure put on them by organized interests such as unions, social movements and employer groups. Politicians and bureaucrats pay close attention to what these groups are saying at any one time and will seek to accommodate as much of their agenda as possible in order to win elections and maintain power. For the pluralists the system of participation therefore depends upon just how well these interests reflect the concerns and priorities of ordinary citizens. So long as there are a great number of such groups, and provided that their strength within the policy system is roughly proportionate to their popular appeal, the system can be said to work well.

Corporatist theory attempts to frame the problem somewhat differently. It takes an empirical view and asserts that many democratic systems tend towards some form of selectivity in the relationship between government and interests. Institutions of participation build up around a few dominant relationships. This is because both sides have a real interest in establishing a stable, well understood method of engagement. This allows deals to be done and honoured without undue strife or costly bouts of open conflict. The most obvious forms of corporatism are those involving unions and business groups, but the same framework can also be applied to the professions and to key environmental groups in some cases.

A third framework, less common now than it was twenty years ago, is class theory. According to this view, public interests are filtered through class positions. And the first among unequals in this game of class conflict is the interest of the capitalist class. In other words, before any other interests can be accommodated by policy makers there must first be an acceptance that governments will take care of the basic things which keep business healthy and thus keep profits strong. It can readily be seen that this is a better argument about the macro-political dynamic of any capitalist society than it is an explanation of the way actual interests are included and excluded in each local case (Lindblom, 1988).

Taking these three approaches in reverse order the participation challenge can be divided into three levels:

- systemic participation
- institutional participation
- local participation.

At the top level we might want to consider the policy consequences for popular interests in the overall architecture of the system and at this level inquire about the extent of political engagement with citizens on basic questions of profit-making, wages, equality and opportunity. It is clearly at this level that elements of the basic social contract between state and citizenry are formed and expressed. In social systems which emphasize hierarchy, patriarchy or other forms of exclusion it will come as no surprise that habits of participation in policy-making are also apt to be tilted towards socially powerful groups. It makes little sense to invite people to come and discuss a new proposal if it is already obvious that only certain leading individuals possess the cultural capital to take advantage of the opportunity.

To assure equal representation might well require unequal efforts. For example, if the Ministry for Health wishes to invite citizens to participate in a process designed to identify recreational needs it could be safe in assuming that organized groups such as football clubs and dance companies will make submissions. It is not so obvious that older citizens will be heard. In this case it will take special effort to go out and collect information and perhaps to support older people to come to meetings to discuss their interests.

Next we might identify the institutionalized forms of engagement of both organized interests and broader categories of citizens. What are the ongoing forms of consultation that are used? Which groups get to sit at the negotiating tables? What is the character of these engagements – deliberation, information sharing, negotiation, arbitration or conflict? Most policy fields or systems have a characteristic pattern of engagement between officials, managers, politicians and interest groups. These will usually range from ministerial councils where policy is regularly discussed, through to industrial relations tribunals where disputes between parties are adjudicated. Not only are these an important source of openness and closure, they also acculturate actors to habitual ways of dealing with each other. A system characterized by an industrial relations style of participation will tend to be based on posturing, over-bidding, open conflict and independent arbitration. A system where the main institutional path is organized around professional regulation will probably have very limited openings for non-professionals to participate, but within the circle of privileged participants issues will be resolved by consensus and appeals to expertise.

Finally, we need to examine the dynamics which drive local episodes or outbreaks of public concern over policy-making issues. How are people mobilized? Do they depend upon a few well-informed individuals to engage them, or does the mass media carry most of the responsibility for informing them? What are the values or norms articulated within the claims and counter-claims being made in any particular case? Is there opportunity for people to learn and adapt, or are positions relatively inflexible? What forums or vehicles are most important to these forms of public speech? Whatever we may think about the larger architecture of interested participation in policy, there remain distinct possibilities that leading groups will lose contact with public opinion, or fail to see new issues emerging. It will take a new problem to bring these to the surface.

The double work of participation

If policy systems are built layer upon layer, circuit after circuit, from the efforts of different kinds of actors, then participation describes the different levels of communication and conflict that it takes to bring these actors into play and to keep them from deserting.

The purpose and effect of communication is not always the same, however. Policy-making always involves a dual structure. It has an instrumental dimension in that it produces decisions, programmes and other outcomes which actors value. It also has a set of developmental relationships in the way it allows for the communication of moral and ethical norms, and the building of trust and solidarity between actors. Conversely, policy has the potential to produce outcomes which produce anti-values such as dominance or non-developmental processes which are divisive (Barber, 1984; Putnam, 1971).

Unfortunately, many academic treatments of participation in policy-making undervalue the developmental aspect of individual and group action. They tend either to embrace a simple rationalism which assumes that it is only products which count, or they adopt an elitist political realism which views participation by non-government actors as a source of chaos and overload.

In this treatment, however, participation is viewed as a primary structure within all policy development and implementation episodes. The central propositions of this framework are that participation describes three types of action: it facilitates rational deliberation, it creates and communicates moral principles, and it expresses personal and group affects and needs. When all three forms of action are available then participation provides a means for the creation of the social capital from which all central democratic objectives spring, including legitimacy, cooperation and innovation (Bernardy, Boisgoutier and Goyet, 1993).

Participation needs therefore to be viewed as both an *instrumental* and a *developmental* value. It is judged as a means to improve decision-making or implementation, and as a process for creating the community of shared understandings which are the prerequisite of any society.

The instrumental value of participation is the observable effect it has upon the improvement of any single decision or plan. Issues which were hidden or undervalued now come to the surface as a result of a wider public being involved. This means the decision reached will better address the core problem under review. The developmental value of participation is the effect it has upon persistent capacities within a system or community. When leaders speak of the need for capacity-building in a given system they are generally referring to this dual nature of participation.

Developmental values include increased knowledge, greater understanding of others, improved tolerance, increased solidarity or sense of joint purpose, greater trust and sympathy. Even if the decision reached is not a good one, the effect of becoming involved may stimulate the various publics to think more deeply about policy matters, to give greater attention to the views of others, or to simply become better informed about the best ways to resolve such problems. Such civic values remain to be tapped in future episodes, provided new forms of exclusion do not run down this civic capital in the meantime.

Of course it is no simple matter to design a policy system with the exact properties likely to engender trust and effectiveness. We certainly know from experience that designing too much uniformity into a system, or expecting people to have common demands and needs, is more than likely to arrest development, not enhance it. In other words both the instrumental and developmental values need to be seen as conditional norms, not as absolutes. No one really knows what a fully developed system would look like, but most of us can outline the conditions that should be met to become more developed than we are now. Similarly, there are no absolutely efficient decisions in most policy domains, only decisions that are more efficient than others we could identify.

These two dimensions of participation and the conditional nature of their enhancement can perhaps be grasped most effectively through a simple illustration.

Traffic problems

Imagine a local neighbourhood experiencing problems with severe traffic congestion. This brings with it noise, pollution and the danger of accidents. As a result of complaints or their own observations, city officials recognize that action needs to be taken. If the policy task is defined as reducing the number of cars on designated streets in the neighbourhood, an obvious set of solutions will emerge. City engineers will be asked to measure the volume and flow of cars and trucks and will then prepare options for government decision makers. A choice will then be made based upon the cheapest method for inducing the largest traffic reduction, subject to any other policy goals which decision makers might have. Residents will be invited to comment on the proposed speed humps and stop signs and then a decision will be made. Some time later the engineers may check the new pattern of traffic flow to make certain that the new policy is working in the manner planned. In this case policy is a question of choosing the right instrument and the choice process itself is based on the selection from known traffic measures – civil engineering techniques in this case.

An alternative approach might view the issue as part of a continuing set of problems which residents have with their local environment. The invasion of cars and trucks now appears as a problem of domination and the goals of residents are viewed as only partly to do with the measured flow of traffic. If their protests are seen as complaints about lack of control and autonomy to live as they wish, policy-making becomes an effort to restore local forms of influence. To achieve this, city officials will wish to engage in regular communication with residents and to discuss the permanent problem of establishing boundaries between their local interests and the ever-persistent needs of other external interests. The process of meaningful involvement in policy-making will almost certainly change attitudes and demands by residents, officials and other groups. Decisions will not complete this learning process so much as punctuate it with a series of agreements which are open to further amendment.

In the first scenario policy seeks to limit and complete action, and participation is primarily a means to gain clearance for an efficient official decision, or is perhaps a method for communicating decisions to those who need to accept them in order for them to function. In the second scenario the policy-making process is itself a valued relationship. Whether or not the participation of groups transforms the process from an instrumental exchange to a developmental relationship will depend upon the way the already established mechanisms for involvement are structured. This will depend upon:

- how well the process includes all those affected
- the preparation that goes into informing people about the issues

- the willingness to identify and deal with conflicting positions
- the capacity to negotiate
- the time allowed for people to assess issues and solutions
- the willingness of decision makers to share ownership of the solution.

Not all communities come to the negotiating table fully equipped to participate effectively. It is therefore a measure of the seriousness of decision makers that they invest effort in preparing an issue for public consultation. The methods used to create such engagement vary a great deal. The following three scenarios illustrate this diversity.

> The Ministry for Education has a statutory responsibility to advise residents when it plans to change the school system in a local area. This includes any decision to alter school hours, to change the location of schools or to close schools.
> To achieve consistency of practice the ministry has devised a three-level system. In level one which we might term 'weak information sharing' they simply take an advertisement in the local paper and announce that school term will finish two days early the following year due to a teacher curriculum conference. Parents may write letters of protest but unless there is a major response no one expects this approach to result in anything other than compliance.
> At level two the ministry writes to parents of currently enrolled students to tell them that a new programme is being introduced and inviting them to speak with teachers or their principal if they are interested. This form of 'weak engagement' at least identifies a path which people may take to advance their interests, even if the path is clearly at a relatively low level in the organization.
> The level three approach is when the ministry grants authority to the local school council to resolve its own budget for the year and to decide whether to employ two specialist teachers or to use the money to send the children to other activities. When the council decides to invite parents to come to a meeting to discuss the options it takes a step towards 'shared decision-making'.

Why would we not expect all policy makers to work for shared decision-making? Like everything else we deal with in public life,

even a virtuous goal such as increased participation has its problematic dimension. The chief threats to participation come from
three criticisms: that it creates an overload in the work that public
programmes must do, that it leads to capture of public organizations by vested interests, and that it is subject to the 'free rider'
problem, leaving most of the work to be done by an unrepresentative minority.

Overload

A major objection to developmental participation is its cost. Any
form of participation will increase the demands which individuals and groups make, it is argued. This excess of demands is then
identified as the prime cause of 'overload', a condition in which
governments are thought to become exhausted by the many programmes they are required to run (Birch, 1984; Murray, 1984).
The proponents of this view point out that new programmes are
often added without consideration of which ones should be
closed. We can certainly see how the dynamic might work in practice. In any community there will be a range of public services.
Different population groups have their favourites which serve
their special needs. They are willing to protest if these are disturbed, but they pay less attention to other services which they
do not themselves use. New groups form around demands for new
services and these attract the interest of leaders wishing to get
elected. It is generally easier to get elected by promising something new.

Other political entrepreneurs also have a natural incentive to
want to add things to the menu. However they get no immediate
value from making promises to cut programmes out, since all that
does is create immediate dissent and lose them votes. So instead
they try to add without deleting. By this method the services
menu keeps expanding to the limits of prudent budgeting, and
even beyond if a way can be found to borrow funds to accommodate these short-term pressures. Now once in office and faced
with responsibility for balancing the books the leadership must
either turn nasty and start offending part of its own support base,

or if it takes a middle path it will simply apportion available resources across a larger number of programmes, each getting a smaller amount than they need to be effective. We can see that the overload scenario is a serious threat to good government and that it may be a greater threat in those systems where participation is based on a crude set of bidding wars amongst entrepreneurs. That in turn will be a consequence of the kind of institutional context structuring interventions.

Capture

A related problem is the one raised by Stigler (1949, 1982) who claims that the involvement of interest groups in policy-making results in the 'capture' of government regulatory institutions by the major interests they are established to control. Producer interests such as manufacturers and professions are Stigler's primary targets. Although they pretend to oppose government regulatory policy, he says, they actually become its main beneficiaries through restrictive rules which prevent competition and consumer choice.

Regulation can mean any sustained effort to control behaviour. Taxation is a form of regulation. So is requiring children to attend school. Putting warning labels on cigarette packs is a regulatory strategy and so is limiting exhaust emissions from city buses.

Capture occurs for several reasons. The first of these is that those being regulated have a greater interest than everyone else in paying close attention to the specific actions of the regulator. It makes sense for them to spend a lot of time and money watching and anticipating the moves being made by politicians, bureaucrats and other interests. This concentration of attention is a sizeable advantage in a policy system where most leaders and communities are struggling with expanding agendas.

Generally speaking, those being regulated soon become better informed than everyone else. In part this is because they begin with more information. Cigarette manufacturers must know quite a lot about their product in order to produce it. The knowledge is intrinsic to the act of production. For the regulator this is not the case. The regulator must go out and seek information about how things are produced and must often rely on what the manufacturer says.

A second information imbalance occurs because the group being regulated suffers some cost as a result of being regulated and they are always prepared to find ways to reduce or avoid this cost. So spending money gathering new information always offers a potential pay off. But for the regulator the best that can be achieved by spending funds on information gathering is that the *status quo* regulations will remain in force.

Closely related to the information problem is the fact that the regulatory system may become captured because the expertise needed to be an effective regulator can only be found in the industry being regulated. If government needs doctors to regulate other doctors then perhaps the system of regulation will always favour a medical outlook.

The reason capture is seen as a problem for theories of participation is that these are generally opportunities for these interests to close an agenda that others might want opened. A public process to discuss renewable energy options will likely be dominated by power companies and the research organizations they help fund. It will also be difficult to keep these interests off any board or commission devised to express public opinion.

What the Stigler case points to is a form of organizational pathology in which regulation may begin well but then become corrupted. The solution therefore lies in refreshing the mandate of the regulator from time to time. Once again, this cannot happen if the form of participation employed allows interest groups to dominate.

Free riding

The third threat to effective participation comes from the rational choice claim that we examined in chapter 8 that most people will 'free ride' on the efforts of others rather than participate themselves. The kernel of this criticism is the idea that citizens will find it more rational to let others agitate for change or voice opinions because the costs of participating are higher than the likely benefits. Furthermore, an entrepreneurial class will generally bring forward ideas that express the general interests of citizens such that by staying home the average person can enjoy the benefits and suffer few of the costs of getting involved.

Mancur Olson (1971), in *The Logic of Collective Action*, explains why not everyone needs to join the union in order to get the benefits of a pay rise. If the benefit to be achieved cannot be localized to those responsible for achieving it, then it will be in the rational self-interest of the majority not to participate, and simply to let others put themselves out to press the case for change. The same case can be made for joining an environmental group such as Greenpeace. Throwing oneself in front of whaling boats in a boiling sea can be costly, certainly more costly than sitting at home. And since everyone can go to the seaside and view the whales after they are saved from extermination, it seems to make sense to let a few Greenpeace agitators do the hard work.

This is very much an instrumental view of political participation. It assumes that participation is itself a cost with no intrinsic benefits. One does not have fun while participating. Rather one is giving up something in order to participate. Almost all forms of participation by citizens collapse under the weight of this logic if this first principle is accepted. Even the small cost associated with exercising one's vote on election day appears as a bad trade given the chances of getting what you really want from your local member.

Why then are there so many people investing time and effort in different forms of group membership? Olson's answer is that they must be getting something else. There must be some other pay off, other than the primary issue. He makes a distinction between different kinds of benefits available to people in groups. The main economic benefits, or collective goods, are supplemented in the case of large groups with non-economic benefits. Olson uses the case of large trade unions to illustrate the point. If they relied on their ability to secure wage improvements alone, large unions might find it difficult to attract members. So they provide insurance, welfare services and superannuation benefits as a supplement.

One need not accept Olson's exclusive focus on economic pay offs in order to see that he is allowing different sources of benefit to result from participation of this kind. If we stretch his logic to include the developmental values discussed above we might argue that for some people the act of involvement might have an intrinsic utility. It might for example help them feel more attached to their fellow human beings, neighbours or co-workers.

Similarly one might view government as facing equally complex problems of gaining the support and participation of their citizens. Simple rules of cost-benefit might suggest that no citizen ought to participate in anything. Indeed the most rational course of action, following Olson, might be for individual citizens to sell their right to vote to entrepreneurs capable of collecting sufficient support to enact policies. However if voting is taken as a developmental activity as well as an instrumental one, the benefits to be derived will include a sense of belonging, fostering of civic responsibility and increased knowledge on the part of ordinary citizens (Putnam, 1993).

Ultimately, whether or not these forms of participation lead to increased demand, overload or capture will depend upon the institutions used to facilitate such participation. Rules and rituals establish the expectations which participants have, the range of issues that can legitimately be discussed, and the kinds of bids that will be viewed as possible. Since all systems require some form of participation (at a minimum by elites and interest groups) the question is not so much whether to foster participation, but what kind is appropriate to different public policy issues and to different visions of contemporary democracy.

Threats to effective participation

Very few policy processes are resourced to the level needed to allow everyone to participate; less than a few employ sufficient time for people to become informed; and only a minority grant real authority to the views expressed in consultation processes. A further threat comes from the potential which these public processes generate for elites, including political elites, to block, stall, coopt and deflect worthwhile proposals for action. We might summarize these as four key threats – lack of resources, insufficient time, tokenism and manipulation.

Under the heading of resource constraints we observe that many exercises in participation limit popular engagement to a brief exchange of established positions and perhaps a round of submission-writing by the already informed. The hallmark of such cases is the advertisement in the press asking members of the public to submit written papers to a parliamentary inquiry or bureaucratic review. For decision makers the yield from such a process might include early warning of major problems but if so this is the only likely source of significant learning. As a pressure valve such strategies have some modest value but beyond this they are almost worthless. Such submissions as are received are bound to be unrepresentative. They may also be partial, or biased towards existing interests.

A more subtle but equally problematic influence is the limitation often placed upon the time available for people to become involved. Once-off inquiries are perhaps the most limiting. To begin from a standing start, become informed, consult others and then reach the point of being ready to offer a view may take weeks or even months. If becoming informed also involves gaining access to expertise, or conducting a study of one's own, several months may well be a minimum. In countries like the Netherlands where high levels of social consensus are sought for any major policy change, it may take more than a year for everyone to have their say and for an agreed piece of legislation to be drafted. Good consultation strategies therefore have time budgets which deal directly with the conditions faced by those from whom feedback is sought.

Perhaps the most persistent complaint about governmental consultation is that decisions are being taken elsewhere and the process for public participation therefore has no authority. Arnstein's (1969) ladder of participation describes this lower level form as 'therapy' or 'manipulation'. What is implied here is that the organization conducting the consultation has a motive and an interest that is likely to be very different to that of the general public, or the local interest groups.

We could perhaps see this as the negative value of participation. A minister might announce a consultation in order to keep an aggrieved interest group or community from taking direct action while he or she works on their own plan to solve the problem. Another strategy which gives the consultees no real power is one in which the minister or department expects the various interests to attack one another and to fail to agree on anything. This is often a method for lowering expectations by showing the public that no agreed solution can be found. Sometimes political leaders will use consultations or public inquiries as a means to get their own officials to take an issue more seriously. By pushing the bureaucrats out into the public gaze they hope to soften internal opposition to their own agenda. Here again the authority given to public participants is minimal.

Citizenship and responsive rule

In all policy systems based on democratic norms the citizen remains the primary source of sovereignty. In practice citizens adopt different roles in each system. Each has its own dynamic and is capable of influencing the policy development process in characteristic ways. For example, individuals act as:

- voters
- political party members
- community activists
- protesters
- campaign workers
- petition signers
- workplace opinion leaders
- respondents to opinion surveys
- union or association members
- audience members for the mass media.

Until recently, the prevailing assessment of the citizen so far as social science was concerned was that he or she was a case of ignorance and apathy punctuated by occasional outbursts of active prejudice. Rarely did the ordinary citizen meet liberal intellectual standards of civility or rational deliberation. As survey techniques caught on as a prime method in the 1950s disillusionment grew. Berelson et al. (1954) summed up the post-war consensus:

> Our data reveal that certain requirements commonly assumed for the successful operation of democracy are not met by the behaviour of the 'average' citizen . . . Many vote without real involvement in the election . . . The citizen is not highly informed on the details of the campaign . . . In any rigorous or narrow sense the voters are not highly rational.

The highly acclaimed study of public involvement in politics produced by Almond and Verba (1963) generalized these findings through a five-nation comparison of Britain, Italy, West Germany, Mexico and the US. Most citizens were not involved in parties and nor were they active in political associations. Only a minority said they discussed politics frequently, and most agreed that they did not pay attention to media reports of government actions on a regular basis. Clearly this expression of disappointment displays as much about the social scientist's preconceptions as it does about citizen politics. What is defined as a political act or political involvement? Many of those who are not members of the major parties may have been active in other ways. Membership of local clubs and cultural groups might have been considered as a means for the creation of important social values. Family, clan and neighbourhood politics might have served as a base from which other politically relevant values and action strategies could develop. And participation could have been understood as a changing historical process, rather than a single census based on one-off measures.

Dalton (1988:65), for example, shows that protest activities have been increasing in most Western countries. Involvement in demonstrations grew to 10 per cent or more in these countries and reached 26 per cent in France during this same time period. In 1974 some 58 per cent of US citizens signed petitions and by 1981 this had grown to 61 per cent. In Britain the growth was from 22 per cent to 63 per cent and in West Germany from 30 per cent up to 46 per cent.

The Dalton study (1988:71) showed that the form of participation had been changing in most Western societies. 'Participation in citizen-initiated and policy-oriented forms of political activity is increasing . . . Political input is not limited to the issues and institutionalised channels determined by elites.' The increased use being made of direct forms of democracy, protest and community-based action by citizens provides new forms of policy influence, different in scope and method from more traditional channels provided through parties, elections and interest groups.

This categorization was heavily influenced by both the optimism and the frustrations of the 1960 programmes of urban renewal and poverty relief in the US. It provides a clear definition of citizen involvement which puts its emphasis on the redistribution of political power:

> It is the strategy by which the have-nots join in determining how information is shared, goals and policies are set, tax resources are allocated, programs are operated, and benefits like contracts and patronage are parcelled out. (Arnstein, 1969:216)

Of course the great difficulty in making a priori assessments of participation strategies is that intentions may not determine outcomes. The best-laid plans of a secretive bureaucracy may come to nothing if a well-organized citizenry uses a weak form of participation such as invitations to make submissions to gather strong support for a new policy. Similarly, a town meeting designed merely to inform people about policy can quickly get out of control if community leaders come prepared with motions of dissent, press releases and counter-information.

But a far more significant problem with the shared-power assumption implicit in Arnstein's and in many other communitarian positions is that with the exception of referenda, much democratic theory is silent on the question of citizen activism outside the electoral process (see table 11.1). While we may wish to see a maximum effort being made to listen to citizens and to use this information as a reference point in decision-making, is it

Table 11.1 Sherry Arnstein's ladder of citizen participation

Citizen control	Degree of citizen power
Delegated power	
Partnership	
Placation	Degree of tokenism
Consultation	
Informing	
Therapy	Non-participation
Manipulation	

Source: Sherry Arnstein, 1969. 'A ladder of citizen participation', *AIP Journal*, July.

really all that democratic to imagine leaving the actual decision-making to a local meeting of interested individuals? If so, why bother with electing legislators?

One useful answer to this is to avoid the either-or distinction in debates about direct democracy and representative democracy and instead to embed participation within a theory of responsive rule (May, 1978; Seward, 1998). In the pioneering work in this field J.D. May (1978:1) defined responsive rule as

[the] necessary correspondence between acts of governance and the wishes with respect to those acts of the persons who are affected.

Every person in a group, community or system has, according to this ideal, to have an equal input or contribution to decisions affecting their common future. Implicit in this ideal is the claim that each individual is the best judge of his or her wishes and that this knowledge can only be transmitted through others; it cannot be known by them independent of information from the individual. There is thus no getting around the fact that democracy requires officials to do what people want, not what they believe may be good for them where these two are different. A further application of this aspect of the principle is that it gives no special weight to expertise. Those with superior knowledge of, say, the technical aspects of nuclear power, get no extra vote in a debate about the site for a new reactor.

What the responsive rule ideal means in practice is that rulers are obliged to take regular account of the preferences and concerns of the public. This makes democracy a process-based model rather than a rule-based regime. If we simply obey rules we can soon imagine a situation in which an elected group of politicians may choose to take no heed of public views until an approaching election makes this desirable. And as Seward (1998:61) argues, 'the moment of decision can have little real democratic substance if there is systematic inequality in citizens' opportunities to influence the shaping of the political agenda'.

The procedures which necessarily go along with the idea of responsiveness therefore include a requirement to inform people about intended actions, to allow freedom of information, to sponsor opportunities for dialogue between citizens and state; and finally, the process for aggregating votes or opinions should allow for a degree of reflexivity or learning and not simply produce majoritarian domination. The simplest example of the latter is logrolling of issues and votes to force voters to accept unwanted and extraneous decisions as the price for having their own preference accepted. Responsiveness, in other words, leads to strong accountability.

12

Policy Interventions and Accountability

Hardly a day passes without some claim of failure, scandal or crisis in a public programme. A patient in a public hospital is given the wrong treatment. A prisoner escapes from jail. A teacher is accused of abusing a pupil. Companies involved in highway construction are found to have entertained public officials at an expensive resort. A politician is accused of having an affair with a junior member of staff.

To what extent are such issues an important consideration in the evaluation of public policies? Can we expect to make policies and programmes better by taking into account the possibility of poor judgement, opportunism and graft on the part of policy actors? And if the answer to this is yes, how can we identify appropriate standards of accountability that satisfy good ethical principles and are also practicable? Once we have some sense of appropriate standards we can then consider the institutional implications – to whom should the public official be accountable, and for what aspects of his or her role?

In the standard works, accountability is defined as the legal obligation to be responsive to the legitimate interests of those affected by decisions, programmes, and interventions (Waldo, 1956; Wilson, 1887). To be responsive includes the duty of care and the requirement that information concerning expenditure of public funds and the exercise of public authority should be given to the individuals affected, including legislators. As such, the issue of accountability forms a central part of a wider issue of public agency: the authority of state actors to compel compliance and to exercise power.

Functions and ethics

Two different considerations drive this concern to improve accountability. First of all we expect that the purposes for which policies are enacted will be achieved and that someone will take responsibility if they are not – let's call this functional accountability. Second, however, is the idea that being public policies, these actions ought to obey some accepted moral standard – we might call this ethical accountability.

In both these cases the question of accountability requires that we be able to apportion responsibility to real actors, including organizations. For example, if voters have elected a government on a platform to reduce unemployment and no such improvement occurs, it should be possible for them to punish those who are to blame. Otherwise the trust which voters place in the electoral system will be undermined. Equally, if taxpayers discover that their funds are being skimmed off by contractors who are found to have inflated their costs or charged for work they have not done, we would expect strong legal sanctions to be employed to punish the wrongdoing.

Concealed within these common-sense propositions are a number of challenging problems for policy analysts. These relate to the questions we examined earlier in the book when we considered the problems of 'free riding' and 'opportunism' in different forms of collective action. We now turn to a number of claims about accountability and responsibility.

First of all we must confront the problem of sorting out the *contributions* to any policy or to any problem arising from a public programme. This is what Hardin (1995:126) has in mind when he deals with the 'question of composition: Who is how much responsible for which part of what?' In the case of functional accountability the agency needs to identify contributions in order to rectify the problem. But this need not be an exact science. For example, it is often the case that when consultants are called in to analyse a policy failure or organizational problem they will identify several contributing factors and recommend that they all be fixed. If matters then improve we will be satisfied that the requirements of functional accountability have been met. No one need trouble themselves about which factor was most to blame so long as improvement is achieved.

Blame

In the case of ethical accountability the problem is less easily treated as an organizational issue. To avoid blame shifting and unjust sanctioning we will usually want to know that those individuals who actually contributed most to the problem are sanctioned in a proportionate way. This question of blame therefore imposes a more demanding test than is usually the case in the functional sphere. Let us look at an example that is all too common in complex welfare systems. Due to a wide range of family problems a small child is placed in the care of a state welfare agency. Social workers, teachers, administrators and court officials work out a schedule whereby the child spends some time with her family and some time under supervision by the agency. After a year or so the regulations concerning home visits are relaxed and on an unsupervised weekend visit a domestic dispute occurs between the mother and stepfather resulting in the child being badly beaten. Newspaper reports carry photographs of the brutal injuries suffered by the child alongside editorials calling for the bureaucrats 'responsible' to be sacked.

There are now three possibilities for us to consider. First is the question of whether or not the actors in this chain of interventions acted properly. That is, whether they exercised due care for the child when they were in a position to do so, whether they informed others of their actions so that they could take appropriate steps, and whether their knowledge of the child's interests was adequate for them to discharge their duties in an appropriate manner. In most cases it is possible to discover who did what. In many such episodes it is also possible to identify places where responsible actors failed to act. So we may seek to determine this first level of accountability by an audit of contributions.

A second level of accountability is the one governing supervisors and senior managers. They are likely to have had no direct contact with the case and so their contributions (and failures to contribute) are one step removed. For example, if it turns out that the manager in the agency gave this case to a first-year social work graduate and then failed to provide any case supervision, we might want to shift the proportion of blame off the shoulders of the caseworker and onto the desk of her manager. In a sense this second level requires that we make judgements based upon a hypothetical – what might have happened had a better system been put in place? To hold a manager accountable in such a case we would want to establish that he knew, or could have known, the risks of not supervising the caseworker adequately. If it was his job to know such things then he was surely implicated in the failure which resulted. Blame is a critical step in any attempt to apportion responsibility because it requires that we identify real actors and not just abstract processes or whole institutions.

The third level of accountability is political. Where failures are a result of human systems (and not natural disasters) and where these have serious consequences, we expect a minister or cabinet secretary to accept responsibility. In the Westminster parliaments there is a convention that ministers will resign if their departments are implicated in serious wrongdoing. Although this tradition has weakened considerably over the past fifty years, its purpose is to draw a connection between the political level and the administrative sphere, which lies beneath. This is not merely a form of incentive to keep ministers alert; it is also a way to establish that parliaments and not just courts are responsible for the conduct of public programmes. So while we may regard the law as the ultimate protection for public ethics there is also good reason to consider how political institutions and organizations contribute to ethical problems and their possible solution.

These conventions also produce unique pathologies. In order to shield themselves from blame politicians may seek to erect barriers between themselves and the operational parts of the policy system. So, for example, in the Next Steps reforms in the UK in the 1980s discussed earlier as a form of clarification of policy roles, a secondary effect was to distance senior ministers from blame. Under the new arrangements it was the chief executive of the agency who carried explicit responsibility for performance issues and ministers were only to be blamed for poor policy direction, not for foul ups or corruption further down the line.

Sanctions

The two main spheres of accountability – functional and ethical – often involve the use of sanctions to encourage preferred behaviour and to punish wrongdoing. In the case of functional failures the sanctions tend to be professional and organizational. In programmes that fail to meet their objectives staff may lose pay or promotion opportunities. Loss of reputation is also an informal sanction.

In the case of ethical failure the sanctions are likely to be more precise and as a result the process for delivering them will generally be more legalistic. Where failure results in harm to another person there is the very real prospect of civil or criminal action against the agency for negligence. Each legal system has its own rules for apportioning blame between individuals and other legal persons such as corporations. The important point here is that the presence of legally enforceable sanctions changes the discussion of ethical conduct from one of local design or lore to one of formal legal action, subject to more complex institutional requirements.

Intervention issues

With these distinctions in mind we can now turn to the policy maker's central question: how are functional and ethical accountability built into policies and the programmes devised to deliver them?

While these questions should seem perfectly reasonable to anyone interested in public policy, it is important to note that although accountability is a virtue it is also a cost. The time and effort spent holding people and programmes accountable will cost money, time and commitment in some cases. Auditors take the programme's time away from serving clients in order to collect, calculate and formalize results. Making officials do too much form

filling can clog up the works, diverting resources and opening organizations to perverse pressures. Like that other popular organizational good, coordination, its costs are always less visible than
its benefits. For example, Campbell and Szablowski (1980:203)
spoke of an 'accountability crisis in bureaucracy' in Canada, but
also argued that 'very much stricter checks on government could
lead to unstable governments or short-lived ministers or both,
and to a weakening of prime-ministerial leadership and control'.
Similar dilemmas concerning the nature of accountability were
implied in the National Performance Review (NPR) effort to
separate 'steering' and 'rowing'. In this case politicians were
explicitly barred from looking too closely at the activities of
public managers and their organizations. These contemporary
views about the nature of political management include the
assertion that politicians should craft performance agreements
with agency heads, but these agreements 'should not microman-
age the work of the agency heads. They do not row the boat.
They should set the course' (Gore, 1993:75; quoted in Moe,
1994:116).

   These observations help caution us against too simplistic a view
of the means available for increasing either functional or ethical
accountability. This is not to say we should not try, only that we
should be mindful of how we estimate the costs.

For what, to whom?

The public official performing a public service has a duty to act
in accord with a code of behaviour defined through a hierarchy
of responsibilities. In classical accounts of the 'chain of command'
derived from both military practice and traditional church organization, it is expected that these organizations will rank and
divide tasks in a way that limits those at the bottom to direct
instruction and those above to more discretionary conduct. In the
Weberian bureaucracy this takes the form of clearly defined offices
within which the individual official obeys the protocol and accepts
supervision. More complex tasks are performed by better trained
staff and those with greater experience. Training and supervision

limit the possibility of errors, or at the very least confine them to an expected (hopefully minor) type. Functional accountability in this system can be shared by the whole organization, since the protocols belong to the system. Ethical accountability follows the chain of command, with those at the front line being protected from most of the blame provided they followed the rules.

However, this traditional line authority is now contradicted everywhere by the demands of entrepreneurship and output-based performance. In the past ten years, the public services of many advanced systems have been reinvented according to a new orthodoxy that requires enlarged management prerogative as a means to induce higher outputs. Input controls, precedent, and due process are consequently viewed as a source of organizational rigidity, goal displacement, and red tape (Lane, 1993; Osborne and Gaebler, 1992; Walsh, 1995). In the new world of enterprising government, the public official is expected both to honour his or her official mandate and to move freely outside the hierarchical constraints of government in search of collaborative and quasi-market relationships with contractors, competitors, and copro-ducers (Considine, 2002).

This multi-dimensional aspect of power suggests that account-ability cannot be defined either as the following of rules or as honest communication with one's superiors. Doing these things might be part of an accountability process, but they are not on their own sufficient conditions for establishing real responsiveness. Rather, accountability nowadays involves what might be thought of as the appropriate exercise of a navigational competence: that is, the proper use of authority to range freely across a multi-relationship terrain in search of the most advantageous path to success. This so-called steering mandate involves different relationships and trade-offs from those defined by constitutional convention and classical organization theory. And this is not merely a problem of theory. Real actors stand behind these novel definitions of accountability. Real institutions ask questions about how they perform. Courts still wish to see the letter of the statute honoured and due process followed. Parliaments still expect detailed, descriptive reports which name and shame programmes. Citizen groups still press ministers and civil servants to take responsibility for public programmes, even if the programmes are delivered by contractors.

We therefore need to approach the accountability issue as a problem with multiple levels and more than one possible meaning. Of course this has always been the case to some extent. Public servants managing large programmes have often had to balance demands for accountability from the executive branch, from congressional committees, from ministers outside their portfolio and from different organizations representing parts of the citizenry. However, until recently, these pressures were generally defined within the remit of a single public ministry or agency. With the advent of entrepreneurial government expressed most obviously in extensive forms of contracting out, these organizational boundaries and identities are less able to contain or limit the accountability issue. Recent changes have stretched the elasticity of our received notions of accountability to the breaking point.

Vertical and horizontal power

In making a distinction between vertical (traditional) and horizontal (new governance) accountabilities we can see that the key to making agents responsive is that we first identify what kind of power or agency they exercise. Rather than a theory of hierarchy, accountability necessarily becomes a core property of the systemic interactions between *different and separate actors sharing responsibility* for policy outcomes. In other words, the formal rules and agreements become embedded in sets of routines and conventions, which create a culture of responsibility and thus give the real meaning to accountability.

This involves a different approach to that which seeks to define accountability as a functional value owned within the defined competence of an office or institution. Instead of a 'line of accountability' (Thynne and Goldring, 1987:6), we have to think in terms of a climate or culture of responsibility.

It is also necessary in this light to explore the extent of conflict or dissonance between these different dimensions of accountability in service delivery systems undergoing various forms of 'new governance' (or NPM) reform. The underlying assumption here is that the dimensions will not necessarily converge around a single form of accountability, nor will they always produce consistent patterns of accountability. We may see programmes performing well in responding to their clients, but failing to follow policies coming from the minister's office. Equally, it is possible to imagine a situation in which a programme does what its legislation demands, yet has callous disregard for issues and values not recognized when the programme's authorization was developed.

Vertical accountability

Traditional legal instruments used in policy-making concern themselves with questions of *authorization*, including definitions that propose a line of accountability in which each institution or actor is linked to a defined mandate established by a congress, a parliament or the courts. This line of authority also becomes the line of accountability; making a unified chain of command, as we have observed above, the key to almost every classical treatment of this issue.

For the most part the modern history of the accountability debate (and the related discourse of deniability) must be understood as an effort to improve the behaviour of ministers and senior managers. Much of the argument about political responsibility and accountability has been focused upon the legislature, where a formidable array of checks and balances has emerged in most systems.

But because the accountability of the rest of the policy-making system has been deemed in constitutional terms to derive from the authority of the political executive, managerial accountability has been underdeveloped. Only the most general legal precepts have traditionally been available to check the work of bureaucrats, advisers, regulators and the various classes of public trustee.

For example, the Fulton Report argued that Whitehall had become too involved in providing policy advice and had neglected service delivery responsibilities. Fulton proposed a form of accountable management derived from General Motors. In essence, this involved identifying the costs of individual sub-units and matching these against their measured output so that performance could be assessed. Each sub-unit could then be better managed if the organization as a whole would only specify programme sub-goals that reflected some logical part of an overall corporate objective. At the other end of the vertical line, most accounts of the role of citizens simply reverse the direction of accountability and ask how a parliament serves its 'shareholders', or how bureaucrats serve their 'customers'.

Liberal political theory provides both a means to assert the superiority of claims by citizens (via consent, social contract and representation) and a set of recommended mechanisms to subordinate elected and appointed officials to various forms of popular will. However, reversing the direction of traffic along this vertical line does not necessarily satisfy all the requirements of a robust theory of accountability. Many key public agencies simply have no clearly defined place in this vertical line. For example, as Rose (1989:325) points out, in England, 'many public-sector agencies are not directly accountable to the electorate'. Nor does the traditional view make room for the accountability challenges inherent in contracting out or the development of strategic partnerships with nonprofits and firms.

The second part of the vertical tradition has its roots in organizational economics (OE) and seeks to deal with accountability as a control loss problem (Bamey and Ouchi, 1986; Donaldson, 1995). We have discussed this earlier in the book when dealing with the origins of 'new governance' and new public management (NPM). The OE tradition seeks to solve such problems with the use of strong material incentives and open competition between protagonists. Lex Donaldson has called these the anti-management theories of organization and rightly points out that they see the administrative world primarily as a game played by cheats and opportunists. Senior managers cheat their boards, operatives cheat their senior managers, and everyone cheats the consumer. Since rules become the easiest device of all to circumvent, this tradition prefers material incentives of one kind or another.

This is a version of the 'control loss' problem discussed in the previous chapter.

The OE approach actually posits two different control loss issues, one for top managers and another for operatives. The solution for those at the top is to pay them more but make their tenure less secure. This increases the range of incentives available to shareholders, or so the theory goes. However, the solution is not so straightforward for operatives or front line staff. It is generally seen as too costly to pay them more. Indeed, one of the reasons put forward for the loss of efficiency in bureaucracies is that labour productivity is too low, so these OE strategies generally seek to cut pay and remove tenure. In the process, this tradition has brought to the fore a revised approach to inter-agency production. The use of contracts and contracting is viewed as an efficient alternative to legal mandates, value-based collaboration and hierarchy. However, in both practice and theory, the act of imagination that sees complex public organizations reinvented as a chain of contracts actually unites aspects of both vertical traditions (Ormsby, 1998). The lawyers become the key agents in writing contracts and advising on their possible litigation. The economists provide the measures and output targets.

A good deal of ink is now being spilt showing how awkward is the marriage between these two different vertical approaches. For example, Hondegham's collection of European essays points to gaps in accountability being created by new forms of devolution and performance management, which give greater power to officials but do not increase the institutional means to have them account for what they do. Rhodes (1997:21) also acknowledges that this new world of shared accountability involving networks of interdependent organizations 'undervalues the traditional mechanisms of representative democracy'.

Without dismissing the achievements of performance-based budgets and management regimes, we can see that these strategies for bringing order to a far more complex public sector do seem to create important gaps and inconsistencies. The so-called line between shareholder and consumer, or between legislature and citizen, is neither straight nor continuous. It is not so much that other institutions get in the way as it is that there are actually several 'competing' lines of accountability involved (Ciborra, 1996; Considine and Painter, 1997). Even the apparently straightforward link between ministers and senior bureaucrats or between departmental secretaries and the political executive often fails to submit to this logic.

Horizontal accountability

Consideration of a horizontal axis is therefore needed to open up the question of relationships between co-authorized actors. These include two types – public agencies who cooperate to produce a service and hybrid systems involving public and private agencies. This is the axis upon which questions of environmental or ecological relations are often identified in organization theory. This dimension would encompass the broad traditions of structural contingency (SC) theory (Chandler, 1977; Emery and Trist, 1965; Perrow, 1986), the major alternative to OE. The idea that structure should follow strategy really means that vertical issues (hierarchy, divisions, matrix structures) should ultimately be resolved in reference to horizontal problems and opportunities (competition, integration, relations with suppliers, and so on). This horizontal dimension raises key questions about the nature of agency power and thus the accountability of agencies not lined up under a vertical 'chain of command' mandate. A diffusion of goals and interests complicates any assumption regarding the purpose of action itself. Such differences also call for different instruments to exact whatever accountability is deemed important. In this environment, contracts may become more important than commands, and performance may be measured as output rather than as process (Walsh, 1995).

In this sense, the accountability issue for ministers or cabinet secretaries is now far more complex than on the vertical axis, where finding the line of command also means identifying the line of responsibility. Where co-responsibility and overlap prevail, accountability becomes a structural contingency problem; accountability codes and rules must then constantly be adjusted to reflect actual conditions in the environment. Interdependence in achieving shared outcomes should therefore lead to willingness to share accountability. Alternatively, conflicting mandates and resource competition could be expected to result in accountability conflicts and vetoes. The 'fuzzy' boundaries between public and private agencies and their overlapping mandates demonstrate the potential for pathological conflict along this horizontal axis.

However, there is also a positive side: horizontal accountability issues can be seen as those able to invite and authorize the contributions of social partners, community interests, other levels of government and other autonomous contributors. As the Blair government has shown, this 'joined-up' approach may actually raise the public legitimacy of the whole governance system, including the public agencies, providing questions of mandate and responsibility are kept in the public domain. Overlap also contributes to forms of redundancy that reduce risk. The question, then, becomes one of tailoring accountability arrangements to reflect a mix of vertical and horizontal imperatives, depending on how much consensus and how much risk is to be accepted.

Accountability as a process

Many governments are willing to pay the price of granting increased sovereignty to semi-independent agents in order to maximize output efficiency. While no one can seriously doubt the importance of output-based performance measurement as a tool for improving public programmes, the costs occasioned by poor accountability also need to be assessed. There is little doubt that the new preoccupation with outputs has solved some older problems by creating new accountability gaps and failures. This concern is raised in regard to the vertical line of accountability whenever public organizations are thought not to be directly subject to legislative oversight. It is even more profound when, on the horizontal axis, we observe private and semipublic agencies spending public funds on activities that are all but immune from public review.

Attempts to solve such horizontal accountability problems by moving away from both law and markets and to embrace network relations can be found in some recent accounts (Barker, 1982; Considine and Lewis, 1999; Fox and Miller, 1995; Rhodes, 1997). These network theories include various forms of strategic partnerships, cluster development, business alliances, and coproduction systems. In these cases the question of accountability goes beyond being a matter of compliance (legal strategy) or performance (economic strategy) and becomes a matter of organizational convergence (cultural strategy).

The French system of *affermage*, or leasing, in which private companies run public services according to public service principles (such as in water treatment and supply), comprises an example of such convergence. This suggests that the form of service remains the same, with private firms making profit without changing the nature of the service or altering its distribution towards those more able to pay (Amsier, 1995). Though they are promising, these new network theories still lack tools and techniques for making these cultural processes visible and measurable. However, they do help in one important respect. By emphasizing the role of organizational culture, they force us to reconsider the role of processes, not as a means to re-regulate but as a device for feedback and learning.

A key aspect of the accountability problem, therefore, is to reconceptualize the 'due process' elements on the input or supply side of the organizational system. To illustrate with an extreme view, being accountable might even be widened to mean providing some things that were not asked for, or for which there were not yet targets and for which no indicator had yet been identified. In management-speak, this involves a shift beyond 'performance-against-plan' accounting.

In considering this question of 'performance-beyond-plan', we need to place the questions of measurement within a larger theory of agency that can accommodate organizational learning. To consider functional accountability merely as a signing off on predetermined targets is to ignore the highly dynamic and interdependent character of both vertical and horizontal relationships.

Organizational learning theory deals with the process by which a system takes account of new information in order to better adjust its activities to core values. Thus, in addition to showing that resources are accounted for, this part of the accountability process involves acts of creativity and innovation. Central to this is Argyris and Schon's (1996:21) notion of double-loop learning. This is derived from Ashby's cybernetic theory, in particular his concept of second-order variation. In this framework, any organizational system learns both by working out how to return itself to stability and by altering the conditions of the state of stability itself in accord with new information about the world. In contemporary social theory, the link between first- and second-order variations would be understood as system reflexivity.

As an organizational process, this form of creative change remains accountable insofar as it continues to reflect core values and agreed principles, even if the action itself is not specifically predictable. This is close to the notion of improvisation, which organization theorists use to explain the way creativity emerges within disciplined artistic space. For example, in a study of members of a jazz band, Preston (1987:95) shows how understood arrangements allow each participant to 'know at least roughly what other members of the setting will be doing' – yet these arrangements are themselves subject to improvisation. Maugham calls these 'rules in progress' and attributes to them the means by which order is both maintained and re-established in a creative way.

If we apply this to our two dimensions of accountability, we can see that most discussions of performance only relate to the manufacture of standard outputs and therefore treat only the single-loop adaptations or variations by which errors are corrected. However, when NPM reforms impose multilevel complexity upon public institutions, this form of simple feedback is plainly inadequate. And if Rhodes (1997:5) is right to complain that these changes lead to the formation of 'self-steering inter-organizational policy networks [that] confound democratic accountability', then definitions of accountability might be extended to explicitly include the form and extent of double-loop, or improvisation. If shared mandates are a key aspect of institutional life under NPM, then traditional line accountability must be accompanied by a cultural framework of obligations. This might be defined as a willingness to regard other actors as sharing in a wider agency right or responsibility for a particular service or group of services.

Mapping different accountabilities

Accountability refers to the degree to which public servants and others providing public programmes are responsive to those they serve. We obviously require multi-dimensional methods to see how the different institutional arrangements advantage different forms and degrees of responsiveness to different stakeholders. But accountability is far more than just responsiveness. The warrant for action must be founded on legal and democratic rights to act. So when it involves multiple agents and more than one 'line' we need to imagine a chain of elements which, when put together, lead to high or low levels of responsiveness to both functional and ethical standards. These elements include:

1   Assignability – of goals and standards:
   When programmes are devised it is incumbent upon government to identify the purpose they are intended to serve, including nomination of the groups they hope to satisfy.
2   Transparency – publicity of results:
   In order for citizens, legislators and courts to verify that governments are doing what they promise, including taking responsibility that their contractors do what they are employed to do, the programmes must be open to scrutiny.
3   Knowability – of consequences:
   For responsibility to be assigned to those involved in producing benefits and costs within a programme, it must be possible for any reasonable observer to see the connection between the policy action and its consequences.
4   Reviewability – by supervisors and courts:
   Clients and citizens must be able to take any complaints they have about programmes to an authoritative agency inside or outside the policy organization. The greater the impact of pro-

grammes, the greater the need for this reviewer to be independent of the agency that produced the programme.

5 Answerability – for failure:
There cannot be full accountability if no person in office is sanctioned when a knowable error or fault results in harm or lost opportunity. Sanctions must be proportionate to errors and must meet the transparency requirement.

6 Revisability – of programmes:
Taking responsibility for policy failure includes a requirement that programmes or policies be changed as soon as it is known that they have failed to meet the conditions of accountability.

As service delivery systems move to more complex forms of agency, we must expect accountability to undergo a dynamic process of evolution, adaptation, and – in some cases – crisis. It is clearly not enough to bemoan the decline of parliament or the weakness of the consumer. Institutional development must fit each case. Vertical strength can be improved with stronger roles for parliamentary committees, ombudsmen and so on. Tools for greater horizontal accountability will need to be different for competitive systems and for those using more collaborative methods. In both cases, a focus upon the role of reflexive feedback or improvisation offers a means to reopen the organizational process box without the perils of re-regulation. This new domain of accountability will take some time to develop its own regime of measures, standards and rules. Perhaps the most important step needed is the recognition that multi-dimensionality means both multiple measures and new forms of intervention.

13

Conclusions: Understanding Interactions, Devising Interventions

The policy maker's world in the twenty-first century is founded upon a new complexity. Things are considered complex not because the systems defining them contain many variables. That condition is simply complicated. But when the relationship between variables is dynamic, causing waves of change to flow back and forth among component parts of the system or field, it is regarded as complex. As Simon (1957), Luhmann (1985) and March and Olsen (1984) have demonstrated, the first task of policy institutions is to contain and reduce such complexity. In the new environment, this cannot be achieved by a general recourse to rule-centred bureaucracy, nor to leaving social life to dissolve into markets. I have followed Royall (1993:51) in agreeing that 'solutions may or may not be fully brought about in the traditional central rule, hierarchical government-centered approach'.

Instead, the new focus is upon the interactions between current problems and their contexts, and between actors and institutions. This includes government and non-government agencies. This 'new interactionism' is an attempt to define government as a key player seeking to broker better relations ('joining up') among the actors who may best be able to resolve problems, deliver services and create value. But inevitably this also involves learning how to govern 'at a distance' (Kickert, 1992).

Obviously it is not a simple matter to comprehend the dynamics of all these intersecting processes and semi-autonomous contributions. Unlike industrial bureaucracy, these new systems do not necessarily adopt a generally recognized code of behaviour. So, as Kooiman (1993:38–9) points out, for 'governance it is of great importance to get theoretical and empirical insight into the many forms interactions can assume'.

In this sense I have treated policy interventions as forms of deliberate institutional action that seek to improve outcomes for individuals and communities. To create a deeper understanding of such interventions we can think of each policy question as a tri-structured puzzle. Three domains are usually involved in creating this structure: First comes the political economy of particular resources and interests, then we observe the normative map of ideas in good standing and special vocabularies, and thirdly we identify the institutional path laid out by previous generations of interventionists, and by those opposing such reforms.

There is not much that is either mechanical or linear about the way these three intersect. Context, language and institution each help define one another, but on terms that are themselves quite dynamic. Each policy field or sub-system tends to have its own time-specific mixture of these contributions. Even apparently settled fields such as health, where doctors and hospitals enjoy a fortified dominance, outbreaks of instability, social change and political opportunism still throw some basic relationships into doubt.

Public hospitals may then lose ground to private clinics. Traditional medicine may have its power eroded by alternative therapies. In other words the existence of long-established structures is not of itself a guarantee of continuity, only of the likelihood that these structures will have a sizeable role in shaping what comes next. Such structures must continue to answer the questions raised by current problems.

With this in mind we return to the three scenarios that began the book.

A year has passed since Bill Walker and his neighbours set out to stop an office development from changing the character of their leafy suburb in London's south. The planning tribunal heard their objection and then granted the developer a modified permit. The chair, Maria Rivers, summarized her decision as one seeking 'concessions for both the need for development and the rights for residents to enjoy the amenity of their neighbourhood'. The nine-storey office block was reduced to six stories and a larger set-back from the road was offered as a means to soften the visual impact.

The residents decided they could not afford an appeal to the higher courts and instead have begun to put their efforts into changing the political colour of the local council. Bill has recently won his local ward and has become a champion of the 'Save Our Neighbourhood' group. He is using his role on the council to slow down the approval of undesirable applications and is a regular contributor to local papers and radio debates.

Bruno Hella has also enjoyed modest success and some reversals over the past two years. After a series of violent confrontations between Bruno's fleet and rogue boats from North Africa, the provincial government established a regulatory regime managed by a new Office for Aquaculture (*AquaCare*). Quotas and fishing zones were created and exclusive licences were issued to existing boat owners. This new bureaucracy soon became the focus of complaints as the 'fish police' began to be drawn into new issues. In addition to checking the size of the catch, they were soon having to report on the occupational health and safety of workers on the boats and the environmental management of fishing by-products. Owners of nearby holiday cottages also complained about the seagulls attracted to the new inspection dock, and to the surrounding rooftops.

After a year of disputes and several high-profile cases of local boats being caught trying to circumvent the inspection system, the provincial government offered to contract out *AquaCare* to a legal partnership (*AquaPartner*) with a board composed of four delegates elected by the fishing fleet cooperative, and two local government politicians chosen by the two municipalities. The new self-regulation system has now been working effectively for almost a year.

A different process of change emerged in Anna Trikolidis's IVF case. The legislation enacted to control access to test-tube babies failed to stop doctors from recommending treatment to patients who were outside the official guidelines. Older women, single women and gay couples launched successful legal challenges to force clinics to treat them. Church groups and other conservative associations put strong pressure on the government and activated upper house independents to threaten funding to hospitals and universities engaged in developing new treatments.

The response of the government was to undertake a major public review and to include in the terms of reference a request that the reviewers examine methods for including ordinary citizens in discussion of new technology and ways for them to participate in the regulatory process. After a protracted parliamentary debate and several upper house amendments, a new IVF Regulation Office was created with a Community Advisory Panel empowered to elect two of the eight office board members and to develop and implement community consultation and education plans, and to require scientists and clinics to do the same.

In each of these scenarios there was significant policy change and in two of the cases (Bruno and Anna) this also involved changes to institutional structures. In none of the cases was the policy decision a complete or final resolution. Rather, the actual decisions might be viewed as punctuation points in a longer engagement between these actors. This is common to most real-world situations. Only a minority of policy interventions are achieved within existing structures. Most require new institutions, or at the very least, new instruments to drive existing ones.

In the first scenario Bill's outcome resulted from arbitrated incremental adjustment. This was framed by deep conflict between developers and residents. No one had all their needs met through the outcome and this was not because the policy process was poor, or because the deliberations were biased, nor yet because the actors were incompetent or malevolent. Rather it was because the conflicting interests had little common ground. One wanted what could only be taken from the other. Quite a lot of public policy is like this. We do not have to go to Palestine to find cases of deep, irreconcilable conflict. What we see in this case is that institutions must work quite hard to contain such conflicts. This usually means finding a pathway that encourages both open expressions of conflict and sympathetic hearings of grievances, followed then by dispassionate decision-making within a known set of rules.

What we find in these property development disputes and in similar zero-sum conflicts, is that arbitration becomes the only institutional instrument capable of holding the parties in a stable relationship with government. The tribunal methodology involves establishing a planning code, requiring formal building applications, publicizing proposed permits, and then providing for objections. It gives formal roles to each side. This also helps keep politicians away from the strife by handing the arbitration of individual cases to a judge. Politicians are unlikely to have the right kind of authority to resolve zero-sum disputes and will tend to take sides, making the ultimate decision more costly. But problems can also arise if the tribunal's authority is compromised by poorly drafted planning codes and constant appeals to higher courts.

The second point to note in this scenario is that concession does not guarantee quiescence. Bill is now using political office and committee politics to send developers the message that residents want to hear. Unlike the planning appeal system, the committees are deliberative and openly partisan and therefore much better at expressing stronger views. While judges are usually deflected away from making policy decisions by legislation steering them towards case-by-case adjudication, deliberative committees have no such brake on them. Rather than arbitration, this pathway is structured around deliberative pressure and the imposition of costs on opponents.

Of course, the fact that other committee members support the developers limits the use Bill can make of his power. In other words the safety valve in the council system is the fact that each councillor has an equal and independent power to support whichever community interest group they like, subject only to their ability to keep getting elected. In Bill's case the wards are single member constituencies so he has no running mate or group to whom he must answer inside the council chamber. This widens the scope of his own potential agenda, while narrowing the chances that he will prevail against his fellow councillors on any given issue.

In Bruno's case the institutional dynamics were very different. In the first instance his group of fishers and fish processors were treated by government as part of the problem. While there was some sympathy for their loss of livelihood there was also a strong element of blame. Had they not taken too much out of the local fish stock? Why should government bail them out for consequences of their own bad behaviour? This response during early negotiations with government drew attention to the fact that the village had rather weak organizational structures for dealing with this issue. The fishing cooperative was limited to boat owners and its mandate was for landing and marketing the catch, not for rationing fleet activity. The crews and their families were not members, and nor were other local stakeholders such as those in the processing plant, the transport industry, local shops and restaurants.

The first response by the provincial government was logical, rational and ultimately ineffective. The establishment of a new agency, *AquaCare*, increased authority over the fleet and put expert resources in place to carry out inspections, sanctions and dispute resolution. But once on the dock *AquaCare* could not resist pressure from other interests. For example, their colleagues in the Department of Health had been forced to contribute to the budget for the new agency and used this as leverage to demand that they do something about the high level of accidents and illnesses among crew members and those in the processing plants. And having acquiesced on this point, the agency was then under pressure from the national border control agency to assist with monitoring illegal immigration.

Owners of holiday houses also found the *AquaCare* mandate for regulation in the 'interest of all' an easy door through which to push their demands about noise, seagull mess and visual amenity. While some of this was no more than opportunism, some of the residents had a strong case – the charming docks and headlands were important assets and some controls on development were needed. Building new public agencies means establishing careful boundaries to prevent goal displacement and overload. It also involves great skill by those sponsoring and leading such organizations to manage expectations inside and outside government.

The decision to scrap the bureaucratic agency and replace it with a partnership heralded a more astute episode of institutional design. This time the focus was less about rules and sanctions and more about relationships and interactions between the players. By giving them shares and bringing the fishing industry onto the board of *AquaPartner*, it was now possible to utilize the embedded resources of the industry. Their knowledge of best practice, their observation of one another's fishing times and catch, and their ability to self-regulate were all mobilized.

The weakness of the new design was the potential for some boat owners to cheat. If this happened while the industry itself was helping to manage the regulatory system, the public outcry would be significant and the potential for the whole industry to collapse would be high. In the previous public system there was an inbuilt assumption of defaulting and a public expectation that a certain amount of 'cops and robbers' conflict would be a measure of the effectiveness of the system. But defaulting by those with formal power to run the system would be much more dangerous to the legitimacy and sustainability of the industry.

While the new agency relied upon trust and internal transparency to overcome these problems it was not altogether sanguine about the likelihood of some forms of cheating. Its mandate included the same prosecutorial provisions previously available to *AquaCare*. However, it added to this armoury a rule that those found fishing outside the limits would be expelled from the cooperative and prevented from using the cooperative's processing plants. Since these were internal rules of the association they did not require lengthy court proceedings before implementation. So when Carlo Zena's boat was found fishing after-hours the board of *AquaCare* recommended his membership of the cooperative be immediately suspended pending the result of the formal prosecution. Word soon travelled through the industry and there were no more violations.

The other challenging aspect of this resolution was the need for local leaders to gain new skills in agency management. In the first generation of leaders there were sufficient skills for the establishment of a strong board with a cohesive outlook. However it soon became evident that the workload involved was high and the need for new management expertise was great. With the help of the two local municipalities, *AquaPartner* had to engage in regular capacity-building exercises to maintain good relations with the industry and the community.

In Anna's case the context was highly unstable. This was because of the speed of scientific breakthroughs in the IVF area, coupled with the challenges they posed for definitions of life, family and individual rights. This meant that government policy was under constant siege. The regulatory institution that had been first developed to deal with these problems was only partially successful. It contained the scientists and kept the public hospitals under control. But the implicit pact with the scientists was that they could keep doing new work provided they did not move into controversial areas of clinical practice such as cloning and farming foetal stem cells. In return the regulatory regime promised to protect the scientists from media pressure, scaremongering, campaigns by conservative church groups and the complaints of ethicists. Similarly, the hospitals were happy only so long as the regulatory regime helped restrain demands by non-traditional couples and singles.

The fractures in this system came from two directions. Scientists wanted to stay in front of international developments in the field and pushed ahead of the agreed boundaries. And the courts favoured individual rights to therapy, thus breaching the boundary between traditional couples and other users of the new techniques. These were tensions within the field that were never going to be eliminated. Failure to contain them meant that new institutions would soon be needed. The use of a wide-ranging review spoke to the government's reluctance to expend its own limited authority on such a dangerous enterprise as predicting community opinion and tolerance of the new science.

A public review is first and foremost an exercise in burden-sharing. The subsequent decision to include a community advisory panel in the new organizational architecture was evidence of ongoing doubts about the effectiveness of either a regulatory board, or a precise legislative mandate. Neither seemed to offer the necessary flexibility to respond to new developments and educate different interests about the public interest directions being set. The risk with both instruments was that government could have lost control of the agenda altogether and then been blamed by everyone for not having led from the front.

The method used to avoid this outcome was for the government to cultivate an alliance between the leading scientists and the review chair, a moderate church leader. During successive briefing sessions the key bureaucrats from the old regulatory agency rehearsed different scenarios with these leaders and by the time they were out in the community taking submissions, the basic contours of the new strategy were already understood.

What each of these three cases has in common is the reliance of actors on good strategic judgement. Policy interventions have a large potential to run out of control and become colonized by opportunistic interests, including those inside government. Understanding how the same kinds of instruments can be used as veto points as well as action channels is a first step in steering successfully. Some instruments are better at creating consensus than others, but raise the potential for time loss and open conflict. Others are good at settling disputes, but only so long as they are presented on a case-by-case basis. Fitting policies inside the right institutional setting is therefore much harder than just choosing between policy options on the basis of cost-benefit ratios. Judgements must be made about the way context and discourse already prioritize some institutional settings over others.

Theorizing policy interventions

These discussions of interactivity and complexity bring to the surface a series of larger theoretical puzzles. One relatively simple way to see this is to look at one of the most famous problems introduced into policy studies from game theory, the theorization of a core question about social institutions, framed as a puzzle for two players. The puzzle is about the traps egoistic individuals face when trying to fit individual self-interest into an account of community or public interest.

Like the economist's model of perfect market competition and the capacity of its 'hidden hand' to turn private self-interest into a motor force for common prosperity, the Prisoner's Dilemma is a fable about how individuals unintentionally create or weaken social institutions.

Discovered in 1952 by Flood and Dresher, and given its name by A.W. Tucker (Hardin,1995:32), the Prisoner's Dilemma is almost the antithesis of Adam Smith's 'hidden hand'. It shows that when left to calculate their own individual self-interest, individuals will choose a path that makes matters worse than would have been achieved had they cooperated.

The rules of the game are very simple. Two prisoners are being interrogated in separate rooms in regard to a single crime they are accused of having committed. They are each offered a lesser sentence if they confess and implicate the other, who will then take the full sentence. If neither confesses there will be insufficient evidence for any conviction. If they trust one another and stay silent they maximize the outcome for both of them. If both confess they both get sentenced. In various empirical enactments with different individuals the players tend to 'defect' and try to obtain their freedom at the other's expense, and miss the optimal outcome – freedom for both.

The underlying assumptions of the game are meant to remind us of life in a mass society. First, the two prisoners are held apart and cannot communicate. Second, the game is played as a once-only interaction, there is no chance to learn from one another's behaviour. Third, the pay offs are tilted towards scarcity, and therefore to the idea that one person's gain is likely to be another person's loss. Finally, we can notice that the strategic behaviour of the defector who confesses and hands all the costs to his fellow prisoner, delivers a 'free ride'.

Stinchcombe (1980) has shown that the Prisoner's Dilemma infects many social questions in large, complex societies. Anonymous interactions, interactions which occur only once, and interactions where the costs of opting out are low and the opportunities to 'free ride' are plentiful can all be seen in schools and workplaces in every modern society. As we saw earlier, Mancur Olson (1971) applied this logic to trade unions and argued that where non-members receive the same pay rise as members, it will be rational for most employees to free ride on the union's hard work.

This idea of creating incentives to help individuals calculate their way towards a more successful solution is the economist's resolution of the dilemma. If we want to stop individuals 'free riding' we should either pay them or punish them. Let's take the simplest form of collective action – the parents' committee at the local school. Since all children will benefit from the new playground the parents' committee is building, any individual parent may choose not to come to the working-bee and to allow others to create the benefit that all will enjoy. The economist's solution is then to do one of two things. The school may elect to impose a levy on all parents and to exempt those who contribute their labour instead. Or the parents' committee might put on a social event after the working-bee for the participants.

In the first solution – an imposed tax – the school takes on a burden of administering the new arrangements and the cost of this must be included in the tax. This means the resulting burden will be higher than if everyone had cooperated without being compelled. In the case of the extra social event we can also see that extra costs have been created. A meal and entertainment have to be paid for and extra effort will be required from the committee members to organize the event.

An alternative to the economist's solution is what we might call the sociologist's solution: If social ties or commitments exist between people, the cost of getting them to cooperate will be lower than in the economist's solution and the original tendency to defect, or 'free ride', will be much lower.

In one sense this solution implies that we change the basic rules of the game. Instead of a blind encounter in a one-off situation, the sociologist asks us to imagine that the prisoners are members of a society in which certain forms of cooperation are taught and reinforced by cultural institutions. The sense of duty to one's fellow citizens or to members of the same neighbourhood will impel individuals to come to the working-bee or suspend aspects of their immediate self-interest so that a larger community value can be created.

Of course this idea of duty assumes that individuals are in fact facing situations that were anticipated by their earlier social training. Being taught by one's parents that it was important to contribute to the church fete might predispose someone to join the working-bee at the school, and so on. If these social norms are disturbed by major changes in society, such as urbanization and declining contact between neighbours, we might expect the cooperative spirit to default back to the prisoner's state.

In addition to thinking about the role of social norms the sociologist's solution also implies that we consider the game as one played over and over, not just as a single iteration. If the prisoners know they are likely to meet again under similar situations they will realize that the other can punish them for defaulting. This changes the calculus quite a lot and makes cooperation far more likely.

Ayers and Braithwaite (1992) have shown how this assumption of continuity of involvement will make even quite self-interested actors more interested in collective solutions. Companies seek the creation of a regulatory framework to stop opportunistic members of their own industry from behaving in ways that would discredit them all. These regulations are then internalized by members who see them as valuable. Of course it would be naïve to think that no firm would ever default, so in these regimes the work of voluntary adoption is supplemented by some form of sanction. This is the situation Bruno and his colleagues faced.

We can now move from the theory of cooperation to the practical questions of policy intervention. How does the Prisoner's Dilemma impact upon the policy processes of contemporary systems?

It will have become obvious by now that the use of some form of central regulation is the standard solution usually put forward for resolving this dilemma. The state becomes the actor charged with arranging sanctions and pay offs that maximize the benefits of cooperation. If some firms will not treat customers with minimal respect, a consumer protection authority must be instituted to impose penalties for lying, cheating or refusing to make good when new products fail.

The problems with the state-regulator solution are manifold. It is unlikely that any institution will be able to keep intractable egoists from defaulting without considerable (and expensive) effort. The consumer protection agency will not cost very much if it only has to investigate a few bad firms, but it will eat up large reserves of taxpayer money if it has to investigate and prosecute large numbers of cases. These costs will be handed back to taxpayers, consumers and firms. A related problem in this solution is that the level of state surveillance and power may become more extensive than we would want, either for efficiency or civil rights reasons.

The optimal solution to the economics of the collective action problem will therefore tend to involve a mix of self-regulation by actors, supported by sanctions from government when defaulting looks like becoming a problem. If there are no penalties for opportunistic behaviour then even those who prefer to cooperate will start to feel exploited by those who 'free ride' and they too will then begin to default. But is the economic framework sophisticated enough to deal with the underlying question – why individuals are more or less likely to treat fellow citizens and social groups as mere opportunities for profit and loss? Here we must note that institutions may contribute far more than simple devices for punishment and reward. Languages and meaning systems may do more than register preferences. Under the conditions discussed in the earlier chapters, such arrangements can help reinforce the bonds of affection and commitment that exist between citizens, may strengthen the forms of community and engagement that allow conflicts to be resolved, and in certain circumstances may also open creative new pathways for action not available to individuals acting alone.

Summing up

The book has explored these central dynamics by considering policy intervention as part of a larger game of institutional complexity and interaction. It has indicated how we might ask better questions about the way governments define problems and the way governmental institutions set the scene for conflict and cooperation.

The things we call public policies are actions in a larger pattern of institution-building that determines how individuals are drawn together by certain common forms of inter-dependence. When a given community decides that all its children must be inoculated against polio or smallpox and that the state will pay for doctors to administer this programme through local clinics, a certain ideal of common rights and entitlements has been established. The authority of the state has been mobilized to direct resources to defend a specific idea about the rights of individuals to be free from certain forms of disease. For simplicity's sake we can break this action into three common elements: authority, resources and discourses.

Authority is the core ingredient of all public policy-making. At its most basic a policy is an authoritative allocation of effort which determines how individuals and groups will relate to one another. A law prohibiting the building of office blocks in suburban streets is an exercise of authority. So is the granting of fishing licences. So too is a rule which says women over fifty will not be permitted to use technologically assisted reproduction or surrogacy.

Where does this authority come from? There can be a number of answers to this question. Since we are interested in public policy the first thing to notice is that authority is the rule-making power of public institutions and as such is ultimately a form of actual or implied legal force. Having the capacity to impose costs and benefits on a group of participants in a policy-making field means having the legal power to create compliance. Even where the form of coercion is mild and remote, action is guaranteed by the simple fact that those who defect from any rule or procedure can be coerced and punished. All public institutions involved in the making of policy have some ultimate power to reward and punish. By understanding how this happens we take an important step in explaining why individuals and groups behave as they do.

The second thing policy depends upon is resources. Material opportunities and conflicts over scarce resources underpin struggles to define and resolve policy-making problems. And because resources are typically created, shared and exchanged in systems of relationships involving producers, suppliers, regulators and consumers, when we speak of resources we also begin to notice the roles of elites, classes, cartels and other organized interests. The resources which governments deploy are considerable in both depth and scope. Taxes, grants, services and public goods underpin all forms of modern life. While we may distinguish some states by the fact that they do less than others, we also notice that they still hold critically important functions within their control.

Next, we observe that even though certain patterns of conduct are evident in the way things like the health system work, we see that this is more than merely a consequence of material scarcity or underdevelopment. After all, a health system only knows how to organize itself because certain objectives are shared and some forms of conduct have priority over others. This could be as simple as the idea that doctors are powerful and use their material resources to out-flank competitors. It could also be due to the fact that medicine grants priority to the ideas of health and cure that result from a medical knowledge base. This may give priority to certain forms of disease and to established methods of treatment. It will also tend to define the way doctors interact with their patients and with key institutions such as hospitals. Such norms help drive and justify the way authority is brought to bear upon the distribution of resources.

These patterns in the way these three factors are combined yield a picture of an overall system of public commitments. If instead of empowering public clinics to administer the smallpox inoculation the programme says that citizens will be given a voucher for health services which parents can spend at any public or private clinic they choose, a different system of services and treatments will soon emerge. Some parents may choose not to use the service at all. Others might prefer to use the voucher for vitamin supplements or dental services. When individuals have more choices about how they will behave we can expect greater diversity in outcomes and in the way resources are distributed. This in turn raises questions about exactly who is best placed to decide what happens to patients in hospitals or children in schools.

So to summarize, we started with some questions about the way public action and complex institutions become structured and configured. We now see various generalizations about the kind of priority or underlying structure evident in different systems. This concept of structure is easily over-used and so it is worth pausing to consider what theoretical assumptions it may involve. Structure in human interactions is quite different from the structures we see in other realms of life. A building has a structure that is plain to see. This involves a settled order of materials that are arranged in a defined and (hopefully) stable relationship to one another. The laws of gravity and mechanics help explain how these relationships work.

Biological structures are more dynamic and this leads to forms of relationship which evolve, develop and decline according to an interactive dynamic. But we still observe certain rules about the patterns of this development. Human structures involve an arrangement of individual parts linked by relationships. Families, political parties and schools are examples where certain known contributors (parents, leaders, teachers, etc.) adopt defined roles which are meaningful to them and to those around them.

We need a different concept of structure in order to explain the ongoing patterns in human systems such as policy-making. Without it the complex mix of participants becomes too chaotic to comprehend. Without it we are forced to regard every action and episode as a completely unique event. So in seeking the structure of things we focus our attention upon certain real-world actions which we observe as having a recognizable pattern or regularity. This is where things get difficult. By imposing a certain pattern upon events and issues we perform a cognitive act which is open to question. Are we seeing an actual regularity, or is our analysis merely a subjective convention which others might regard as a fabrication? Since we cannot escape the necessity of building any analysis from some set of assumptions the task we face is to try to make these basic assumptions as clear and open to debate as possible.

For our purposes these ontological challenges involve being clear about what it is that we see driving the relationships which contribute to structured arrangements. For example, do we see the role of government as founded upon democratic assumptions? Do we assume that human nature is a condition which is open to improvement through rational dialogue, or limited to base instincts? Few policy issues are free of such questions and we must proceed with caution before generalizing about the way solutions to problems can be devised.

In addition to searching for the basic assumptions being made about the nature of human conduct we also approach the task of generalizing about structures by asking how much we can know about their properties and dynamics. It is not sufficient to say we know a thing just because we think it or have a strong opinion about it. We also need to develop our analysis and intervention strategy by establishing how the observer gathers and interprets information, weighs evidence and justifies conclusions.

Some branches of policy theory employ the model of scientific deduction used in some of the natural sciences. This is sometimes called positivism. This approach begins with the assumption that there is a definite structure behind all events. With careful reasoning and inquiry, this can be uncovered. By making all potential truth statements subject to tests which can be proved false, this method aims to remove the likelihood that the observer will come to a conclusion simply because they hold a belief about how things should be.

An alternative approach is to treat data much more provisionally. This approach recognizes that independent proof is often absent when we seek to draw conclusions about human conduct. All the players, including the scientists, may have a vested interest in the outcome, or at the very least a habituated vocabulary and vision for observing the system. In these situations we must seek truth through interpretation. Here the objective of inquiry is to explain sets of events and particular outcomes rather than to define a whole class of behaviours and to predict all future events of this type. As the Geertz (2001:1) quote from chapter 1 put it, 'First you do it, then you name it, then you try and determine what sort of "family resemblance" if any, holds it intelligibly together.'

Only rarely can this evidence-based approach be based on the kinds of independent observations that inform parts of medicine and engineering. Human society and the policy challenges it throws up are far more complex than the structure of a physical machine or biological organ (Kline, 1995). The difficulty in creating policy solutions is 'that there are strong constraints associated with the capabilities and wills and beliefs of the people whose actions somehow must be enlisted, coordinated, or managed' (Nelson, 2003:920).

The burden of effort in the interpretive approach is therefore upon the interpreter. She must cross the boundary between herself and the audience, taking on board any available data concerning the way the audience hears and listens. In this sense we can conclude that interventions must not simply be the best fit with known facts, they must also be intelligible to those whose support is needed for successful implementation, a condition that will always make good policy interventions an interactive skill.

Bibliography

Alford, John and O'Neill, Deirdre (eds), 1994. *The Contract State: Public Management and the Kennett Government*. Geelong: Deakin University Press.

Alford, R.R. and Friedland R., 1985. *Powers of Theory: Capitalism, the State, and Democracy*. Cambridge: Cambridge University Press.

Allison, Graham T., 1971. *Essence of Decision: Explaining the Cuban Missile Crisis*. Boston: Little, Brown.

Almond, Gabriel A. and Verba, Sidney, 1963. *The Civic Culture: Political Attitudes and Democracy in Five Nations*. Princeton, NJ: Princeton University Press.

Amsier, Yves, 1995. *Private Financing of Public Infrastructure: the French Experience*. Paris: DAEI, Ministry of Regional Development, Public Works and Transportation.

Argyris, Chris and Schon, Donald A., 1996. *Organizational Learning II: Theory, Method, and Practice*. Reading, MA: Addison-Wesley.

Arnstein, Sherry R., 1969. 'A ladder of citizen participation', *AIP Journal*, July.

Aronowitz, S. 1990. *The Crisis in Historical Materialism*. London: Macmillan.

Atkinson, Michael M. and Coleman, William D., 1989. *The State, Business, and Industrial Change in Canada*. Toronto: University of Toronto Press.

Axelrod, Robert, 1984. *The Evolution of Cooperation*. New York: Basic Books.

Ayers, Ian and Braithwaite, John, 1992. *Responsive Regulation: Transcending the Deregulation Debate*. New York: Oxford University Press.

Baecker, Dirk, 1999. *Problems of Form*. Stanford, CA: Stanford University Press.

Bailey, F.G., 1977. *Stratagems and Spoils: a Social Anthropology of Politics.* Oxford: Basil Blackwell.

Barber, Benjamin, 1984. *Strong Democracy: Participatory Politics for a New Age.* Berkeley: University of California Press.

Bardach, E., 2000. *A Practical Guide for Policy Analysis: the Eightfold Path to Successful Problem-Solving.* New York: Chatham House.

Barker, A., 1982. *Governmental Bodies and Networks of Mutual Accountability. Quangos in Britain.* London: Macmillan.

Barns, Ian, Dudley, Janice, Harris, Patricia and Petersen, Alan, 1999. *'Introduction' Poststructuralism, Citizenship and Social Policy.* London: Routledge.

Barzelay, Michael, 1992. *Breaking through Bureaucracy: a New Vision for Managing in Government.* Berkeley: University of California Press.

Barzelay, Michael and Campbell, Colin, 2003. *Preparing for the Future: Strategic Planning in the US Air Force.* Washington: Brookings Institution.

Baumgartner, Frank R. and Jones, Bryan D., 1993. *Agendas and Instability in American Politics.* Chicago: University of Illinois Press.

Beck, Ulrich, 1997. *The Reinvention of Politics: Rethinking Modernity in the Global Social Order.* Cambridge: Polity.

Beck, Ulrich, 2000. 'Living your own life in a runaway world: individualisation, globalisation and politics', in Will Hutton and Anthony Giddens (eds), *On the Edge: Living with Global Capitalism.* London: Jonathan Cape, 164–74.

Benhabib, Seyla, 2002. *The Claims of Culture.* Princeton: Princeton University Press.

Benson, Kenneth J., 1977. 'Organisations: a dialectical view', *Administrative Science Quarterly*, 22.

Benson, K.J., 1982. 'A framework for policy analysis', in D. Rogers, D. Witten and assoc., *Interorganisational Coordination.* Ames: Iowa State University Press, 137–76.

Bentley, Arthur F. (ed. P. Odegard), 1949. *The Process of Government.* Evanston: Principia Press of Illinois.

Benveniste, Guy, 1987. *Professionalising the Organisation: Reducing Bureaucracy to Enhance Effectiveness.* San Francisco: Jossey-Bass, 147–9.

Berelson, Bernard, Lazarsfeld, Paul and McPhee, William, 1954. *Voting.* Chicago: University of Chicago Press, 307–10.

Berman, Paul and McLaughlin, Milbrey, 1975. *Federal Programs Supporting Educational Change, Vol. IV: the Findings of the Review.* Santa Monica, CA: Rand Corporation.

Bernardy, Michel de, Boisgoutier, Pierre and Goyet, Georges, 1993. 'The ecology of innovation: the cultural substratum and sustainable development', *International Social Science Journal*, 135, 55–66.

Best, S. and Kellner, D., 1991. *Post-modern Theory: Critical Interrogations*. New York: Guilford Press.

Birch, Anthony, 1984. 'Overload, ungovernability and delegitimation: the theories and the British case', *British Journal of Political Science*, 14, 135–60.

Black, R.D.C., 1979. 'Introduction', in W. Stanley Jevons, *The Theory of Political Economy*, ed. R.D.C. Black. Harmondsworth: Penguin.

Blodgett, Terrell, 1987. *Contracting Selected State Government Functions: Legislation and Implementation*. Austin: University of Texas.

Boston, Jonathan, Martin, John, Pallot, June and Walsh, Pat (eds), 1991. *Reshaping the State: New Zealand's Bureaucratic Revolution*. Auckland: Oxford University Press.

Boston, Jonathan (ed.), 1995. *The State under Contract. 'Inherently Governmental Functions and the Limits to Contracting Out'*. Auckland: Bridget Williams Books.

Bourdieu, Pierre, 1990. *The Logic of Practice*. Cambridge, UK: Polity.

Braun, Deitmar and Busch, Andreas (eds), 1999. *Public Policy and Political Ideas*. Cheltenham, UK: Edward Elgar.

Brown, W., 1986. 'Professional language: words that succeed', *Radical History Review*, 34, 33–51.

Brustein, William, 1988. *The Social Origins of Political Regionalism: France 1849–1981*. University of California Press.

Burchell, Graham, Gordon, Colin and Miller, Peter (eds), 1991. *The Foucault Effect: Studies in Governmentality*. London: Harvester Wheatsheaf.

Burrell, Gibson and Morgan, Gareth, 1980. *Sociological Paradigms and Organisational Analysis*. London: Heinemann.

Butt, Henry and Palmer, Bob, 1985. *Value for Money in the Public Sector: The Decision Maker's Guide*. Oxford: Blackwell.

Camdessus, Michael, 1997. *Good Governance: The IMF's Role. Address to the United Nations Economic and Social Council*. International Monetary Fund, 2 July, Washington DC.

Campbell, Colin and Halligan, John, 1992. *Political Leadership in an Age of Constraint: Bureaucratic Politics under Hawke and Keating*. St Leonards, NSW: Allen and Unwin.

Campbell, Colin and Szablowski, George, 1980. *The Super-Bureaucrats: Structure and Behaviour in Central Agencies*. Toronto: Sage.

Capling, Ann M., 2001. *Australia and the Global Trade System: from Havana to Seattle*. Cambridge: Cambridge University Press.

Capling, Ann and Galligan, Brian, 1992. *Beyond the Protective State*. Cambridge: Cambridge University Press.

Capling, Ann, Considine, Mark and Crozier, Michael, 1998. *Australian Politics in the Global Era*. Melbourne: Addison Wesley Longman.

Chandler, Alfred, 1977. *The Visible Hand: the Managerial Revolution in American Business*. Cambridge, MA: Belknap Press, Harvard University Press.

Ciborra, Claudio U., 1996. *Teams, Markets, and Systems: Business Innovation and Information Technology*. Cambridge, UK: Cambridge University Press.

Cohen, Michael D., March, James G. and Olsen, Johan P., 1972. 'A garbage can model of organisational choice', *Administrative Science Quarterly*, 17, 1–25.

Coleman, James S., 1990. *Foundations of Social Theory*. Cambridge, MA: Harvard University Press.

Connell, R.W. and Irving, T.H., 1980. *Class Structure and Australian History*. Melbourne: Longman Cheshire.

Considine, Mark, 1990. 'Managerialism strikes out', *Australian Journal of Public Administration*, 49(2), 166–78.

Considine, Mark, 1992. 'Alternatives to hierarchy: the role and performance of lateral structures in bureaucracies', *Australian Journal of Public Administration*, 51(3), September, 309–20.

Considine, Mark, 1994. *Public Policy: a Critical Approach*. Melbourne: Macmillan.

Considine, M., 1998. 'Making up the government's mind: agenda setting in a parliamentary system', *Governance*, 11, 297–317.

Considine, Mark, 2001. *Enterprising States: the Public Management of Welfare-to-Work*. Cambridge, UK: Cambridge University Press.

Considine, Mark, 2002. 'The end of the line? Accountable governance in the age of networks, partnerships and joined-up services', *Governance*, 15(1), 19–40.

Considine, Mark and Costar, Brian (eds) 1992. *Trials in Power: Cain, Kirner and Victoria 1982–92*. Melbourne: Melbourne University Press.

Considine, Mark and Deutchman, Iva Ellen, 1992. 'The gendering of political institutions: a comparison of American and Australian state legislatures', paper presented to the annual meeting of the American Political Science Association, Chicago.

Considine, M. and Lewis, J.M., 1999. 'Governance at ground level: the front-line bureaucrat in the age of markets and networks', *Public Administration Review*, 59(6), 467–80.

Considine, Mark and Painter, Martin (eds) 1997. *Managerialism: the Great Debate*. Melbourne: University of Melbourne Press.

Corbett, David, 1992. *Australian Public Sector Management*. Sydney: Allen and Unwin, ch. 5.

Corbett, Richard, Jacobs, Francis and Shackleton, Michael, 2003. *The European Parliament*, 5th edn. London: John Harper Publishing.

Crisp, Mr Justice, 1973. Quoted in A.F. Davies, *Politics as Work*. Melbourne Politics Monographs, May. Melbourne: University of Melbourne Press.

Crouch, Colin, 1985. 'Conditions for trade union wage restraint', in L.N. Lindberg and C.S. Maier (eds), *The Politics of Inflation and Economic Stagnation*. Washington: Brookings Institution, 105–39.

Crouch, Colin and Farrell, Henry, 2002. 'Breaking the path of institutional development? Alternatives to the new determinism'. European University Institute, Working Paper, SPS 2002/4.

Culpitt, Ian, 1999. *Social Policy and Risk*. London: Sage.

Daguerre, Anne, 2000. 'Policy networks in England and France: the case of child care policy 1980–1989, *Journal of European Public Policy*, 7(2), 244–60.

Dahl, R.A., 1961. *Who Governs?* New Haven: Yale University Press.

Dahl, R.A., 1982. *Dilemmas of Pluralist Democracy: Autonomy versus Control*. New Haven: Yale University Press.

Dalton, Russell J., 1988. *Citizen Politics in Western Democracies*. Chatham, NJ: Chatham House Publishers.

DiMaggio, Paul, 1983. 'State expansion and organisational fields', in Richard Hall and Robert Quinn (eds), *Organisational Theory and Public Policy*. Beverly Hills: Sage.

DiMaggio, Paul J. and Powell, Walter, W., 1983. '"The Iron Cage" revisited: institutional isomorphism and collective rationality in organisational fields', *American Sociological Review*, 48(2), 147–60.

Donaldson, Lex, 1995. *American Antimanagement Theories of Organization*. Cambridge: Cambridge University Press.

Douglas, Mary, 1987. *How Institutions Think*. London: Routledge and Kegan Paul.

Dowding, K., 1995. 'Model or metaphor? A critical review of the policy network approach', *Political Studies*, 53, 136–58.

Downs, A., 1957. *An Economic Theory of Democracy*. New York: Harper & Row.

Downs, A., 1972. 'Up and down with ecology: the issue attention cycle', *The Public Interest*, 28, 38–50.

Drucker, Peter F., 1961. *The Practice of Management*. London: Mercury Books.

Drucker, Peter, 1985. *The Changing World of the Executive*. New York: Times Books.

Dryzek, John, 1990. *Discursive Democracy: Politics, Policy and Political Science*. Cambridge: Cambridge University Press.

Du Gay, P. and Salaman, Graeme, 1996. 'The cult(ure) of the customer', *Journal of Management Studies*, 29(5), 615–33.

Durkheim, Emile, [1912] 1965. *The Elementary Forms of the Religious Life*, New York: Free Press.

Durkheim, Emile, [1893] 1984. *The Division of Labour in Society*, trans. W.D. Halls. London.

Easton, David, 1965. *A Framework for Political Analysis*. Englewood Cliffs, NJ: Prentice-Hall.

Eckstein, Harry and Apter, David, 1963. *Comparative Politics: a Reader*. New York: Free Press.

Edelman, Murray, 1977. *Political Language: Words that Succeed and Policies that Fail*. New York: Academic Press.

Elkin, Stephen L., 1987. *City and Regime in the American Republic*. Chicago: University of Chicago Press.

Elster, Jon, 1989. *Nuts and Bolts for the Social Sciences*. Cambridge: Cambridge University Press.

Emery, F.E. and Trist, E.L., 1965. 'The causal texture of organisational environments', *Human Relations*, 18(1), 21–31.

Emery, F.E. and Trist, E.L., 1966. 'The causal texture of organizational environments', in Walter A. Hill and Douglas Egan (eds), *Readings in Organization Theory: a Behavioral Approach*. Boston: Allyn and Bacon.

Fama, Eugene F., 1980. 'Agency problems and the theory of the firm', *Journal of Political Economy*, 88, 288–305.

Fayol, Henri, 1925. *Industrial and General Administration*. Paris: Dunod.

Fisher, Sue and Todd, Alexandra (eds), 1986. *Discourse and Institutional Authority: Medicine, Education and Law*. Norwood, NJ: Ablex.

Ford, Henry, 1924. *My Life and Work*, 7th edn. Sydney: Cornstalk Publishing.

Foucault, Michel, 1991. 'Politics and the study of discourse', in Burchell et al., op cit.

Fournier, Valerie and Grey, Christopher, 1999. 'Too much, too little and too often: a critique of du Gay's Analysis of Enterprise', *Organisation*, 6(1), 107–28.

Fox, Charles J. and Miller, Hugh T., 1995. *Postmodern Public Administration: Towards Discourse*. Thousand Oaks, CA: Sage.

Frake, C., 1969. 'The ethnographic study of cognitive systems', in S.A. Taylor (ed.), *Cognitive Anthropology*. New York: Holt, Rinehart & Winston, 28–39.

Galbraith, J.K., 1952. *American Capitalism: the Concept of Countervailing Power*. London: Hamish Hamilton.

Game, Ann and Pringle, Rosemary, 1983. *Gender at Work*. Sydney: Allen & Unwin.

Geertz, Clifford, 2001. 'School building: a retrospective preface', in Joan W. Scott and Debra Keates (eds), *Schools of Thought: Twenty-Five Years of Interpretive Social Science*. Princeton: Princeton University Press.

Genschel, Phillipp, 1997. 'The dynamics of inertia: institutional persistence and change in telecommunications and health care', *Governance*, 10(1), 43–66.

Giddens, Anthony and Hutton, Will, 2000. 'In conversation'. In W. Hutton and A. Giddens (eds), *On the Edge: Living with Global Capitalism*. London: Jonathan Cape, 1–51.

Goodin, R.E. (ed.), 1996. *The Theory of Institutional Design*. Cambridge: Cambridge University Press.

Gordon, Colin, 1991. 'Governmental rationality: an introduction', in Burchell et al., *The Foucault Effect: Studies in Governmentality*, 1–52.

Gore, Al, 1993. 'From red tape to results: creating a government that works better and costs less'. *Report of the National Performance Review*. Washington, DC: Times Books.

Grice, H.P., 1975. 'Logic and conversation', in Peter Cole and Jerry Morgan (eds), *Syntax and Semantics 3*. New York: Academic Press.

Gulick, Luther, 1937. 'Notes on the theory of organisation', in Luther Gulick and Lyndall F. Urwick (eds), *Papers on the Science of Administration*. New York: Institute of Public Administration, Columbia University.

Haas, P., 1992. 'Introduction: epistemic communities and international policy co-ordination', *International Organisation*, 49(1), 1–35.

Habermas, J., 1986. *Autonomy and Solidarity: Interviews*. London: Verso.

Hacking, Ian, 1986. 'Making up people', in Thomas C. Heller et al. (eds), *Reconstructing Individualism*. Stanford, CA: Stanford University Press.

Harden, Ian, Lewis, Norman and Graham, Cosmo, 1992. *The Contracting State*. Buckingham: Open University Press.

Hardin G., 1968. 'The tragedy of the commons', *Science*, 162, 1243–8.

Hardin, Russell, 1995. *One for All: the Logic of Group Conflict*. Princeton: Princeton University Press.

Harsanyi, John, 1969. 'Rational choice models of behaviour versus functionalist and conformist theories', *World Politics*, 22, 513–38.

Haveman, Robert H. and Margolis, Julius (eds), 1977. *Public Expenditure and Policy Analysis*, 2nd edn. Chicago: Rand McNally College Publishing.

Hawley, A.H., 1950. *Human Ecology*. New York: Ronald Press.

Hayek, F.A., von (ed.), 1935. *Collectivist Economic Planning*. London: Routledge & Kegan Paul.

Hazareesingh, Sudhir, 1994. *Political Traditions in Modern France*. Oxford: Oxford University Press.

Hechter, Michael (ed.), 1983. *The Microfoundations of Macrosociology*. Philadelphia: Temple University Press.

Hennessy, Peter, 1986. *Cabinet*. Cambridge: Basil Blackwell.

Herzberg, Fredrick, 1966. *Work and the Nature of Man*. New York: Crowell.

Hogwood, Brian W. and Gunn, Lewis A., 1984. *Policy Analysis for the Real World*. Oxford: Oxford University Press.

Indyk, Martin, 1975. 'Establishment and nouveau capitalists: power and conflict in big business', *Australian and New Zealand Journal of Sociology*, 10(2), 128–34.

Jensen, Michael and Meckling, William, 1976. 'Theory of the firm: managerial behaviour, agency costs and ownership structure', *Journal of Financial Economics*, 3(October), 305–60.

Jessop, Bob, 1990. *State Theory: Putting the Capitalist State in its Place*. Cambridge: Polity.

Jobert, Bruno and Miller, Pierre, 1987. *L'Etat en action: politiques publiques et corporatisme*. Paris: Presses Universitaires de France.

John, Peter, 1998. *Analysing Public Policy*. London: Pinter.

Katz, R.S., 1980. *A Theory of Parties and Electoral Systems*. Baltimore and London: Johns Hopkins University Press.

Kelsey, Jane, 1995. *The New Zealand Experiment: a World Model for Structural Adjustment?* Auckland: Auckland University Press and Bridget Williams Books.

Kickert, W.J.M., 1993. 'Complexity, governance and dynamics: conceptual explorations of public network management', in Jan Kooiman (ed.), *Modern Governance: New Government-Society Interactions*. London: Sage, 191–204.

Kickert, W.J.M., 1995. 'Steering at a distance', *Governance*, 8, 135–57.

Kingdon, John W., 1984. *Agendas, Alternatives and Public Policies*. Boston: Little, Brown & Co.

Kline, S., 1995. *Conceptual Foundations for Multidisciplinary Thinking*. Stanford, CA: Stanford University Press.

Knill, Christopher, 2001.*The Europeanization of National Administrations*. New York: Cambridge University Press.

Kochen, Manfred (ed.), 1989. *The Small World*. Norwood, NJ: Ablex Publishing.

Kooiman, Jan, 1993. 'Governance and governability, using complexity, dynamics and diversity', in Jan Kooiman (ed.), *Modern Governance: New Government-Society Interactions*. London: Sage.

Kubler, Daniel, 1999. 'Ideas as catalytic elements for policy change: advocacy coalitions and drug policy in Switzerland', in Deitmar Braun and Andreas Busch (eds), op. cit.

Lakatos, Imre, 1971. 'History of science and its rational reconstructions', in R. Buck and Robert Cohen (eds), *Boston Studies in the Philosophy of Science*, vol. VIII. Dordrecht, Holland: Reidel, 91–182.

Lane, Jan-Erik, 1993. *The Public Sector: Concepts, Models and Approaches*. London: Sage.

Larner, Wendy, 1997. 'The legacy of the social: market governance and the consumer', *Economy and Society*, 26(3), 373–99.

Laumann, Edward O. and Knoke, David, 1987. *The Organisational State: Social Choice International Policy Domains*. Madison, WI: University of Wisconsin Press.

Laver, Michael, 1986. *Social Choice and Public Policy*. Oxford: Blackwell.

Lee, R. and Morgan, D. (eds), 1989. *Birthrights. Law and Ethics at the Beginning of Life*. London: Routledge.

LeGrand, Julian and Bartlett, Will (eds), 1993. *Quasi-markets and Social Policy*. London: Macmillan.

Lehmbruch, Gerhard, 1984. 'Concertation and the structure of corporatist networks', in J.H. Goldthorpe (ed.), *Order and Conflict in Contemporary Capitalism*. Oxford: Clarendon Press.

Lehmbruch, Gerhard and Schmitter, Phillipe, C. (eds), 1982. *Patterns of Corporatist Policy-making*. London: Sage.

Levi, Margaret, 1997. 'A model, a method, and a map: rational choice in comparative and historical analysis', in Mark I. Lichbach and Alan S. Zuckerman (eds), *Comparative Politics: Rationality, Culture and Structure*. New York: Cambridge University Press, 19–41.

Lewis, J.M. and Considine, M., 1999. 'Medicine, economics and agenda setting', *Social Science and Medicine*, 48(3), 393–405.

Lijphart, Arend, 1999. *Patterns of Democracy: Government and Performance in Thirty-six Countries*. New Haven: Yale University Press.

Lijphart, Arend, Rogowski, R. and Weaver, R. Kent, 1993. 'Separation of powers and cleavage management', in R. Weaver and B. Rockman, *Do*

Institutions Matter? Government Capabilities in the United States and Abroad. Washington DC: Brookings Institution.

Lindblom, Charles E., 1959. 'The "science" of muddling through', *Public Administration Review*, 19, 79–88.

Lindblom, Charles E., 1965. *The Intelligence of Democracy: Decision Making Through Partisan Mutual Adjustment*. New York: Free Press.

Lindblom, Charles E., 1988. *Democracy and the Market System*. Oslo: Norwegian University Press.

Linder, Stephen H. and Peters, B. Guy, 1989. 'Instruments of government: perceptions and contexts', *Journal of Public Policy*, 9, 35–58.

Lipset, S.M. and Rokkan, S., 1967. *Party Systems and Voter Alignment*. New York: Free Press.

Lockwood, David, 1956. 'Some remarks on "the social system"', *British Journal of Sociology*, 7, 134–43.

Lowi, Theodore J., 1970. 'Decision-making vs. policy-making: toward an antidote for technocracy', *Public Administration Review*, 30, May/June, 314–25.

Lowi, Theodore J., 1972. 'Four systems of policy, politics and choice', *Public Administration Review*, 32, 308.

Luhmann, Niklas, 1995. *The Social System*, trans. John Bednarz with Dirk Baecker. Stanford, CA: Stanford University Press.

Lyon, David, 1988. *The Information Society: Issues and Illusions*. Cambridge: Polity.

Malatesta, Dominique, 1993. 'Le side et les consommateurs de drogue: la prévention à l'épreuve de la ville', *Ethological Helvetica*, 17/18, 201–18.

March, James, G. and Olsen, Johen P., 1984. 'The new institutionalism: organisational factors in political life', *American Political Science Review*, 78, 734–49.

March, J.G. and Olsen, J.P., 1989. *Rediscovering Institutions: the Organisational Basis of Politics*. New York: Free Press.

Marsh, D. and Rhodes, R.A.W., 1990. 'Policy networks: a British perspective', *Journal of Theoretical Politics*, 2(3), 293–317.

Marsh, D. and Rhodes, R.A.W., 1992. 'Policy communities and issue networks: beyond typology', in D. Marsh and R.A.W. Rhodes (eds), *Policy Networks in British Government*. Oxford: Clarendon Press.

Maugham, Iain, 1979. *The Politics of Organisational Change*. London: Associated Business Press.

May, J.D., 1978. 'Defining democracy: a bid for coherence and consensus', *Political Studies*, 26(1), 1–14.

Mayntz, Renate, 1993. 'Policy-Netwerke und die Logik von Verhand-
lungssystemen', in Adriene Heretier (ed.), *Policy-Analyse*. Opladen:
Westdeutscher Verlag, 19–41.

Milgram, Stanley, 1967. 'The small world problem', *Psychology Today*, 1,
60–7.

Mises, L. von, 1962. *Bureaucracy*. Westport, CT: Arlington House.

Mishler, Elliot G., 1984. *The Discourse of Medicine*. Norwood, NJ: Ablex.

Moe, Terry, 1984. 'The new economics of organisation', *American Journal
of Political Science*, 28(4), 739–77.

Morgan, Gareth, 1986. *Images of Organisation*. London: Sage.

Mosca, Gaetano, 1939. *The Ruling Class*. New York: McGraw-Hill.

Mulgan, Geoff, 1997. 'Introduction', in G. Mulgan (ed.), *Life after Politics: New Thinking for the Twenty-first Century*. London: Fontana Press.

Murray, Charles, 1984. *Losing Ground: American Social Policy
1950–1980*. New York: Basic Books.

Nelson, Richard R., 2003. 'On the uneven evolution of human know-
how', *Research Policy*, 32, 909–22.

Nelson, R. and Sampat, B., 2001. 'Making sense of institutions as a factor
in economic growth', *Journal of Economic Organisation and Behaviour*,
44, 31–54.

Neureither, K., 1999. 'The European parliament,' in N. Nugent (ed.),
Developments in the European Union. London: Macmillan.

North, Douglass, C., 1990. *Institutions, Institutional Change and Economic
Performance*. Cambridge: Cambridge University Press.

Offe, Claus, 1984. *Contradictions of the Welfare State*. London: Hutchinson.

Offe, Claus, 1985. 'The political economy of the labour market', in *Dis-
organised Capitalism*. Cambridge: Polity.

Olson, Mancur, 1971. *The Logic of Collective Action*. Cambridge, MA:
Harvard University Press.

Olson, David M., 1980. *The Legislative Process: a Comparative Approach*.
New York: Harper and Row.

Olson, David M. and Mezey, Michael L., 1991. *Legislatures in the Policy
Process: the Dilemmas of Economic Policy*. Cambridge: Cambridge University Press.

Ormsby, Maurice J., 1998. 'The provider/purchaser split: a report from
New Zealand', *Governance*, 11, 357–87.

Osborne, David, and Gaebler, Ted, 1992. *Reinventing Government: How
the Entrepreneurial Spirit is Transforming the Public Sector*. New York:
Plume.

Ostrom, Elinor, 1990. *Governing the Commons: the Evolution of Institutions for Collective Action*. New York: Cambridge University Press.

Ostrom, Elinor, 1992. *Crafting Institutions for Self-governing Irrigation Systems*. San Francisco: Institute for Contemporary Studies Press.

Ostrom, Elinor, 1998. 'A behaviouralist approach to rational choice theories of collective action', *American Political Science Review*, 92 (March), 1–22.

O'Toole, L.J., 1997. 'Treating networks seriously: practical and research-based agendas in public administration', *Public Administration Review*, 57(1), 45–52.

Parsons, Talcott and Bales, Robert F., 1956. *Family: Socialisation and Interaction Process*. London: Routledge and Kegan Paul.

Pasquino, G., 1990. 'Party elites and democratic consolidation: cross-national comparison of Southern European experience', in G. Pridham (ed.), *Securing Democracy*. London: Routledge and Kegan Paul.

Perrow, Charles, 1970. *Organisational Analysis: a Sociological View*. London: Tavistock Publications.

Perrow, Charles, 1986. *Complex Organizations: a Critical Essay*, 3rd edn. New York: Random House.

Peters, B. Guy, 1998. 'Policy networks, myth, metaphor and reality', in D. Marsh (ed.), *Comparing Policy Networks*. Buckingham: Open University Press.

Peters, B.G., Doughty, J.C. and McCulloch, M.K., 1977. 'Types of democratic systems and types of public policy', *Comparative Politics*, 9, 237–55.

Pfeffer, Jeffrey and Salancik, Gerald R., 1978. *The External Control of Organisations*. New York: Harper and Row.

Pierson, Paul, 2000. 'Increasing returns, path dependence, and the study of politics', *American Political Science Review*, 94(2), 803–32.

Poggi, Gianfranco, 1978. *The Development of the Modern State*. London: Hutchinson.

Pollitt, Christopher, 1993. *Managerialism and the Public Services: Cuts or Cultural Change in the 1990s*. Oxford: Blackwell Business.

Polsby, N.W., 1960. 'How to study community power: the pluralist alternative', *Journal of Politics*, 22(August), 474–84.

Polsby, N.W., 1980. *Community Power and Political Theory*, 2nd edn. New Haven: Yale University Press.

Postman, Neil, 1992. *Technology*. New York: Pantheon.

Powell, William and DiMaggio, P. (eds), 1991. *The New Institutionalism in Organizational Analysis*. Chicago: University of Chicago Press.

Putnam, Robert D., 1971. 'Studying elite political culture: the case of ideology', *American Political Science Review*, 65 (September), 651–81.

Putnam, Robert D., 1993. *Making Democracy Work: Civic Traditions in Modern Italy*. Princeton, NJ: Princeton University Press.

Rein, Martin and Schon, Donald, 1991. 'Frame-reflective policy discourse', in Peter Wagner, Bjorn Wittock and Helmut Wollman (eds), *Social Science and Modern States: National Experiences and Theoretical Crossroads*. Cambridge: Cambridge University Press, 262–89.

Rhodes, R.A.W., 1990. 'Policy networks: a British perspective', *Journal of Theoretical Politics*, 2(3), 293–317.

Rhodes, R.A.W., 1997. *Understanding Governance: Policy Networks, Governance, Reflexivity and Accountability*. Buckingham: Open University Press.

Rhodes, R.A.W. and Marsh, D., 1992. 'Policy networks in British politics: a critique of existing approaches', in R.A.W. Rhodes and D. Marsh (eds), *Policy Networks in British Government*. Oxford: Clarendon Press.

Ringland, Gill, 1998. 'Scenarios to influence public attitudes', in G. Ringland, *Scenario Planning: Managing for the Future*. London: John Wiley.

Robson, William A., 1956. *The Civil Service in Britain and France*. London: Macmillan.

Rockman, Bert A., 1997. 'Institutions, democratic stability, and performance', in Metin Heper, Ali Kazancigil and Bert A. Rockman (eds), *Institutions and Democratic Statecraft*. Boulder, CO: Westview Press.

Rose, Nikolas, 1996. *Inventing our Selves: Psychology, Power and Personhood*. Cambridge: Cambridge University Press.

Rose, Richard, 1974. *The Problems of Party Government*. London: Macmillan.

Rose, Richard, 1989. *Politics in England: Change and Persistence*, 5th edn. Basingstoke: Macmillan.

Royall, Frederic, 1993. 'Lost opportunity: the case of labour market management in the republic of Ireland', in Kooiman (ed.), op. cit.

Ryan, W.P., 1999. 'The new landscape for nonprofits', *Harvard Business Review*, 77(1), 127–36.

Sabatier, Paul A., 1993. 'Policy changes over a decade or more', in Sabatier and Jenkins-Smith (eds), op. cit.

Sabatier, Paul A. and Jenkins-Smith, Hank (eds), 1993. *Policy Change and Learning: the Advocacy Coalition Approach*. Boulder, CO: Westview Press.

Sabetti, Filippo, 2000. *The Search for Good Government: Understanding the Paradox of Italian Democracy*. Montreal & Kingston: McGill-Queen's University Press.

Samuelson, Paul A., 1985. *Economics*, 12th edn. New York: McGraw-Hill.

Schattschneider, E.E., 1960. *The Semi-Sovereign People: a Realist's Guide to Democracy in America*. New York: Reinhart & Winston.

Schmitter, Phillipe, 1974. 'Still the century of corporatism?', *The Review of Politics*, 36, 85–131.

Schmitter, Phillipe C., 1977. 'Notes towards a political economic conceptualisation of policy-making in Latin America', unpublished manuscript, quoted in Leon N. Lindberg, Robert Alford, Colin Crouch and Claus Offe (eds), *Stress and Contradiction in Modern Capitalism: Public Policy and the Theory of the State*. Lexington, MA: D.C. Heath.

Schmitter, Phillipe, 1992. 'Interest systems and the consolidation of democracy', in G. Marks and L. Diamond (eds), *Reexamining Democracy*. London: Sage.

Schmitter, P. and Lehmbruch, G. (eds), 1982. *Trends Toward Corporatist Intermediation*. London: Sage.

Schoonmaker, Donald, 1988. 'The challenge of the Greens to the West German party system', in Kay Lawson and Peter Merkl (eds), *When Parties Fail: Emerging Alternative Organisations*. Princeton, NJ: Princeton University Press, 41–75.

Schutz, Alfred, 1953. 'Common-sense and scientific interpretation of human action', *Philosophy and Phenomenological Research*, 14, September, 1–37.

Scott, Joan W. and Keates, Debra (eds), 2001. *Schools of Thought: Twenty-five Years in Interpretive Social Science*. Princeton: Princeton University Press.

Seward, Michael, 1998. *The Terms of Democracy*. Cambridge: Polity.

Silverman, David, 1970. *The Theory of Organisations*. London: Heinemann.

Simmel, Georg, 1950. *Conflict and the Web of Group Affiliations*. Glencoe: Green Press.

Simon, Herbert, 1957. *Administrative Behaviour: a Study of Decision Making Processes in Administrative Organisation*, 2nd edn. New York: Macmillan.

Skocpol, Theda, 1996. *Boomerang: Health Care Reform and the Turn Against Government*. New York: W.W. Norton.

Smart, B., 1993. *Post Modernity*. London: Routledge and Kegan Paul.

Smith, Adam, 1910. *The Wealth of Nations*. London: Dent.

Sol, Els, 2000. *Arbeidsvoorzieningsbeleid in Nederland: De rol van de overhead en de sociale partners*. Den Haag: Sdu Uitgevers.

Steinbrunner, John [1960], 1974. *The Cybernetic Theory of Decision: New Dimensions of Political Analysis*. Princeton: Princeton University Press.

Steinem, Gloria, 1974. 'The myth of masculine mystique', in Joseph H. Pleck and Jack Sawyer (eds), *Men and Masculinity*. Englewood Cliffs, NJ: Prentice-Hall, 134–9.

Stichweh, Rudolf, 1999. 'The form of the university', in Baecker (ed.), op. cit. 121–41.

Stidham, R. and Carp, Robert A., 1987. 'Judges, presidents and policy choices: exploring the linkage', *Social Science Quarterly*, 68 (June), 395–404.

Stigler, George, 1949. *Five Lectures on Economic Problems*. London: Longman.

Stigler, George, 1982. 'The pleasures and pains of modern capitalism', Occasional Paper No. 64, London: Institute of Economic Affairs.

Stinchcombe, A., 1975. 'Merton's theory of social structure', in Lewis Coser (ed.), *The Idea of Social Structure*. New York: Harcourt Brace Jovanovich.

Stinchcombe, Arthur L., 1980. 'Is the Prisoner's Dilemma all of sociology', *Inquiry*, 23, 187–92.

Strange, Susan, 1988. *States and Markets*, 2nd edn. London: Pinter.

Streeck, Wolfgang, 1992. *Social Institutions and Economic Performance: Studies of Industrial Relations in Advanced Capitalist Economies*. London: Sage.

Streeck, W. and Schmitter, P.C. (eds), 1985. *Private Interest Government: Beyond Market and State*. London: Sage.

Termeer, C.J.A.M. and Koppenjan, J.F.M., 1997. 'Managing perceptions in networks', in W.J.M. Kickert, E.H. Klijn and J.F.M. Koppenjan (eds), *Managing Complex Networks: Strategies for the Public Sector*. London: Sage.

Thynne, Ian and Goldring, John, 1987. *Accountability and Control: Government Officials and the Exercise of Power*. Sydney: Law Book Co.

Tocqueville, Alexis de, 1835 and 1840. *Democracy in America*, 2 vols, 1962. New York: Vintage Books.

Touraine, Alain, 2000. *Can We Live Together? Equality and Difference*. Cambridge: Polity.

Truman, David B., 1958. *The Governmental Process*. New York: Alfred Knopf.

United Nations, 1999. 'Public enterprise reform and performance contracting', New York Conference Proceedings.

Van der Heijden, Kees, 1996. *Scenarios: the Art of Strategic Conversation*. Chichester: John Wiley.

Van Dyck, J., 1995. *Manufacturing Babies and Public Consent*. Basingstoke: Macmillan.

Verba, Sidney, 1961. *Small Groups and Political Behaviour*. Princeton, NJ: Princeton University Press.

Von Hippel, E., 1988. *The Sources of Innovation*. New York: Oxford University Press.

Waldo, Dwight, 1956. *Perspectives on Administration*. Tuscaloosa: University of Alabama.

Wallace, Helen, 1980. *Budgetary Politics: the Finances of the European Communities*. London: George Allen and Unwin.

Walsh, K., 1995. *Public Services and Market Mechanisms: Competition, Contracting, and the New Public Management*. Basingstoke: Macmillan.

Walter, James, 1986. *The Minister's Minders*. Melbourne: Oxford University Press.

Weaver, R. Kent and Rockman, Bert, 1993. *Do Institutions Matter? Government Capabilities in the United States and Abroad*. Washington DC: The Brookings Institution.

Weber, Max, 1968. *Economy and Society*, G. Roth and C. Wittich (eds). New York: Bedminster Press.

Wildavsky, Aaron, 1962. 'The analysis of issue-contexts in the study of decision-making', *The Journal of Politics*, 24(4), November, 717–32.

Wildavsky, Aaron, 1964. *The Politics of the Budgetary Process*. Boston: Little, Brown.

Wildavsky, Aaron, 1987. 'Choosing preferences by constructing institutions: a cultural theory of preference formation', *American Political Science Review*, 81, 3–22.

Williamson, Oliver E., 1975. *Markets and Hierarchies: Analysis and Antitrust Implications*. New York: Free Press.

Williamson, Oliver E., 1983. 'Organisational innovations: the transaction-cost approach', in J. Rohen (ed.), *Entrepreneurship*. Lexington, MA: Heath Lexington, 101–34.

Wilson, Woodrow [1887], 1978. *The Study of Public Administration*, reprinted in Jay M. Shafritz and Albert C. Hyde (eds), *Classics of Public Administration*. Oak Park, IL: Moore Publishing.

Wiseman, H.V., 1966. *Political Systems: Some Sociological Approaches*. London: Routledge & Kegan Paul.

Index